THE BIG BOOK OF
MYSTERIES

Also by Lionel and Patricia Fanthorpe

THE BIG BOOK OF
MYSTERIES

LIONEL AND PATRICIA
FANTHORPE

DUNDURN PRESS
TORONTO

Editor: Allison Hirst
Design: Jesse Hooper
Printer: Transcontinental

Library and Archives Canada Cataloguing in Publication

Fanthorpe, R. Lionel
    The big book of mysteries / by Lionel and Patricia Fanthorpe.

Issued also in an electronic format.
ISBN 978-1-55488-779-8

    1. Curiosities and wonders. I. Fanthorpe, Patricia II. Title.

AG243.F34 2010   001.94   C2010-902419-2

1   2   3   4   5   14   13   12   11   10

We acknowledge the support of the **Canada Council for the Arts** and the **Ontario Arts Council** for our publishing program. We also acknowledge the financial support of the **Government of Canada** through the **Canada Book Fund** and **The Association for the Export of Canadian Books**, and the **Government of Ontario** through the **Ontario Book Publishers Tax Credit program**, and the **Ontario Media Development Corporation**.

Printed and bound in Canada.
www.dundurn.com

Dundurn Press	Gazelle Book Services Limited	Dundurn Press
3 Church Street, Suite 500	White Cross Mills	2250 Military Road
Toronto, Ontario, Canada	High Town, Lancaster, England	Tonawanda, NY
M5E 1M2	LA1 4XS	U.S.A. 14150

This book is dedicated to our family and friends all over the world who share our interest in the paranormal and the unexplained and who encourage us in our research and exploration.

CONTENTS

FOREWORD

All humans are born with the same shared physical attributes. It doesn't follow, of course, that we are therefore all like "peas in a pod." In fact, we appear in endless variety: some taller or broader than others, some more handsome than the rest. Physical differences there may be, but we are all constructed of the same parts.

Temperamentally, however, it's another story. Here we are often poles apart. To some of us the engine of a car, or the workings of a clock, is a fascinating piece of work. These enthusiasts love nothing better than taking the engine or clock to pieces, working out how the disparate pieces all work together, and then are capable of putting every one of the pieces back together. Others couldn't care less how mechanical things work: we only get bad-tempered when they don't.

This complex world of ours has even more for us to wonder about. There is something almost miraculous about the way it works. Equally miraculous are the lengths of daring, of achievement, that some people reach. Wondering at it all is where most of us are content to leave it. If there are scenes of beauty, we simply stand back and admire them. If something seems a mystery to us, we accept it for what it is. Where treasures are known to have once existed and are now lost, we leave others to find them. Where areas of the world are as yet undiscovered, someone else will be the pioneer. Captain Cook, many generations ago, was a man apart. He resolved, cost what it may, to sail where others had never been, to find and chart lands as yet unknown. His voyages made him a national and lifelong hero, but few of us, if offered the chance, would have signed on as one of his crew! Howard Carter spent more than twenty years of his life and vast sums of his partner's money searching in vain in the vast stretches of the Egyptian deserts until he unearthed the secrets of Tutankhamen's tomb. Few of us would ever have stood up to so many of those fruitless, disappointing, costly years. Most of us leave the search for truth to others and marvel at their dedication.

The Fanthorpes, certainly, are not like the rest of us. They long to know about the world we share. Indeed, if there was a Nobel Prize to be awarded for those bent on researching the mysteries of this world, they would be candidates for it. They have devoted much of their lives to a search for truth and understanding. They have journeyed many times to that area of France where Bérenger Saunière was once parish priest to trace the source of his unexplained access to immense wealth. They have flown to Canada to the money pit of Oak Island to see if, where so many others have failed, they can recover the treasure it is believed to be protecting. They have spent lonely hours in so-called "haunted houses," or eerie graveyards, not merely unafraid of apparitions but longing to encounter them. With hindsight, knowing what happened to the *Mary Celeste*, they would probably have gladly booked a passage on that ill-fated vessel, simply to see for themselves what happened to cause the crew and passengers to disappear.

The Fanthorpes are no doubt both pleased and proud to have some of their work and their investigations included in this book. It may tempt others to follow in their footsteps. If they do, they will need to be stout-hearted and single-minded to match or outdo Lionel and Patricia Fanthorpe, whose friendship I have shared over many years.

— Canon Stanley Mogford, MA

INTRODUCTION

We live in an incredibly strange universe. From the tiniest of its subatomic particles to the farthest of its ever-accelerating galaxies, it challenges the most daringly imaginative scientists and philosophers to make some sort of sense of it.

We have been investigating and researching all kinds of unsolved mysteries, paranormal and anomalous phenomena for the best part of a half-century. Whenever possible, we have interviewed eyewitnesses and visited the sites where the mysteries were reported: Oak Island, Nova Scotia; Rennes-le-Château in France; the Chase Elliot Vault in Barbados (where heavy lead coffins moved around); and Croglin Grange, with its sinister vampire traditions. Unsolved mysteries still intrigue us today as much as they did when we took on the very first investigation.

Charles Fort (1874–1932) had the right attitude toward the unexplained: nothing is so firmly proved that it can't be re-examined — and nothing is so ridiculously improbable that it isn't worth looking into.

There is a serious side to investigating the paranormal, in addition to the sheer fascination of exploring the unknown for its own sake. If we want to find out more about what's *really* out there, then looking in the strangest places is more likely to yield new data than going over familiar territory.

In our adventures into the anomalous we always try to be as objective, as open-minded, and as scientific as possible. We collect the data, examine it critically, evaluate it, categorize it, and formulate a theory or two and test them in so far as it's possible to test them. If they stand up to every test we can devise — promote them to the rank of *possible* explanations of the phenomenon being investigated. If more data comes along, then pop the old theories into retirement and formulate some new ones.

We greatly hope that our readers will enjoy exploring the mysteries in this *Big Book of Mysteries* as much as we have enjoyed anthologizing them.

The authors are deeply indebted to Canon Stanley Mogford for contributing the Foreword. He is rightly regarded as one of the foremost scholars in Wales.

1 PREHISTORIC MYSTERIES

Every so often strange things — Fortean things — turn up and smudge the elaborate picture that most of us are busily painting on the flimsy canvas of common-sense reality (which screens us from the "Ultimate Reality" that we know is waiting out there somewhere).

They may be anachronistic fossils, odd drawings, or carvings that have survived for thousands of years — huge lines carved across a flat plain so that they make much more sense from the air than from ground level, or semi-legendary, semi-mythical accounts of angels and demons, monsters and demigods, who could by a slight tweak of the text be better understood as extraterrestrials, or as the weird, vestigial survivors of strange pre-human civilizations.

In Giza, to the west of Cairo, is the site of the vast and formidable Sphinx with its human head and lion's body. Nearby are the three great pyramids of Menkaura, Khafra, and Khufu. Usually regarded by Egyptologists as the oldest and biggest of the statues surviving from the Old Kingdom, which began approximately five thousand years ago, the Sphinx's human face may be meant to represent Pharaoh Chephren, although the Sphinx was also regarded as an image of the benign god, Horus. Did its strange and sinister design perhaps originate in lost Atlantis?

The oldest known sphinx is far more ancient than the one in Giza. It is situated in Gobekli Tepe in Turkey and is believed to date back as far as 9500 B.C.

Small, delicate ancient mysteries can sometimes be harder to solve than those on a vast scale like the Sphinx. In 1901, divers working near the island of Antikythera found a very strange little metal device. It was well preserved and thought to have survived for two millennia at least. Careful examination by expert archaeologists, engineers, and historians led to the conclusion that it was a very early computer-type device intended for calculating the positions of the zodiac signs.

The so-called Babylonian electric cells were found by Austrian archaeologist Wilhelm Konig in 1931. He later became director of the Baghdad Antiquities Administration, working from the Iraq Museum. Digging at a Parthian site in Khujut Rubu'a, he came across a small ceramic container with a copper cylinder inside it. This had been soldered with an alloy of tin and lead, topped by a copper disc, and sealed with bitumen. An iron rod showing acidic damage was secured within the copper cylinder. In Konig's opinion, the only possible explanation of the artifact was that it was an electric cell, and his theory was justified when working reproductions of it produced a potential difference of about one volt.

Konig's example from Khujut was by no means unique: Numerous other examples were found in the region — all dating from the Parthian period between 300 B.C and A.D. 300. A significant part of the mystery is *why* the Parthians were using electric cells over two thousand years ago. No devices have yet been found that Konig's cells may have powered.

Without travelling to Babylon, Egypt, or Greece, strange ancient mysteries abound in Britain — and few are stranger than Stonehenge in Wiltshire. These great trilithons with their thirty upright stones, each nearly four metres tall and weighing a good twenty-five tons, stand in a circle on Salisbury Plain. There are lintel stones balanced horizontally above these massive uprights, and the technical term "trilithon" refers to all three stones together.

The so-called blue stones of the structure seem to have been brought all the way across from Wales. Another interesting feature of Stonehenge is the Heel Stone (Heelstone). This is a block measuring nearly five metres in height, leaning at an angle of almost thirty degrees. There is an interesting legend attached to it: the devil is supposed to have used it to attack a monk, or friar, whose heel was struck by the stone. Other experts think that the word translated as "friar" in the Middle Ages was actually *Freyja*, the Norse goddess, and that the original purpose of the stone was connected with her worship.

Another mysterious site, Woodhenge, is not far away, and although little remains of the original wood today. Some experts believe that it was used as the model, or trial design, for Stonehenge itself. Others suggest that it was constructed later — during the Bronze Age — and based on the Stonehenge design.

Other ancient mysteries involve curiously ambiguous statuettes, such as the famous Woman of Willendorf, or Venus of Willendorf.

The statuette is just less than twelve centimetres high and is reckoned to be well over twenty thousand years old. Willendorf is in Austria, and when archaeologist Josef Szombathy was working at a paleolithic site there in 1908, he discovered the remarkable little statuette carved out of oolitic limestone and tinted with red ochre. Among the many suggestions about her meaning and origin is that what looks like her hair is actually a space helmet — implying that she is really an extraterrestrial!

The idea of highly technical visitors from space (if that's what she was) is supported by the fact that there are numerous ancient buildings and subterranean labyrinths that the best modern machinery would be hard-pressed to construct: and there are very old maps, copies of even older maps, which show the detail of coastlines and geographical features that have been totally inaccessible for millennia because of a thick covering of ice.

In July 1960, United States Air Force lieutenant Colonel Harold Z. Ohlmeyer of the 8th Reconnaissance Technical Squadron, Westover, Massachusetts, wrote a devastatingly important letter to Professor Charles H. Hapgood. Hapgood had asked Ohlmeyer to study the Piri Reis map drawn by that famous old Turkish admiral in 1513, and Ohlmeyer's

Stonehenge.

15

answer was that the seismic work of the 1949 Anglo-Swedish Expedition showed that Reis's coastline, far below the present Antarctic ice sheet, *was accurate*. Ohlmeyer concluded that the coastline in question had been mapped *before* the ice covered it.

Who was Piri Reis, and how did he get that accurate geographical information in the early sixteenth century? He was a high-ranking officer in the Ottoman Turkish Empire, and, as far as can be judged, a particularly honest and open character. He did not claim to have compiled his map by his own unaided efforts or his own practical cartographic expeditions, although he was an excellent sailor who travelled far and wide, and had written a textbook about sailing. Notes in his own handwriting

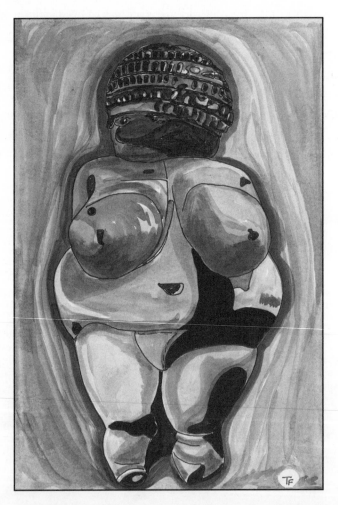

The Venus of Willendorf in Austria. Is she wearing a space helmet?

explain how he compiled his map from many sources — some of them as recent as Christopher Columbus, others going back to at least 400 B.C. Somehow or another he clashed with the Ottoman High Command and was beheaded around 1555. His precious map drawn on gazelle skin was rediscovered in the old Imperial Palace in Constantinople in 1929.

Hapgood's work in 1963 envisaged Reis working away among the ancient documents preserved at Constantinople, which were themselves based on far older sources, compiled in turn from older sources still … and going back beyond 4000 B.C. This argument implied that a very advanced technological civilization had existed at a far more distant date than was generally accepted by most prehistorians. Hapgood traced this channel of geographical and navigational information through the Minoan and Phoenician cultures, through ancient Egypt, and back beyond that. How far was ancient Atlantis connected with these mysterious, old maps?

One map alone, however interesting its history, and however accurate its details of the Antarctic coastline, could be regarded as nothing more than a strange coincidence. If *another* old map turned up *independently*, that would be much more significant. Well, such a map did in fact appear: it is known as the Oronteus Finaeus map and was drawn in 1531–32. It depicts mountain ranges as well as a surprisingly accurate Antarctic coastline, and realistic rivers draining down from the mountains. It is also significant that the central area nearest to the South Pole itself has been left blank — as though the accurate and honest cartographer who drew it has acknowledged that this central region is heavily shrouded in ice so that no details of mountains or rivers can be surveyed or measured.

THREADS OF TIME

There is one anachronistic mystery that concerned a length of gold thread that was found inside a lump of coal estimated at three hundred million years old. Had a time traveller lost it when that piece of coal was growing as a green and fertile tree?

A major discrepancy on the Oronteus Finaeus map is that the Antarctic Peninsula goes too far north, almost touching Cape Horn. But a closer scrutiny of the *whole* of Oronteus's representation of the Antarctic continent shows that *all* of it extends too far from the centre, too far north, in fact, in every direction. It is not *inaccurate* — it's simply drawn to the *wrong scale* for the rest of the Finaeus map. Whoever first made the scaling error, it was made in the distant past and copied by a succession of cartographers, including Piri Reis.

The very old portolanos on which the medieval navigators depended did not carry regular grid lines like our modern lines of latitude and longitude. Instead they tended to use central points — located at various positions on the map — from which lines radiated like the closely fitting spokes of a bicycle wheel. The centres may have been meant to reproduce the directions of a primitive mariner's compass, and navigation would probably have proceeded by attempting to recognize the ship's location by the position of various landmarks, islands, cliffs, bays, and headlands. Having established his present position, the navigator would possibly have tried to line up the ship's course along the grid line which would have taken it nearest to his intended destination.

A.E. Nordenskiöld, who was an acknowledged world authority in this area, compiled an atlas from the many portolanos he studied, and concluded that they were based on much older and far more accurate maps. He argued that the Dulcert Portolano of 1339 was particularly accurate beyond the capabilities of typical fourteenth century navigators and cartographers. He thought that there was no observable *development* in the maps and charts that appeared from the fourteenth to the sixteenth centuries. Two hundred years of sailing, exploration, and discovery was not reflected in the maps. He concluded that this was because someone in the early 1300s had discovered an exceptionally accurate map, one that was destined not to be surpassed for the next two centuries at least. It also seemed to Nordenskiöld that there was only one such excellent original and that all the good and reliable portolanos had been copied from it.

His measurements revealed that as far as the Mediterranean and the Black Sea were concerned, all the portolanos were practically identical, and the same scale was used on all.

Nordenskiöld was intrigued to find that the scale used was not obviously linked with the customary Mediterranean units of measurement, except for those found in Catalonia. He suggested that the historical link between

Catalan and the ancient Phoenicians and Carthaginians could well account for this. If the units of measurement and the scale were Carthaginian, then there was a strong possibility that the original, accurate map from which the good portolanos had been copied, had also been known to the Carthaginians — even if it had not originated with them.

Nordenskiöld then examined the role of Marinus of Tyre, a navigator who lived during the second century A.D. and was the predecessor of the famous Ptolemy.

Theodorus Meliteniota of Byzantium, from whom most of the information about the great scholar's life is derived, suggests that Claudius Ptolemaus, popularly known as Ptolemy, was born in the Greek city of Ptolemais Hermii, and did most of his scientific, astronomical, and mathematical work in Alexandria. He was certainly making astronomical observations between the years A.D. 127 and 151, and may still have been working as late as 155. There is also an Arabian tradition that Ptolemy died at the age of seventy-eight.

From his studies of the portolanos, Nordenskiöld felt that the units of measurement used could not have been from a time later than that of Marinus of Tyre, and were probably far earlier. Comparing them with Ptolemy's work, he saw clearly that the original source from which the portolanos had been copied was greatly superior.

To give Ptolemy the credit he richly deserves, he was the most famous geographer of his time. He had access to the greatest library of the ancient world, and all its geographical documents and records. He was a fine mathematician and posessed a modern, scientific attitude to the phenomena he observed and studied. As Hapgood so rightly argues in *Maps of the Ancient Sea-Kings*, it is very unlikely that medieval sailors during the fourteenth century *without* the advantages of Ptolemy's reference library and high mathematical skills could have produced charts superior to his.

Assuming that it was the Carthaginians and Phoenicians who had access to much older and more accurate charts than Ptolemy was able to produce, and assuming again that these reappeared after an interval of well over a thousand years to form the basis of the portolanos, why did they vanish, and where might they have been hidden? The answer could lie in the grim and chronic struggle between Rome and Carthage known as the Punic Wars.

To understand the hatred and rivalry between these two great ancient powers, it is necessary to look briefly at their respective histories.

The first legend of the foundation of Rome relates how Aeneas, the Trojan prince, escaped from the ruin of Troy, married a Latin princess, and founded the city of Rome and the Julian Dynasty. The second legend concerns Romulus and Remus, descendants of Aeneas on their mother's side, and, in the myth, the sons of Mars, god of war. Thrown into the Tiber by an unfriendly king of Latium, they drifted to Capitol Hill, were raised by a she-wolf, and founded Rome in 753 B.C. — a date from which all Roman history traditionally begins.

The most likely historical origin is that clusters of settlements on Rome's seven hills got together to form a city state round about 1000 B.C. Having been involved in various battles with fierce Celtic neighbours and Gauls, "Rome conquered the world in self-defence!"

The Roman Empire was a great trading organization, and freedom of the seas was vitally important to her both commercially and militarily. The Carthaginians were the major maritime problem for Roman ships in the Mediterranean. It was inevitable that one power or the other would have to go down.

The history of Carthage begins with Phoenician colonists from Lebanon and Syria 1,600 kilometres to the east. Lacking the manpower to establish large settlements, they set up a few coastal cities as trading posts. The silver and tin of southern Spain were a great attraction for them. Phoenicians looked for places easily accessible from the sea but not open to hostile tribes from the hinterland: they liked offshore islands, rocky peninsulas, and sandy bays to facilitate beaching their ships. Carthage conformed to this pattern. It was also in a good position to expand into the fertile areas around it. The name itself derives from two Phoenician words *kart hadasht*, which means "new city."

The implacable attitude separating the two great Mediterranean powers is clearly illustrated by the bitter words of the grim old Roman senator Marcus Porcius Cato (234–149 B.C.) *"Delenda est Carthago"* — "Carthage must be destroyed."

The first Punic War (264–261 B.C.) started because of problems in Sicily. The second (218–201 B.C.) ended with Scipio Africanus's triumph over Hannibal, the Carthaginian general at the epoch-making Battle of Zama in what is now Tunisia. The third and final round (149–146 B.C.) ended with the total destruction of Carthage and her people.

Did the precious old maps survive the destruction of Carthage, or were they safely onboard a Carthaginian ship that somehow evaded the Roman blockade and made its way east, back toward the old Phoenician homelands from which the ill-fated colony at Carthage had originally sprung?

It is interesting to speculate that *if* the precious and highly accurate old map did find its way back to the Middle East before the final destruction of Carthage, it could well have surfaced again during the Crusades, the period prior to 1307 during which the indomitable Templars were in the ascendancy. They were great sailors as well as great soldiers: were their successes at sea due in part to their possession of superior maps and charts, copied from highly accurate originals that predated the maritime Phoenicians and Carthaginians?

So one possible scenario suggests that some very ancient but unknown source produced maps of high quality, which in turn came into the hands of the Phoenicians, and passed from them — indirectly — to the Templars, and so to European navigators in the thirteenth and fourteenth centuries.

Where could the advanced technical knowledge behind those maps have come from in the first place? Assuming that Graham Hancock's thoroughly researched and well-reasoned theories have the sound basis in fact that they certainly appear to have, then Antarctica would be as good a starting place as any.

If Hapgood's deductions about the ability of continental land masses to slide over the Earth's surface — that is, if the crust is able to move independently of the core beneath it — are correct, then areas that once occupied warm or temperate zones may find themselves relatively quickly inside polar circles, and vice versa.

Hapgood and his colleague, James Campbell, put forward the theory that the Earth's crust rests on a very weak layer below — a layer that is virtually liquid. Following an idea suggested to them by Hugh Auchincloss Brown, an engineer, they investigated the possibility that a force powerful enough to move the entire crust of the Earth over this weak, quasi-liquid layer, could be generated by the mass of the polar ice-caps themselves, and their centrifugal effects arising from the Earth's own rotation.

The centre of gravity of the Antarctic ice-cap, for example, is approximately 483 kilometres from the South Pole: "As the Earth rotates," suggests Hapgood, "the eccentricity creates a centrifugal effect that works horizontally on the crust, tending to displace it toward the equator."

Einstein himself supported this theory: in the introduction to Hapgood's *Earth's Shifting Crust*, Einstein wrote, "His (Hapgood's) idea is original, of great simplicity, and — if it continues to prove itself — of great importance to everything that is related to the history of the Earth's surface."

Following Hapgood's hypothesis, if there was an advanced civilization living on Antarctica before it moved into a polar position where it would rapidly become ice-locked, what would such people do to save themselves, their children, and their culture?

Such cataclysmic shifting of the Earth's crust would inevitably be accompanied by dynamic geological and meteorological phenomena. There would be earthquakes, volcanic disturbances, fierce storms, destructive winds, and tidal waves. Those who could — those who had ships strong and buoyant enough to survive the devastation and the accelerating onset of the paralyzing cold — would head north toward warmer zones. Where might those fortunate few refugees and survivors have landed?

Heading north from all sides of the ice-doomed Antarctic continent would bring the desperate travellers to either Cape Horn, the Cape of Good Hope, New Zealand's South Island, the southern coast of Australia, or — if they travelled far enough due north along the 109 degrees west longitude — to the remote mysteries of Easter Island.

Is there the faintest possibility that the indecipherable *rongo-rongo* script and the inexplicable stone heads of Easter Island are thousands of years older than is generally thought to be the case?

Just suppose that a highly advanced civilization once flourished on the land that is now buried under hundreds of metres of Antarctic ice. Those of their refugees who travelled up the East African coast could eventually have reached Egypt. Was it their skill, perhaps, that designed and constructed the Sphinx and many of the other massive structures that are still defying time?

Did another group of them reach South America and leave indelible traces of their architectural knowledge and structural expertise there as well?

When the oldest indigenous Australians talk of the *Dream Time* does their mysticism go right back to another half-remembered place from which they came millennia ago, and will paintings one day be discovered under the ice of Antarctica that bear an uncanny resemblance to the oldest Australian rock and cave art?

Puzzling legends of lost civilizations persist all over the world. The vanishing of a once great Antarctic civilization below the ice of the present South Pole might reveal the history behind those legends.

We now move from the frozen wastes of Antarctica to the oppressive heat of the African sun for the next of the ancient mysteries — the Blombos Cave in South Africa. The caves contain a variety of wall carvings, many thousands of years old, that some experts believe could be the famous square and compasses symbol of the Masonic Order. There are daringly speculative historians and antiquarians who have suggested that the Order is far, far older than is generally recognized, and that modern Freemasonry is descended from a group of Guardians who have protected human beings for many millennia.

ANCIENT AIR TRAVEL?

Some very strange, ancient gold ornaments from Venezuela, Costa Rica, and Columbia made by Mochica or Chimú people were thought by Fortean investigator Ivan Sanderson to resemble model airplanes, and, as the illustration shows, there was good reason for his hypothesis.

2 MYSTERIES
OF THE MOUNTAINS

There is a subtle difference between asking whether Bigfoot or Sasquatch is real and asking whether the phenomenon associated with that name is real. The phenomenon is certainly real. New reports of sightings or the discovery of footprints come in almost daily. Someone or something — psychic entity, mental aberration, extraterrestrial being, unknown physical lifeform — is triggering the sightings. Someone or something is leaving the footprints. An enormous amount of Sasquatch evidence is accumulating in the Pacific Northwest of Canada and the United States.

On October 20, 1967, just after 1:00 p.m., Bob Gimlin and Roger Patterson managed to take 953 frames of 16mm cine film of something that looked like a very big, hair-covered humanoid. The existence of their film eliminates two theories: whatever they saw was not a hallucination, nor was it the result of auto-suggestion, self-hypnosis, or any sort of psycho-sociological mind trick that they'd accidentally played on themselves. As far as is known, cameras can't record images that exist only in the photographer's mind.

The film wasn't perfect, but it was good enough to dispose of another theory: whatever is on the Gimlin–Patterson film is not a commonly known but misidentified zoological species. This thing wasn't any kind of bear or anthropoid ape seen in strange conditions or from an odd perspective. It could have been one of two things: a hoax, or an unknown creature of some sort that possessed a type of objective reality capable of leaving a photographic record.

The indigenous people of Canada and North America have cultural and traditional histories of Bigfoot that go back several centuries. The oldest written records go back nearly two hundred years, and the sightings are by no means culture specific. Indigenous people as well as European,

African, and Asian immigrants have all been involved in Bigfoot episodes.

Statistical analysis produces interesting correlations. There are, for example, more than six hundred place names in the northwestern United States that are thought to have associations with the Bigfoot or Sasquatch legends. These place names are not positively linked to population density. If hoaxers had been responsible, it would have seemed probable that the more people there were around, the greater the chance of a hoaxer working the area — but not so. What the sightings and place names *do* seem to correlate with positively is mountain ridges and mountain crests: in other words, if there really are such things as Sasquatch or Bigfoot, then they are closely associated with high and inaccessible places — just as the Yeti is in Tibet and Nepal.

Let us relate to you one of these thousands of typical reports. Two hunters from Stewart in British Columbia were travelling at an altitude of over 1,200 metres along an old mine access road. As daylight faded they turned a corner and jumped from their truck thinking that they'd seen a bear moving ahead of them. Setting off in pursuit, they saw that it was walking upright. The creature became aware of them at the same moment and turned to look directly at them. It turned its shoulders and the whole of its upper body, as it didn't seem to have a neck.

The men described a dark face with a small beard and a flattish nose. It seemed as surprised to see them as they were to see it. The last glimpse they had of it, the Sasquatch was vanishing among the trees. The hunters noted particularly that it was very big — over seven feet tall — and heavily built, and that there was a powerfully unpleasant smell around it. They also noticed that the hands swung lower than the knees.

Albert Ostman had a much closer encounter than the Stewart hunters. He reported how in 1924 he was prospecting in Toba Inlet in British Columbia when an eight-foot Sasquatch picked him up like a rucksack and carted him along inside his sleeping bag for about three hours. When dawn broke he found he was in a Sasquatch "homestead" of some description and that it was occupied by the adult male that had kidnapped him, an adult female, and two young ones. Although they prevented his escape for several days, Ostman was unwilling to use his gun on them because they had done him no harm, and clearly intended no harm. He finally escaped by tricking the adult male with some snuff from his pack, and while it was rushing to find water to sooth the irritation, Ostman made a dash for freedom.

Dr. W. Henner Farenbach performed another interesting piece of statistical analysis on a large sample of Sasquatch footprints. The print size of any natural animal species, including human beings, tends to follow a normal bell curve of distribution. Most human beings, for example, have British shoe sizes greater than four but smaller than eleven. The great majority — the apex of that normal distribution bell curve — being between six and nine. A few very small-footed people have sizes two or three, and an equally low number of large-footed people wear sizes eleven or twelve.

When Dr. Farenbach made the calculations, he discovered that the Sasquatch prints adhered well to this normal, natural pattern. If hoaxers were responsible, it seems highly improbable that they could have colluded over such wide distances and over so many years to produce such a realistic sample range.

SASQUATCH SOUNDS

In addition to footprints and occasional hair samples, there are sound recordings in existence that claim to have caught Sasquatch vocalizations. Some of the most interesting of these were made by Al Berry and Ron Morehead in the Sierra Nevada. They can actually be contacted through the Internet at their web site "Sierra Sounds," where CDs or tapes are available.

One question frequently asked by serious Sasquatch researchers is why prominent, orthodox scientists haven't joined their ranks in any perceptible strength. It may be argued that they have, but that the traditionalist and rather cautious academic official media are still reluctant to give much space or weight to Sasquatch research.

The well-balanced information available over the Internet via the Virtual Bigfoot Conference Site organized by Henry Franzoni suggests that part of the problem is to be found in the suspicion among a number of researchers that Bigfoot seems to possess a kind of paranormal sixth sense, and perhaps some additional ultra-human abilities. How else, one might sensibly ask, has it managed to avoid contact with *Homo sapiens* for so long?

Once the question of a sixth sense arises, Franzoni warns, orthodox scientists begin to shy away from delving into a phenomenon. This is probably because of the heavy bias in favour of the mechanistic philosophy of science which appears to have been a dominant influence since the seventeenth century, and the lasting impact of Rene Descartes.

Dr. Rupert Sheldrake's profound and highly readable work entitled *Why Puzzling Powers of Animals Have Been Neglected* makes the point that academic biology has inherited from seventeenth century science a strong faith in reductionism — a technique for explaining complex systems in terms of smaller and simpler parts. For example, it was once believed that atoms formed the fundamental bedrock for all physical explanations, but recent subatomic research has shown that the atoms themselves can be thought of as patterns of vibrations within fields: which more or less dissolves the foundations of the old style materialistic science.

Karl Popper, the great philosopher of science, has said: "Through modern physics, materialism has transcended itself." What seems to have revolutionized the philosophy of science as far as physics is concerned has not yet conquered the stubborn materialism that still persists in some areas of biology. As Dr. Sheldrake says, "Fields of enquiry that are inherently holistic have a low status in the hierarchy of science."

There is, however, another biological philosophy of science known as *vitalism* which suggests that living organisms are *truly* alive, whereas mechanistic and materialistic theories regard them as merely inanimate and soulless.

Because vitalism admits the existence of unknown vital principles, its adherents tended to be open minded about the possibilities of phenomena which were not vulnerable to explanation in mechanistic terms. Vitalists were interested in studying the psychic powers of human beings and uncanny powers in animals — such as the apparent sixth sense of the Sasquatch.

A report from Union Town in Pennsylvania, published in a paper by Stan Gordon for the 1974 UFO Symposium, tells the story of a woman who was sitting at home watching television, when she heard a strange noise coming from her front porch and got up to investigate. Thinking that something dangerous might be out there, she picked up a loaded shotgun first. As she turned on the porch light and stepped out to look, she saw a creature she described as seven feet tall and covered in hair, less than two metres away. She said that it raised its arms above its head, and,

PARANORMAL ABILITIES

J.W. Burns worked for many years as a teacher among the indigenous Chehalis people of Harrison River, close to Harrison Hot Springs. From his Chehalis friends he heard many accounts of the Sasquatch, not as huge, ape-like semi-humans, but as a magically gifted giant race that had clothes, fire, weapons, and basic technology, and lived in villages. They also had paranormal abilities.

thinking it was about to attack, she fired one shot into its body at point blank range. There was a flash of light and the thing simply vanished: no blood, no carcass, no sign of anything.

It may be unkind to suggest that perhaps mechanists are mechanists *because* they are afraid of vitalism and its implications, but it often seems as though they are. As Dr. Sheldrake argues again, for them to admit the reality of anything mysterious or mystical in life would mean abandoning their faith in the hard won certainties of science.

Some embarrassing phenomena are then either attacked or ignored, not because they are unorthodox, illogical, fallacious or ridiculous, but simply because they don't conform to the comforting mechanistic theory which sets out to explain the universe and all it contains.

Sheldrake maintains that a broader alternative to the mechanistic theory of life has grown up in the form of a holistic or organismic philosophy of nature. The whole is *more* than the sum of its parts. Nature is made up of organisms not machines.

Against this more liberal philosophical-biological background, the Sasquatch and his Himalayan cousin the Yeti, have much more opportunity of emerging into the light.

An amazing encounter was reported by nineteen-year-old Lakpa Sherpani in 1974. She said that her yak herd was attacked by a short but immensely powerful yeti, which killed five of them by twisting their horns and then knocked her unconscious. The incident occurred at an altitude of approximately 4.3 kilometres in the vicinity of Mount Everest.

In 1957, Professor V.K. Leontiev was in the Caucasus Mountains near the source of the River Jurmut, when he saw strange tracks in the snow. That night he heard inexplicable sounds, and saw a weird, unknown creature the following day. He described it as over seven feet tall and very broad. The body was covered in hair and it walked upright, not touching the ground with its hands. The professor referred to it as a Kaptar, the name by which it was known locally. He examined its footprints carefully after it had gone, and described them as unlike the prints of any animal he had ever come across previously.

In July of 1924 a party of miners was attacked by a group of Sasquatch in the Mount St. Helen's/Lewis River district in Washington State. The miners had heard strange, frightening sounds for over a week before the Sasquatch actually attacked them. They saw a weird, seven-foot-tall creature and fired at it, then ran to their cabin and barricaded themselves in. All through the night the Sasquatch hurled rocks at the cabin and attempted to break in the door — despite their massive strength, it held. Press men from the *Portland Oregonian* came to investigate and found giant footprints all around the miners' cabin. After the attack, the place was renamed Ape Canyon — a name by which it is still known today.

Artist's impression of Sasquatch or Yeti, based on witnesses' reports.

Ivan Wally of Vancouver was driving his pickup along the Trans-Canada Highway above the River Thompson, five or six kilometres east of Lytton. It was the evening of November 20, 1969. As his vehicle climbed the hill he saw a creature ahead of him on the road. It was approximately seven feet tall; the legs looked long in proportion to the body, and Ivan guessed that it probably weighed more than 136 kilograms. The creature had short greyish-brown hair all over it. As the truck approached, the creature turned to look at it, and raised both arms.

Ivan said later that its face reminded him of a wizened old man. Something about the thing sent Ivan's dog — which was on the seat beside him — half crazy with either fear or anger, maybe a combination of both. At that point the creature loped away on its long legs. Ivan turned around and drove back to Lytton where he reported the incident to the RCMP, who took him seriously and searched for footprints. Unfortunately, the roadside gravel was not conducive to taking impressions, and they found none.

Volumes could easily be filled with similar incidents: hundreds, perhaps thousands, of sensible, truthful and reliable witnesses from Canada, the United States, Tibet, Nepal, China, and Russia have reported sighting after sighting of strange creatures resembling very large men, covered with hair. So what might they be? A significant number of the reports suggest that there is something paranormal about them. Are they simply some unknown but perfectly normal and natural anthropoid? If so, why do we never find their bodies? Perhaps they bury their dead. Perhaps they go off to find a lonely and desolate place — maybe a hidden mountain cave — where they can die with dignity, privacy and secrecy when they feel that their end is near. The strangest theory of all is that they enjoy enormous longevity.

In the Hunza valley, high in the Himalayas, the normal human inhabitants enjoy exceptionally good health and extremely long lifespans — possibly attributable to their pollution free air and a diet rich in apricots and apricot oil. If the Sasquatch and Yeti and their cousins around the world's other mountain ranges also benefit from the pollution free air available at those altitudes, perhaps their life-spans are many times ours.

Some researchers suggest that they may have had an extraterrestrial origin: the jury's still out on that one.

It seems highly unlikely that the Sasquatch and his close relatives are merely myth, legend, hoax or imagination. There have been so many reports of these enigmatical hairy giants that there simply *has* to be someone or something up there in the mountains — the great unsolved mystery is *what*.

PROOF OF THE YETI?

Joshua Gates, a television presenter, came across what seemed to be Yeti footprints in Nepal, not far from Mount Everest, in 2007. Each print was well over thirty centimetres long. The prints had five toes and measured about twenty-five centimetres in width. Casts were taken, and when these were examined by university experts in the United States they were thought to be too anatomically accurate to be fakes. Gates's team also found mysterious hairs on a high-altitude tree. When these were examined, it was concluded that they belonged to a hitherto unknown primate of some kind. In 2008, Japanese researchers led by Yoshiteru Takahashi photographed what looked very much like Yeti prints.

3 BIBLICAL MYSTERIES

T he books of the Bible introduce a host of mysteries to human-kind, and man has for centuries attempted to translate and understand the stories told within its spiritual prose. What better place to start than in the beginning....

The book of Genesis gives an account of the Garden of Eden that suggests a realistic description of an actual historical and geographical location — a real, solid, physical place, rather than the colourful dream landscape of myth or legend. George MacDonald, C.S. Lewis and J.R.R. Tolkien all had the gift of creating imaginary landscapes that possess uncanny realism — as if they had visited the actual locations.

By contrast, the biblical description of Eden seems to possess a sturdy, time-defying realism, a sense of historical and geographical *actuality*, which makes the quest for it well worth pursuing.

The first biblical clue is that the Garden of Eden spread over the sources of four rivers: the Tigris, the Euphrates, the Gihon, and the Pishon. The first two present no difficulties on a modern map, but it's helpful to note that the Hebrew Hiddekel is the same river as the Tigris. The River Aras was called the Gihon-Aras until relatively recent times. To find the fourth river, a little inter-lingual manipulation is needed. Within the area of the Tigris, Euphrates, and Gihon-Aras there is another river named the Uizun. An old scholar named Walker made an interesting etymological suggestion about this a few years ago. He argued that in Hebrew pronunciation the *u* became the labial *p* instead. The *z* of *Uizun* slides into a sibilant *sh* and the final syllable can interchange *a*, *u*, and *o* without difficulty.

There are other possibilities for the Gihon and the Pishon, of course, and these include the theories of scholar/historians Josephus, Eusebius, and Augustine that the Pishon was the Ganges. Other theologians, Jarchi, Gaon, and Nachman, argued that it was the Nile because the etymological root meant "to fill" or "to overflow." Other research in Armenia led researchers to the theory that the Pishon is now called the Halys and the Gihon has been renamed the Araxes.

So the geographical problem posed by the identity of the four rivers of Eden may well be solved eventually, but what of the ancient lands which were said to surround it?

After Abel's murder, his fratricidal brother, Cain, went to the east of Eden to an area known as Nod. Not far to the east of Eden, where Nod was said to lie, is the small contemporary settlement of Noqdi. Could the modern village of Noqdi be all that remains of the ancient, biblical Nod?

The great riddles of Eden, however, are theological and philosophical enigmas rather than geographical and historical ones. If the biblical account of creation is *literally* true — despite the enormous weight of scientific evidence that suggests that it is not: and, after all, even evolution's staunchest supporters will readily refer to it as a *theory* — then the philosopher and theologian are left asking *why* God chose to create our universe in the way that He did, and then to populate it with intelligent, observant beings.

The Yahweh of the Old Testament is described by many of its writers as a jealous guardian of his own power and glory: dominant, majestic, aloof, frequently awe-inspiring and terrifying. Even many centuries later when Christ portrays him as a benign, loving Father, the threat of judgment and condemnation to the everlasting tortures of hell still seem to be there.

The Graeco-Roman pantheon was comprised of gods with human characteristics, separated from us only by their longevity and superior powers. Human suffering could then be explained easily enough by their capriciousness, jealousy, anger, competitiveness, and frequent quarrels. There was no insoluble paradox for the Graeco-Roman theologian when good people suffered.

The difficulty of trying to reconcile the existence of a totally benign and loving God, who also enjoyed absolute power, with medieval torture and burning, the unspeakable horrors of the Holocaust, the atrocities in Kosovo, or the fiendish terrorists in Sierra Leone hacking off innocent victims' limbs to impose their reign of terror, could not exist for them. But it is an unavoidable, mind-splitting dilemma that confronts every honest theist who tries to explain the contradiction of God and human suffering.

There is some useful mileage left in the argument that centres on the essential nature of free will. It can readily and universally be accepted that true and spontaneous love is the greatest good and the greatest joy in the whole of human experience. It is equally true that such genuine love cannot exist without real free will. Love cannot be bought. It cannot be compelled. It cannot be commanded. It can only be given and received *freely* by independent minds, hearts, and spirits. Love is like respect: it can be stimulated, earned, and attracted by kindness, gentleness, mercy, and altruism.

Free will can provide the good, rich, fertile soil in which true love grows. It can also be the toxic waste in which unspeakable evil is spawned. Hitler *could* have chosen goodness. Freewill allowed him to choose the darkest form of evil instead. If the free will argument is valid, God could not prevent Hitler's evil without depriving him of his free will.

But what about hindering or preventing the consequences of Hitler's evil choices? Suppose God had allowed Hitler to think and plan his evil, but had then inspired and empowered heroes to thwart his plans and rescue his victims before that evil could be put into effect. Suppose that this pattern had recurred over and over again since the very beginning, since Eden itself.

But is free will itself diluted or destroyed if the *consequences* of evil choices are neutralized? What if every evil thought is prevented from expressing itself in evil action? Does evil then become an illusion, a hollow sham? Does the would-be murderer look round at the world and say, "There is no point in my shooting, stabbing, strangling or poisoning my victim because whatever evil I *try* to do will not have any *real* effect. God will simply intervene in some marvellous way: my gun will jam, the shot will miss, my knife will be deflected, my hands will be paralyzed just as they encircle the victim's throat, or the man will develop a sudden mysterious immunity to the cyanide capsule I've just dropped into his whisky glass."

If good thoughts and good actions can produce good, solid conse-quences, while evil thoughts and actions are ineffectual, then there is no true freedom of will. The realities of the consequences of good and evil actions must be equal, if the choice between them is to be a genuine choice. If God is totally benign and totally powerful, there can be no room for equivocation or prevarication. The absoluteness of divine goodness must include absolute honesty. A benign God cannot be a cosmic stage illusionist or a celestial confidence trickster.

There is also the argument of stability and consistency. If everything is arbitrary and uncertain, if cause and effect are not parent and child, then learning is impossible and progress nonexistent. If two plus two make three when they feel like it and five when they don't, if gunpowder explodes one day and not another, if arsenic kills today but not tomorrow, if affectionate embraces and a dagger in the heart come arbitrarily from the same unpredictable person, then life is impossible. So dare philosophers and theologians assume that God has made their universe consistent? Humanity can learn and develop only in a consistent environment. We can discover and eventually master the Laws of the Universe only if those laws remain faithful to themselves and to our powers of observation and objective experiment. If *consistency* is as important as *free will*, have we taken the first faltering steps along the road to a partial solution of the problem of suffering and death in a universe ruled by a caring and omnipotent God? Is this the first tentative answer to the Eden problem?

Obsessively puritanical, fanatical, religious sects have almost invariably connected original sin with sex. Phrases like "forbidden fruit" have been understood by them to refer symbolically to sexual activity — often sex in general, sometimes a specific sexual activity or orientation of which cult members disapprove. The curious and irrational belief that total celibacy or, failing that, varying degrees of sexual abstinence or self-denial, are in some inexplicable way pleasing to a loving, joy-giving, and creative God, may also be traced back — at least in part — to this confusion of sex and original sin. It hardly requires the wisdom and courage of Sigmund Freud, or some other pioneering psychoanalyst of his calibre, to suspect with good reason that the most strident advocates of sexual denial and restriction are likely to be those people with the most serious sexual hang-ups and misconceptions. Sex is as good, as natural and as benign as eating, drinking, breathing, and sleeping. It has its safety parameters, of course, just as they have. The wise man or woman does not knowingly eat or drink anything toxic, nor any food infected with salmonella. Neither is it acceptable to steal a neighbour's food. The sensible man or woman does not breathe contaminated air. But to imagine that God *wants* people to give up eating, drinking, or breathing, or wants them to feel guilty about those good and natural biological activities seems as far from the truth as the east is from the west.

So if the "forbidden fruit" has no sexual connotations at all, what might the author of Genesis mean by it? What exactly *was* the "Tree of the Knowledge of Good and Evil" which stood in the Garden of Eden?

Serious students of morality and ethics come up with a number of tantalizingly different answers. The famous Farmingdon Trust, which did outstandingly good work in the field in the late sixties, categorized three types of moral character and attitude. The first was the *psychotic*, whom the Farmingdon researchers described as an "emotional moral cripple." According to them, such people were cognitively aware of good and evil, but could distinguish them only in the way that normal people distinguish colour, size, weight, or shape. The psychotic would know that attacking elderly victims with an iron bar and stealing from them was "wrong" or "bad." He or she would know that housing the homeless or feeding the hungry was "right" and "good." The psychotic's problem is that "right" and "wrong" — "good" and "bad" — have no more *emotional* meaning for him or her than "left" and "right" or "up" or "down." Such distinctions as the psychotic makes are totally devoid of emotional context.

The second Farmingdon category was the *authoritarian moralist*, the man or woman of the sacred book, the unquestioning followers of the guru, of the official rules and regulations, or of the party manifesto. This attitude goes back to — or even far beyond — the days of the ancient Medes and Persians "whose law altereth not." Authoritarian moralists, despite all their inflexible faults and bureaucratic problems are still morally far ahead of the psychotics. Authoritarians are often deeply emotionally involved with their ethics. Good and evil matter to them. Their central weakness and their main focal problem is their inability to understand that what they regard as the ultimate and infallible source of moral authority can often be *wrong* — sometimes so hopelessly wrong that it disguises good as evil and evil as good. The famous Ten Commandments and the ancillary religious laws of the Old Testament — written on their literal and metaphorical Tablets of Stone — are the classical example of what typical authoritarians would recognize as an infallible and immutable ethical source. Tragically, in the name of such laws, authoritarians will resolutely and implacably imprison, torture, stone, or burn those who dare to disagree with them — and will then self-righteously convince themselves that the horrendous and inhuman evil which they are perpetrating is *good*. Matthew Hopkins, the Cromwellian Witchfinder General, was just such a man: as were the witch-finders of Salem.

The third Farmingdon type was referred to as the *autonomous moral thinker*. This is the man or woman who judges every moral situation on its merits, who refuses to jump on any particular ethical bandwagon — however popular or traditionally revered — without reserving the inalienable right to jump off again, if, in his opinion, the wagon appears to be rolling the wrong way. The autonomous moral thinker takes a *general* attitude of *Is this loving? Is this kind? Is this helpful? Will this give pleasure to someone while hurting no one else? Would I want this for myself?* The autonomous moral thinker takes all that he regards as best from every guru and from every rule book, while reserving the intellectual right to disagree. For the autonomous moral thinker, the ultimate source of ethical authority is *his own judgment* about whether a word or an action is acceptable to a God of love and mercy, whether a thought, word, or deed is kind, supportive, and benign. The autonomous moral thinker has the courage to go it alone, to accept full personal responsibility for his decisions. There is no rule book to hide behind. There is no guru to ask. You decide for *yourself* whether a thing is right or wrong — and then you speak or act accordingly.

So how does the Farmingdon analysis relate to the Tree of the Knowledge of Good and Evil in the Garden of Eden? What moral and ethical approach does that Tree represent? What does it symbolize? Did the literal or metaphorical eating of the fruit of that tree take Adam and Eve, as the literal or metaphorical parents of the human race, into a different moral dimension, something beyond a state of young, amoral innocence? Did it mean that after a certain point of development was reached they had to take on the moral responsibility of thinking for themselves — becoming autonomous moral thinkers instead of obeying unquestioningly, conforming unquestioningly?

That raises the great philosophical, theological, moral, and metaphysical question about whether simple obedience and unquestioning loyalty are "better" — more moral, more likely to produce inner peace and happiness — than wanting to think for yourself and make your own independent decisions. If an all-powerful God had wanted obedient robots, androids, or beings incapable of thinking for themselves, it would have been a very simple task to produce them. But if God chose to create free and autonomous beings who could genuinely accept or reject Him because they *wanted* to, who could genuinely choose between good or evil because they understood them, then the Tree and its fruit have profoundly deep meanings. Was that first choice the prototype of all truly autonomous choice? Was it the choice of whether to accept the terrible responsibility of having free will and the power to choose?

Who or what was the literal or metaphorical serpent and its fateful role in the Eden drama? In early Hebrew thought of the kind that must have been familiar to the author of Genesis, the serpent was a subtle, cunning, wily creature — like the fox in medieval western folklore. To what extent was the serpent seen as Satan himself, and to what extent was it thought of as being merely one of his agents or messengers of evil? The Talmudic authorities give the evil spirit, or demon, which tempted Eve a name: they call it Sammâel.

The Phoenicians, however, held the serpent in the highest esteem, and the ancient Chinese regarded it as a symbol of superior wisdom and power. Their early artwork depicted the kings of heaven (*tien-hoangs*) as having the bodies of serpents.

The Egyptians represented the eternal spirit *Kneph*, whom they regarded as the source of all good, in the form of a serpent. Paradoxically, *Tithrambo*, their god of revenge and punishment, was also represented in serpent form, as was *Typhon*, the terrible god of evil and immorality, who also appears in early Greek mythology as the son of Hera.

The serpent was frequently tamed and mummified in ancient Egypt, where it also has a role in the alphabet as a symbol of subtlety, cunning, and sensual pleasure.

The Greeks associated it with Aesculapius and healing, with Ceres, the good provider, and with the swift and benign Hermes or Mercury. On the opposite tack, they also linked it with the evil Furies, and in its Python form as a terrifying monster that only the arrows of the gods could bring down.

It is particularly interesting to note a parallel between the Eden account and the doctrine of Zoroaster, which relates how the evil god Ahriman appeared in the form of a serpent and taught humanity to sin.

In the writings of those researchers who wonder whether the ancient sacred texts like Genesis were partial recollections of extraterrestrial interference in human history, considerable emphasis is placed on the idea of possible rivalry or conflict between two distinct groups of technologically advanced aliens visiting Earth simultaneously. If one such rival group were physically serpentine in form, or, more probably, used a winged serpent as an emblem, information and instructions given to human beings by the *other* group would condemn the serpent as evil. The argument goes on to suggest that genetic engineering by the alien visitors — rather than a natural, Darwinian, evolutionary process — was responsible for the quantum leap in the development of the human mind and brain. Is it also possible that the record of Eve being created from one of Adam's ribs is a dim memory of a very advanced rapid cloning process?

If the Eden narrative is rewritten in terms of a genetic engineering laboratory, and the "forbidden fruit" is seen as exposure to some form of genetic contamination, then the expulsion of the contaminated breeding pair from their original, idyllic, garden laboratory into the dangerous world outside becomes a logical consequence of the contamination.

If one of their offspring, Cain, then demonstrates part of this hypothetical, genetic foul-up by murdering his brother, Abel, that would also seem to harmonize.

The idea that Eden was some sort of isolated, experimental bio-engineering reservation run by extraterrestrial technologists gets around the problem of where the other people came from among whom Cain went on his wanderings. It also goes some way toward offering one possible explanation of the mysterious identity of the "sons of God" who were said to have mated with mortal women in Genesis 6, verse 2, and whose offspring grew up to be "mighty men which were of old men of renown."

Eden is a garden of mystery in every sense. Some recent DNA research suggests that humanity did perhaps have just two ancestors. Were they God's deliberate, miraculous, and specific creation, as Genesis records, and as several other ancient sacred texts partially reinforce? Were they the work of extraterrestrial genetic engineers, and, if so, *why*? Are they likely to come back to see how their experiment is getting along? Or are we under constant observation already? The Eden narrative leaves vast questions unanswered — especially the problems of who God was talking to when He said, "Let *us* make man in *our* own image" (Genesis, chapter 1, verse 26); the identity of the "sons of God," and the origin of the people of Nod, among whom Cain wandered, and from among whom he presumably took his wife, the girl who became Enoch's mother. It is perfectly possible that the Supreme God of the Universe may have chosen to use his genetic engineers from another planet to create intelligent life on this one, just as it is perfectly possible that he used Darwinian evolution — or a modification of it — as one of his instruments. Neither concept raises the slightest theological difficulty nor does it present any challenge to faith: if anything, it makes God even more awesome and powerful than the authors, editors, and translators of Genesis realized.

Genesis, chapter 11, verses 1–9 give the biblical account of the Tower of Babel. At the heart of the story is one of the many quaint and colourful, aetiological or explanatory myths which purport to give reasons for various natural phenomena: thunder is the laughter of the gods — or their game of celestial skittles; the rainbow appeared after the flood as God's promise that the Earth would never again be destroyed by water; the robin has red feathers on its breast because it attempted to take out the crucifixion nails to end Christ's suffering.

The story of the Tower of Babel begins with the assertion that there was only one universal language in the beginning. In the course of their wanderings from the east "they" (an intriguing use of the plural pronoun, which the author of this section of Genesis may well have intended to include all of Adam and Eve's descendants, via Noah and the survivors of the flood), arrived at the Plain of Shinar. It was a pleasant enough spot, and they elected to stay for a while. It was then decided that it would be a good idea to build a permanent city there, and accordingly they set to work.

The Genesis account says that they used brick for stone and "slime" for mortar. There is general agreement among scholars specializing in the period that the word translated "slime" here probably refers to pitch or bitumen.

The Tower of Babel does not provide an explanation for the origins of language but for the differentiation of language. The origins of language do not seem to have concerned the authors, compilers, and redactors of Genesis. It seems probable that the writer's natural assumption was that language had been built into Adam and Eve along with their basic under-standing of themselves and their environment.

Paleolinguistic studies seem to suggest that language and thought patterns evolved in mutually reinforcing roles — like acrobats who raise themselves on piles of wooden blocks by adding a block at a time to each pile on which their hands balance alternately.

Hunting, especially with primitive flint weapons, was likely to prove most successful when groups of hunters co-operated. Co-operation — unless we consider the theory that our earliest ancestors were telepathic — was almost certainly improved by language. The earliest aural signals may have conveyed basic, but vital, hunting messages such as "Go forward. Go back. Move toward me. Move away from me. Keep still and silent. It's coming toward you."

The technique of a skilled shepherd controlling his dogs with simple sounds, elementary proto-words, or whistle signals could be similar to the proto-words with which paleolithic hunting parties coordinated their movements.

The authors and editors of Genesis probably felt that they had to try to provide an explanation for the apparent anomaly: if all persons were descended from Adam and Eve, why did Babylonians, Israelites, and Canaanites speak different languages?

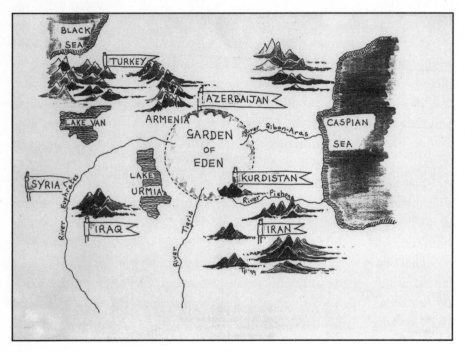

Map of Eden and its location.

There is an interesting and mysterious connection between the Babel story and the Apostles speaking in tongues. On the day of Pentecost, all those to whom the Apostles preached heard the words in their own language — yet the Apostles were Galileans. Some analysts of this "speaking-with-tongues" phenomenon have wondered whether the Apostles were using Koine Greek — a simplified version that resembles classical Greek in much the same way that Pidgin resembles standard English, and which was widely used and understood throughout the Roman Empire.

GLOSSOLALIA

Psycho-linguistics experts have investigated numerous cases of glossolalia, a state in which a subject with no apparent conscious knowledge or recollection of another language can apparently speak it fluently. In the most interesting reports of glossolalia, some subjects have been able to *speak* their mysterious unknown language but have not known the *meaning* of the words they were saying. At other times subjects appear to have been able to understand the *meaning*, but have not been able to *reply* in the strange language.

The precise nature of the neurological and physiological processes involved in speaking and understanding a given set of audible signals (or visual symbols in the case of a written language) is complex and controversial. Most linguistic scientists would probably agree that the process is basically an associative one: a distinct, discrete sound, or sound pattern, becomes associated with an object (noun) or an activity (verb). If different human groups evolved at different sites at different times, their chosen sound patterns for denoting different actions and different objects would in all probability be totally arbitrary, with the exception of certain onomatopoeia.

If, however, the Eden origins of *Homo sapiens* are to be taken literally and historically, then a single "language of Eden" would be the logical sequel.

Investigation seems to suggest, rather tantalizingly, however, that the oldest roots of modern languages *do* tend to converge in the remote past. DNA investigations have also indicated the possibility of a common ancestor — maybe from the vicinity of the Olduvai Gorge.

The word *Babel* seems to have been derived from an ancient Hebrew root meaning "to confound" or "to confuse" and would seem to refer to the story of the tower that was never completed because its builders lost the power to understand one another's languages.

It has been suggested that slaves taken by the Babylonians to carry out their grandiose building projects were dependent upon interpreters among the Babylonian overseers. If a slaves' rebellion — or an outbreak of plague — led to the deaths of these interpreters, almost total confusion would have ensued, leading to probable abandonment of the site.

The Babylonians referred to their city as Bab-ili, Babila, or Babilam, meaning "the gate of God." It was also known as Babilani — "the gate of the gods." The ancient Akkadians called it Ka-dingira, which also meant "the gate of god," as well as Tin-tir —"the seat of life." Its other titles included E or E-ki, meaning "house" or "hollow place." Yet another ancient title was Su-anna, meaning the city with the high defence.

The mysterious "they" of Genesis 2, verses 2–9, may refer solely to the Cushites, followers of Nimrod, the much acclaimed "mighty hunter" of Chapter 10, listed in the ancient genealogies as the great-grandson of Noah through Ham's line. They seem to have referred to themselves as the people of Kingi-Ura, and are known in some scholarly circles as the Sumero-Akkadians. It is likely that they migrated to Shinar from some original location in the northeast of Mesopotamia.

Their building materials were mainly bricks and bitumen, and their earliest city layout seems to have been a relatively basic collection of dwellings scattered around a central temple-tower which they called the Zikkuratu.

Part of the mystery of the city of Babel and its vast tower is its great age. It is mentioned before Erech, Akkad, and Calneh in the account in Genesis 10, and almost certainly predates them by many centuries. The Greek historians of Alexander's time questioned the Babylonians about it, and were given a nominal date of 2230 B.C. The city is undoubtedly much older than that.

The principal god of Babylon was known as Merodach and the city was regarded as his sacred dwelling in a very special and particular way. It was often referred to as "Babilu mahaz Marduk" which translates as "Babylon the stronghold of Merodach."

This Merodach had a consort called Zir-panitum, the principal goddess of Babylon. Innana, Nana, or Ishtar was also regarded as one of the most important patron deities of ancient Babylon.

The great Hammurabi, known in Babylonian as Kimta-rapastum, was king of Babylon round about 2120 B.C., and was a clearly established member of the Babylonian Dynasty.

Throughout the ensuing centuries, there was continual war between Babylon and Assyria. The great city and its magnificent temples were destroyed and rebuilt on numerous occasions, any of which could have been the inspiration of the Tower of Babel story.

Nebuchadnezzar was a particularly vigorous rebuilder and restorer, as Daniel, chapter 4, verse 30, clearly indicates. Antiochus Soter was probably the last Babylonian king to carry out any restorations. The bold and decisive Xerxes plundered Babylon and intrepidly carried away the golden statue from the Temple of Belus, which Darius had hesitated to remove for religious reasons. By the time Alexander the Great got there, the city was in ruins once again. He originally decided to restore Babylon's former glories, but even Alexander's brilliant imagination drew back from the awesome logistics of a task that would have needed ten thousand labourers simply to clear away the rubble before the rebuilding began. After the death of Alexander, the decay and desolation of Babylon continued for many centuries.

TOO MANY RUINED TOWERS?

The biblical mystery of the Tower of Babel and its alleged consequences for global languages remains unsolved. It is not that there are *no* ruined Babylonian towers to which archaeologists can refer: there are, if anything, rather *too many*.

While the Israelites were undertaking their long journey through the wilderness after Moses had led them out of Egypt, their central place of worship was the Tabernacle, and the holiest object within the Tabernacle was the Ark of the Covenant, the Hebrew title of which can also be interpreted as the Ark of the Testimony. Together with the Mercy Seat situated on its lid, this ark was the centre of the Israelites' sacred mystery.

As far as can be ascertained from Exodus, chapter 25, it was cuboid in shape, 1 ½ cubits wide, 1 ½ deep, and 2 ½ long. The biblical cubit was approximately forty-five centimetres or eighteen inches — the length of a human forearm from elbow to fingertips. It was made of fine acacia wood overlaid with gold on both sides.

The Mercy Seat was placed above the ark, and supported a cherub at each end. It was regarded as the symbolic throne of God. When the ark was in place within the Tabernacle, or later within the Holy of Holies in the Temple, a luminous cloud known as the Shechinah was seen to hover above it, and was clearly distinguished from the familiar smoke created by incense.

Tower of Babel.

ACACIA WOOD

Acacia wood, a genus of the mimosa family, or *Mimosaceae*, is found mainly in Africa and Australia, as well as in the Middle East. Acacia flowers tend to be small and fragrant, and are almost always yellow or white. One variety found in the Sudan is the source of gum arabic, used as glue or as an emulsifier in sweets, inks, adhesives, and chemical products. The bark of most acacias is also a rich source of tannin. The acacias yield interesting and unusual wood, particularly appropriate for the sacred Ark of the Covenant.

The Shechinah was reported during the days of the Tabernacle and while Solomon's Temple stood, but apparently it was no longer seen in Zerubbabel's Temple, as it was one of the five things that some Jewish writers maintained was missing from this later temple.

Dr. Bernard in his notes on Josephus disagrees. He argues from Josephus's records that as the mysterious *Urim* and *Thummim* were said to be in Zerubbabel's Temple, the other four significant "missing" things must have been there as well.

The first reference to the Shechinah is found in the Targums. A Targum in Aramaic literally means a translation or an interpretation, so the Targums were translations of portions of the Hebrew Bible — or, indeed, the whole of it — into Aramaic. At one time the word meant a translation of the Old Testament into any language at all, but was honed down over the years to refer specifically to a translation from the old Hebrew into the later Aramaic.

> The word **Shechinah** comes from an old root meaning "to rest," "to settle," or "to dwell." It is not found in the Bible itself, but was widely used by later Jews, and borrowed from them by Christians. It signified the visible majesty of the Divine Presence, particularly when God was thought to be especially there in the area between the Cherubim on the lid of the sacred ark.

The Targums were produced to meet the spiritual and religious needs of the great majority of Jewish worshippers who found it difficult if not impossible to cope with ancient classical Hebrew.

When the Herodian Temple was destroyed in A.D. 70, the Targums came into their own. Synagogues had to replace the lost temple, and the central readings in the synagogue services needed to be translated into Aramaic for the benefit of most of the worshippers. As time went on, the Targums assumed the role of commentaries, and a special meturgeman attempted to explain away any confusions or doubtful meanings.

Wise sayings, proverbs, aphorisms, allegories, and legends crept into the Targums as time went on, so that the later ones were very different from the straightforward translations that had been the main purpose of the originals.

From its special use in the Targums, the concept of Shechinah came to signify the actual *presence* of God on Earth as far as the early Jewish theologians and scholars were concerned. One reason for this was a fear on the part of the writers of the Talmud, Midrash, and Targums that some of the clearly anthropomorphic descriptions of God in the earlier writings might cause serious misunderstandings. The idea of a God who looked like an amorphous cloud of glowing mist — rather than a human being — undoubtedly seemed theologically *safer* to them than the earlier concepts of an undeniably humanoid God who walked in the Garden of Eden in the cool of the evening looking for Adam and Eve.

Some theologians have considered the existence of a parallel between the concept of the Shechinah and the idea of the Holy Spirit. Other, mainly medieval, theologians have tried to work out theories of the Shechinah as a separate Divine Being, *Someone* or *Something* created by God, perhaps a personified representation of Divine Glory or Divine Light.

ARAMAIC

It was after the Exile in Babylon that Aramaic became the preferred spoken language of the Palestinian Jews, and so replaced their original Hebrew. Just as Latin lingered among European academics and ecclesiastical scholars long after it had ceased to be spoken by Roman Legionaries, so Hebrew lingered among Jewish academics and scholars until well after the first century of the Christian era, although by then Aramaic was firmly established in the eastern Mediterranean area.

In one of the sadder short stories of H.G. Wells, a character goes in search of Light but falls to his death in the process — the Wellsian concept of Light in the mind of the tragic hero in this particular story comes surprisingly close to the medieval theological concept of the Shechinah.

Yet another Jewish idea connected with the Shechinah was that it would return when the long-promised Messiah came. In the Gospel account of the Transfiguration of Jesus, when the disciples Peter, James, and John witnessed him shining with his rightful Divine Glory on the mountaintop with Moses and Elijah, the Shechinah could well have been put forward as an explanation.

To what extent can this extremely mysterious and powerful Shechinah light be associated with the records of the Exodus? Many of the biblical accounts surround it with a cloud, so that the brilliant radiance of the Shechinah shines *through* the cloud. In the Exodus account, "The Lord went before the Israelites by day in a pillar of cloud and by night in a pillar of fire." Philo interprets this as, "The fiery appearance of the Deity shone forth from the cloud."

Philo's ideas are always well worth considering. Philo Judaeus, who was also known as Philo of Alexandria, was born in 15 B.C. and died in A.D. 50. He was a brilliantly intelligent, Greek-speaking, Jewish philosopher and theologian, whose great pioneering contribution to human thought was his attempt to reconcile faith with reason — an exceedingly difficult but supremely worthwhile intellectual task. Philo came of an extremely wealthy and influential family in Alexandria. He studied at one of the Greek Gymnasiums, where he mastered mathematics, astronomy, philosophy, grammar, and logic. He also made a deep study of rhetoric, like all other young academics of his time and place.

Unlike his more ascetic scholarly colleagues, Philo had the profound good sense to *enjoy* life as well as to think about its philosophical meaning. He was a keen boxing fan, an enthusiastic theatre-goer, and a devotee of chariot racing. When he wasn't pursuing any of these sensible and healthy interests, he was enjoying an evening of good food and lavish entertainment: he was, in short, a practical *bon viveur* as well as a great thinker. Philo's love of a "middle way" between the extremes of Jewish scriptural fundamentalism on one hand and a liberal disregard of the old laws because they were considered to be "only parables" on the other, would have made him quite a comfortable member of the present-day Anglican Church. He is far and away our most valuable, reliable and informative source of knowledge of the Hellenistic Judaism that was practised in Alexandria in his day.

The highlight of Philo's career, however, was an occasion in the year A.D. 39 on which he displayed great courage and integrity when he dared to lead a delegation of Alexandrian Jews to complain to Caligula about

METURGEMAN

The meturgeman, meaning "interpreter" or "translator," refers to a person who stood beside the reader of the Torah in the ancient synagogue and recited the Aramaic translation of the Bible. Rules set forth in the Talmud and other rabbinic literature state that the meturgeman was to stand upright next to the reader, reciting orally (not from a written text), and not raising his voice louder than that of the reader. These rules were invoked in order to preserve the importance of the original Hebrew text.

a recent pogrom in their city: the ignorant and prejudiced Greek orator Apion, who was opposing Philo, had just delivered a despicable racist attack on the Jews. Philo was on the point of refuting Apion's nonsense when Caligula decided he did not wish to hear any more arguments at that time. Philo, one of those rare beings who dared to risk the wrath of Caligula, told his colleagues not to be disheartened because God would very shortly deal with the insane Roman emperor. Shortly afterward, to everyone's delight, Caligula was assassinated. A man like Philo definitely deserves to be heard.

So what was this strange and mysterious Shechinah that was associated with the even more mysterious Ark of the Covenant?

Looked at disinterestedly and objectively, the ark was not an exclusively Jewish artifact. The ancient Egyptians used Arks for religious purposes, as well, and there is a possibility that when Moses led the Israelite slaves out of bondage in Egypt, the ark and its contents came with them. Had Moses with his secret inner knowledge of the Egyptian Court — he had, after all, been raised as an Egyptian prince — brought some great and powerful ancient treasure away with him? Was that why Pharaoh, upon discovering its loss, had launched his finest chariots suicidally across the treacherous bed of the Red Sea?

If distinguished researchers like Colin Wilson and Graham Hancock are right, and some of the technological wonders of very ancient civilizations escaped terrifying inundations or major disasters caused by ice and polar change, did any of those advanced artifacts find their way to Egypt? Was the dangerously powerful Ark of the Covenant itself one such object, or was it the carefully shielded and insulated *container* for such an object? Was it the operation of a long-forgotten technology rather than the presence of a deity that caused the Shechinah?

The 1999 discoveries by the *Joides Resolution* scientists drilling the bed of the Indian Ocean have tentatively indicated the ancient inundation of a huge land mass almost a third the size of Australia. Fifty million years ago it was a lush and fertile land. Dinosaurs grazed on the abundant vegetation that grew there. Twenty million years ago movements of the Earth's crust started it on its long journey to the ocean bed. If one such great land mass could go down, why not others?

Whether it was the work of Egyptian craftsmen, Israelite craftsmen, survivors of Atlantis, or extraterrestrial aliens, the Ark of the Covenant was described as thickly covered with gold. Apart from its commercial and artistic value, gold has the great practical advantages of being easy to work and massively resistant to corrosion — it also acts as an effective radiation shield. If there was an artifact inside the ark — some sort of weapon, perhaps — was it nuclear powered? Could the Shechinah have been a glow of pure energy, visible only when the machine was operating — in other words, when "God" was present and active?

Alongside the high-profile, magical, miraculous, and historical mysteries recorded in the Bible, there are some equally intriguing low-profile, behavioural mysteries. The strange sequence of events in the exotic house on the walls of Jericho is one of these.

At first glance the story is straightforward enough. Joshua, the brilliant Hebrew general who took over the leadership when Moses died, wisely decided to send two spies to the Canaanite city of Jericho before attacking it.

THE SCARLET CORD

In Middle Eastern cities of that period, inns, taverns, and brothels tended to be situated near the gates so that travellers arriving in the city could locate them easily. A scarlet cord hanging from a window and a scarlet lamp above the door would indicate the nature of the premises.

As the Hebrew spies approached, they saw at once that one particular brothel situated on the city wall would be an ideal vantage point from which to study the gate and other defences.

Once inside, they meet Rahab and arrange to stay. Nerves are on edge in Jericho. News of Joshua's previous military successes against the neighbouring Canaanite strongholds has already reached the city. The arrival of the Hebrew spies has been quietly observed. News of their arrival reaches the king. He sends for Rahab and demands to know where these two dangerous men are.

She reports that they were there earlier, but had slipped away at dusk just before the gates were due to be secured for the night. She assures the king that a swift patrol would almost certainly be able to overtake them.

Meanwhile, she hides them in the flax in case she is not believed and a search party is sent to the house. She begs them to save her and her family when the Hebrew army storms Jericho.

They make her a solemn promise, and instruct her to bring her family together into this house on the wall when the attack starts. They explain that it is vitally important for her to mark the window with the scarlet cord so that the house can be identified.

At the first opportunity, Rahab lowers them down the wall on that same scarlet cord and advises them to make for the mountains and hide there until the patrol gives up the search for them.

The plan works. They remain in the mountains for a day or two, then return safely to the Hebrew camp and report everything to Joshua.

When the attack on Jericho takes place, they go to Rahab's house while the carnage rages all round it. No one else is spared. Jericho is devastated and destroyed. The vow to Rahab and her family is faithfully kept. Intriguingly, Joshua, chapter 6, verse 25, records that "Rahab is with us to this day," indicating that she married a Hebrew and that their descendants were still thriving in the Hebrew nation when the book of Joshua came to be written.

The story as it stands, however, raises several challenging behavioural mysteries. Why did the spies feel sure that they could trust Rahab? Why did she feel certain that she could trust them? They literally trusted one another with their very lives. Do strangers of different nationalities normally offer and accept that kind of ultimate trust?

Their trust was not only mutually offered and accepted: subsequent events proved that it was totally justified by the solid gold integrity of both parties. Spies and prostitutes both live in convoluted serpentine worlds where honesty and integrity are rarer than lap-dancers in a monastery. Rahab herself had no difficulty in telling the king of Jericho a yarn that would have done justice to Baron von Munchausen.

Despite the nature of her work, Rahab was undoubtedly deeply devoted to her family. It wasn't solely her own life she begged for: she wanted to save her parents, brothers, and sisters, as well. And why were the spies so determined to keep their word to her? It's easy enough under the stresses of war for integrity to be the first casualty. Promises are even more vulnerable than flesh and bone when bloodstained swords are swinging in the desperate heat of battle and the only law is kill or be killed. Yet their promise to Rahab and her family was sacrosanct to the two Hebrew spies? Why?

Is it possible that Rahab was a Jewish girl? The well-known account of Joseph and his coat of many colours is a stark reminder that Canaan was infested with opportunist slave traders of the kind who sold Joseph in Egypt. The Hebrew families who straggled out of Egypt with Moses easily became separated from their main column. It would have been the easiest thing in the world for slave traders to abduct Rahab and her family under cover of darkness.

But how to get the best price for them in Jericho? Beautiful young Rahab is undoubtedly the jewel in the crown, and the slavers know exactly where to take her. The proprietor of the house on the wall begins the long, inevitable haggling. No, he has no interest in the others. They might just be worth a handful of silver as domestic servants…. It is only Rahab who is worth gold because she can earn gold. The others are practically a liability. The parents might just as well be killed now. They will not really justify the price of feeding them. If the girl proves difficult and uncooperative, even she may not be worth anything. The slavers understand the haggling arguments only too well.

Then, to everyone's surprise, the spirited and intelligent slave girl intervenes. She understands perfectly well what is going on, what their problems are. Perhaps she can help them all?

Rahab and her family captured by slave traders.

The proprietor and the slavers listen attentively. What if she is willing to be totally committed to her work and to making her customers happy? She could earn far more for him than three or four desperately unhappy girls who have to be starved and beaten into reluctant, passive submission. She will attract extra customers for him. In return, will he allow her family to stay, too, as domestic servants, to gather wood, to fetch water, to prepare flax for linen, to spin, to weave, to clean? One price for the whole family and she will be the best harlot in Jericho.

If he doesn't believe her, would he like to prove it for himself. She will sleep with him here … now … then he can decide if she's worth what she's asking. There are nods and smiles.…

The proprietor leads Rahab to his couch.… He is more than satisfied that she can honour her bargain. Money changes hands. She has won. The family who mean more to her than her own life are safe.… Just as importantly, she has kept them together.

As long as they are alive and together there is always hope of rescue. Joshua will conquer this land before long. They will go back to their people. This house on the wall will be like a nightmare that fades when the sun rises.

One day two strangers come in. Something about them makes her wonder. Dare she ask them who they are and where they're from? Could they possibly be Joshua's men?

She dare not speak to them in Hebrew. The house is full of local clients and local girls. One wrong word and the strangers — if they are Joshua's men — will be captured. Her persistent hope of rescue will be disappointed. One of the men beckons and smiles. Money changes hands. She takes him to her room. As they undress she sees that he is circumcized. Now they are alone she dares to whisper in Hebrew. His eyes brighten. He smiles warmly. He answers her in Hebrew. She tells him her story. He tells her why he and his brother are there.

The attack on Jericho will not be long delayed. They talk urgently about the present danger to him and the imminent danger to her and her family when the great attack begins. In the heat of battle, no Israeli soldier will have time to stay his sword stroke at the urgent pleading of a girl dressed as a Jericho harlot.

Rahab is already very concerned that someone will have reported the spies' presence in the city … even reported that they are in her house on the wall.… It will be best if she hides them among the flax.…

They are no sooner safely hidden than messengers arrive from the king. She plans her story quickly. She's quick-witted as well as beautiful. That's what saved her family after the slavers brought them all to Jericho. Yes, of course, the men were here. One of them was her client. They left soon afterward. She's almost certain that they've left the city. If the king's soldiers pursue them swiftly it should not be difficult to overtake them. It is an honour to be of service to the king.

As soon as it is dark enough, she lowers the men down the same strong red cord that hangs from the window to tell the world what the house on the wall has to offer, the same scarlet cord that is destined to save her life....

So her integrity is absolute, and so is theirs. It is a life for a life, an infinite trust for an infinite trust.

The collapsing walls leave Jericho totally vulnerable. The invincible Israeli army storms through from all directions. The two spies race for the house on the wall. Rahab's family are gathered with her. All are safe. Her courage and intelligence have saved them a second time. The spy she spoke with has his arms protectively around her lovely young shoulders — but not for money this time. There is a powerful bond between people who have saved each other's lives.

So there is a fairy-tale happy ending. They marry. They raise a family.

And at the time when the book of Joshua was written, Rahab's descendants were thriving among their fellow Israelites. Hopefully, they still are.

4 MYSTERIES OF LAKES, SEAS, AND OCEANS

Matthew Arnold (1822–1888), son of the famous Thomas Arnold, Headmaster of Rugby School, graduated from Balliol College, Oxford, and spent more than thirty years as a school inspector. During those decades he also wrote a great deal of excellent and memorable poetry, and was at one time a professor of poetry at Oxford.

His poem "The Forsaken Merman" tells the poignant story of a merman who had married an Earth-girl, who subsequently — so it seems from Arnold's version — left him and their children and returned to her humankind on land. Arnold's poem begins,

> Come, dear children, let us away;
> Down and away below!
> Now my brothers call from the bay,
> Now the great winds shoreward blow,
> Now the salt tides seaward flow;
> Now the wild white horses play,
> Champ and chaff and toss in the spray.
> Children dear, let us away!
> This way, this way …

> … Call her once before you go —
> Call once yet!
> In a voice that she will know:
> "Margaret! Margaret!"

In Arnold's version of the story, however, the faithless Margaret never returns to her Merman and their children. His version ends,

> … Singing: "There dwells a loved one,
> But cruel is she!
> She left lonely forever
> The kings of the sea."

When myths and legends are as persistent as the many stories of mermaids told and retold over thousands of years in song and story, they cannot be dismissed without serious investigation and analysis. A few years before Matthew Arnold was born, another educationalist, William Munro, a schoolmaster from Scotland, wrote a letter to the *Times*, in which he described in great detail a sighting that he himself had made of "a figure resembling an unclothed human female, sitting upon a rock extending into the sea, and apparently in the action of combing its hair, which flowed around its shoulders, and was of a light brown colour …" Munro watched the strange being for some three or four minutes before it slid off its rock and down into the sea. He continued watching carefully, but it never reappeared.

The *London Mirror* of November 16, 1822, reported that John McIsaac from Corphine in Kintyre, Scotland, had made a very similar sighting in 1811. Like the creature that Munro saw, McIsaac's mermaid had long hair which it tended to continually.

Were dugongs like this ever mistaken for mermaids?

Other early-nineteenth-century mermaid observers included a girl named Mackay, whose description of what she had seen along the Caithness coast tallied closely with William Munro's account in his letter to the Times.

In co-author Lionel's poetry anthology, *Earth, Sea and Sky*, there is a different, happier conclusion to the merman's story, entitled "The Merman's Wife Returns":

> There was an answer to the merman's call,
> A faltering step towards the beckoning sea.
> "Wait for me, children. Husband, wait for me."
> The voice they knew and loved, but faint with pain;
> Her children skim the waves to reach the shore.
> Her merman husband bounds across the sands,
> Sweeps her into his arms — his bride once more —
> Strong fingers close around her bleeding hands.
> "What have they done to you, my love, my life?"
> "They could not understand our unity.
> They hated me. They said I was unclean,
> A thing apart, because I lived with you.
> They would not let me go back to the sea,
> Our home of pearl and shell beneath the waves,
> Our lovers' wonderland of coral caves…
> But I broke free… Somehow I found the strength
> To pull my hands clear of their iron bands…
> Their prejudice, their bias and their hate… "
> The merman gently kissed her bleeding hands
> And held her very close, their children too.
> They understood the cost of her escape.
> Rejoicing in the power of her love…
> Safe in their cool, green sea they headed home,
> Their family re-united, strong, complete…
> And in the merman's heart the ocean sang.

Eighteen hundred years before either Munro or Mackay reported their mermaid sightings in Scotland, Gaius Plinius Secundus — better known as Pliny the Elder — was born in A.D. 23 in what was then called Transpadane Gaul: it now forms part of modern Italy. Before his tragic death caused by volcanic fumes from Vesuvius in A.D. 79, Pliny had written a *Natural History* that endured as a standard reference work for centuries — until rational, scientific biologists began to express doubts about some of what they considered to be dubious myths and legends that Pliny had incorporated along with his factual material. In his mermaid section, Pliny wrote,

> Mermaids are not fables. They are, in fact, as the artists depict them. Their bodies, however, are scaly and rough, even where they seem most human. A mermaid was seen by many witnesses close to the shore. It was dying, and the local inhabitants heard it crying pitifully.

Henry Hudson, famous for his heroic but tragic seventeenth-century voyages in quest of the North West Passage, names two of his ship's company, Thomas Hilles and Robert Rayner, as witnesses to a mermaid sighting in an area then known as Novaya Zemlya.

FAROE ISLANDS MERMAN

A Danish Royal Commission went out to make a serious investigation of the mer-folk phenomena in 1723. Not far from the Faroe Islands, members of the commission reported that they had actually seen a merman. It submerged as they approached and then surfaced again, staring at them with a horrible, fixed intensity. This so unnerved the commission that they ordered their skipper to withdraw. Their apparent retreat caused the creature — whatever it was — to give vent to an almighty roar, and submerge again, like an animal that has triumphantly defended its territorial boundaries against intruders.

Sir Richard Whitbourne, who originally came from Exmouth in Devonshire — famous two centuries later for the trail of mysterious footprints crossing the estuary of the River Exe — was practically a contemporary of Hudson. Whitbourne reported sighting something *similar* to a mermaid in 1610, but his report is especially significant in that it describes whatever he saw as having blue streaks around its head, *resembling* hair: but Sir Richard was adamant that these streaks were definitely *not* hair.

Writing about mer-folk in *The Natural History of Norway* (1752–53), no less a dignitary than Bishop Erik Pontoppidan himself declared, "In the Diocese of Bergen, here, and also in the Manor called Nordland, there are many honest and reliable witnesses who most strongly and positively affirm that they have seen creatures of this type."

Various reports of the infamous Amboina mermaids are also worth reporting in outline. Now named Ambon, the Indonesian island once known as Amboina, or Amboyna, is about ten kilometres off the southwestern coast of Seram Island. Its highest point is the summit of Mount Salhatu, and although Ambon is not entirely free from earthquakes, there is no volcanic activity. It does, however, have hot gas vents called *solfataras* as well as hot springs. The climate is tropical, and rainfall is heavy. There are many varieties of fish in Teluk Bay, and some of them are bizarre, which might have given rise to the mermaid sightings.

Dutch writer Francois Valentijn compiled *The Natural History of Amboina*, published in 1726, and containing accounts of mermaids as well as illustrations purporting to illustrate them. He calls them *Zee-Menschen* and *Zee-Wyven*. Valentijn's illustration had already appeared in 1718 in a book called *Poissons, Ecrivisses et Crabes ... des Isles Moluques*. The artist responsible for the picture in both volumes was Samuel Fallours, who held the rank of Official Artist to the Dutch East India Company.

The description accompanying Fallours' illustration said that the creature was about 1.5 metres long and resembled a siren. After being captured, the unlucky *Zee-Wyf* was kept in a barrel of water. Not surprisingly, declining to eat anything, it died about a week later — after making a few faint mewing, squeaking noises that reminded its captors of a mouse.

Tales of the mermaid of Amboina reached the illustrious ears of Tsar Peter the Great, and George III of England, and Valentijn was interrogated further. In response to the imperial interrogation, he came up with an account of an East Indies Company Officer who had seen a pair of the strange mer-folk swimming together near Hennetelo, a village in the Administrative District of Amboina. After several weeks these two creatures were seen again — this time by forty or more witnesses. They were described as being a greyish-green and shaped like human beings from the head down to the waist — after which their bodies tapered like the tail-halves of large fish.

WOODEN MERMAID

On co-author Lionel's Channel 4 U.K. television series, one of the mysteries investigated was what purported to be a wizened, mummified mermaid, but which, under the pathologist's knife, turned out to have been carved entirely from wood. A theory advanced at the time was that these carved figures were meant as votive offerings by Polynesian and other fishing peoples and were cast into the sea at appropriate places to please the gods, so ensuring a profitable catch and a safe return for the fishermen.

Other mermaids in various sideshows and exhibitions where admission fees were charged almost always turned out to have been carefully crafted by skilled taxidermists from the upper body of a monkey and the rear end of a fish.

A rather more detailed and convincing historical account comes from Orford in East Anglia in England, where medieval fishermen apparently caught a merman in 1204. In those days, the port of Orford on England's east coast was relatively prosperous. The event is related by Ralph of Coggeshall, a monastic chronicler of that epoch.

According to Ralph's version of the case, a group of sturdy East Anglian fishermen were having a struggle to get their nets onboard because of a large creature that had somehow become entangled with their catch. When the net finally lay in the bottom of their boat, what looked very much like a man was glaring up at them from among the squirming fish. In Ralph's account, the merman was unclothed but covered in hair — except for the top of his head, which was bald. Another very human feature was his long beard, which was described as straggly. The Orford men tried to talk to their captive, but his best replies were little more than grunting noises. Not knowing what else to do with him, the fishermen took him to the castle and handed him over to the Warden, Bartholomew de Gladville. Gladville wasn't too sure about him either and decided to keep him there as a prisoner. The merman responded positively to a raw fish diet, but still refused to speak — almost certainly because he couldn't. It was noted by his jailers that when he was offered a piece of fish, he squeezed the liquid from it first and drank it.

In desperation, Gladville resorted to torture to try to get some intelligible words from his strange aquatic prisoner, but even when he was hung upside down the merman would not (or could not) talk. On being taken to church, he showed neither knowledge of, nor interest in, religion. The humane side of Gladville coming to the top, however briefly, he ordered his men to sling nets across the harbour mouth and allow the merman to swim for a little while — probably in the hope that if their prisoner felt happier, he might say something. For a swimmer of the merman's ability, the line of nets presented no barrier at all. He simply dived under them and vanished out to sea. After one or two triumphant appearances above the waves, he left the Orford area and was never seen again.

The nature of his real identity remains an unsolved mystery today.

What might still provide clues to the enigma of the mer-folk is what is *alleged* to be the actual grave of a mermaid in the cemetery at Nunton in the Hebrides, off the coast of Scotland. She was found dead on the beach in 1830, and was described in the traditional way — human to the waist and fish from there downward. The human part apparently seemed so human that the sympathetic islanders felt that a decent burial was called for. With the scientific advantages of twenty-first-century DNA analysis, that grave could well be worth very careful investigation.

John Smith — associated with Pocahontas in the rather controversial story of his rescue by the beautiful young indigenous American princess — also features as a reporter of romantic mermaid sightings. In the West Indies in 1614, Smith claimed that he had seen a mermaid so attractive that he had at first mistaken her for a human girl bathing. Closer inspection, however, revealed that she had luxuriant green hair, and in Smith's own phrasing "from below the waist the woman gave way to fish."

Christopher Columbus is also credited with sighting mermaids. He reported seeing no fewer than three of them "leaping out of the water," but it seems much more likely that what Columbus actually observed were dugongs, because he added rather disappointedly that they were "not so fair as they were said to be."

Ovid, the Roman poet, also known as Naso, born in 43 B.C., suggested imaginatively that mermaids were born from the burning galleys of the defeated Trojans. But where did they really come from? Could the manatee and the dugong be all there is at the back of the innumerable mermaid legends? Or is there more to all those reported sightings? The myths and legends of the mer-folk may be connected to the strange and ancient accounts of various marine deities such as Oannes — or demigods like the Tritons — that persist in various shapes and sizes in religious writings all over the world.

Two of the most famous ancient Greek sea monster accounts are remarkably similar: in the first, a fearless hero rescues Princess Hesione from the monster which Poseidon had sent to terrorize Troy; in the second, another hero, Perseus, rescues Andromeda from a parallel fate. So, reports of marine monsters go back a very long way. Early Greek poetry, for example, referred to the battle between the mighty Herakles (Hercules) and one of the terrifying Ketea — the awesome sea monsters under Poseidon's control, sent out by him much as gangland bosses send out their hitmen today.

According to these classical accounts, the creatures were insatiably hungry and resorted to cannibalism when there was no other prey readily available. Oppian, the poet, referred to them frequently and in detail in

Ancient Greek artwork showing Herakles fighting Ketos, a sea monster.

his work *Halieutica* — a treatise on fishing. His book warns that they appear most frequently in the Iberian Sea off the coast of Spain. These ancient Ketea are frequently described as more elongated and serpentine than normal fish.

There is a powerful and persistent nexus between Greek history and mythology and monsters of the deep. One of the most intriguing stories told about Alexander the Great is that he was an intrepid pioneer of the diving bell and that inside a specially constructed glass bell he watched a sea monster so vast that it took three full days to pass his submarine observation post.

Reports of sea monsters are also right up to date. The authors were called in by BBC television to investigate some very interesting reports of sightings in 2003 in Pembroke Dock, Wales. We interviewed four of the eyewitnesses there, and then set out for a couple of hours in the *Cleddau King* — a superb boat for the job, fully equipped with high-tech electronic search gear.

Our first witness was David Crew, Landlord of the Shipwright Inn, Pembroke Dock, Wales. This is what David told us:

> On Wednesday March 5, 2003, at lunchtime, I was in the kitchen. My barmaid, Lesley, was behind the bar and a few of her customers, Peter, Tori and Philip, were in the pub. Lesley looked out of the window overlooking the Milford Haven Estuary and saw something resembling a large fin smashing through the water. She drew our attention to it and when we came out we saw something that we can only describe as a sea-serpent. I would say that it was a long, dark, serpent-shaped object about five to six cars' length. Peter, one of the witnesses, quoted it as having a diamond-shaped head. He saw that diamond-shaped head rear briefly out of the water — it disappeared again just as quickly. I would say it was five or six feet in diameter.

Lesley herself said,

> It was still when I first saw it. It was just motionless in the water at that point. It was a nice bright, clear day. The thing was strange and definitely alive. I felt very shocked when I saw it. It seemed to be a big sea monster.

The next witness was Peter Thomas, a customer who had been in the Shipwright Inn at the time when whatever-it-was was sighted. This is Peter's statement:

> Lesley drew my attention to something she saw in the river and I went to the window and looked out. It was something I estimated to be about ten metres in length. You could see a sort of diamond-shaped head, or what appeared to be a diamond-shaped head, out of the water and you could see the rest of it going back about thirty feet: a body moving through the water — probably about the size of a beer barrel in diameter.

At this point, I asked Peter to sketch what he'd seen.

> When Lesley brought it to my attention, I went to the door and looked between the wall of the port and the Martello tower. You've got the wall down there and the tower this end. All I could see was a diamond-shaped sort of head just above the water — not erect or anything — and then all this turbulence back behind it. It was moving in the river at a fair amount of speed. It was obviously something moving, not anything drifting.

Peter continued: "In a matter of less than a minute it was gone … clean out of sight behind the port wall. It was travelling at about seven or eight knots."

Eyewitness Tori Crawford then said,

> When Lesley told us about the fin, we all proceeded to go outside. We were all together, but I was one of the last ones to get outside. There it was, just as Dave said. It was between three and five car lengths long, and there was definitely a big shadow in the water. I only saw a little bit of the diamond head, not a lot of it — what we think was the head anyway. But it was something that I'd never seen before: never! It certainly wasn't seaweed put together, or anything like that.

After being asked to draw a picture of what she'd seen, Tori provided more information as she sketched it:

> I was one of the last ones to come out, so I hardly saw anything of the head myself. But you have the wall there and the Martello tower here. And it was as if the creature had bumps like this: the large one in the middle and then a small one just coming off here. It looked like a mountain moving along, but it definitely had a smaller bit toward the tail part, and a smaller bit toward the head. The turbulence coming from the back was unbelievable; it made you think it had flippers.

Many years experience as an investigator provides a professional researcher with the ability to weigh up the reliability of witnesses to this kind of reported phenomena. Having spent several hours in their company, the authors are convinced that the witnesses whom we interviewed were very sensible, rational people who had made clear and accurate reports about what they had seen in the estuary by Pembroke Dock: precisely what the creature was remains a mystery. Possibilities range from some large, unknown species of marine animal to a miniature submarine manoeuvring in a difficult, shallow and restricted waterway. There are Ministry of Defence activities in this area from time to time, and unconventional new designs of underwater craft *may* be tested here occasionally.

Reports of sea monsters from the past — centuries before human technology reached a point where the first relatively modern submarines appeared — would seem to require other possible explanations: unless some of the most ancient sea monster myths and legends owe their origin to underwater craft from Atlantis, Lemuria, or the advanced technology of visiting extraterrestrial amphibians. We live in an incredibly strange universe, and the more we learn of its wonders and mysteries, the stranger and more inexplicable it becomes.

What we like to refer to as "good, old-fashioned common-sense" can sometimes be far wide of the mark, but it is always worth looking for simple, common-sense answers *first* before venturing into the misty and uncertain vistas of Von Daniken Land.

William of Occam's famous medieval philosophical Razor taught much the same set of truths! William's basic principle was that we should never make more assumptions than the minimum necessary to explain any phenomenon being studied. It's also referred to as *The Principle of Parsimony*. Despite its medieval origins it underlies much of our contemporary thought. Occam's Razor recommends that we metaphorically shave off anything that isn't absolutely essential to explain the phenomenon we're investigating — or the model of it that we're building.

Although the widely and persistently reported Loch Ness phenomena do not strictly relate to *sea* monsters, the Loch Ness sightings are too important to be omitted from any serious study of marine cryptozoology. If sea monsters in general really exist, a detailed survey of Loch Ness will provide the researcher with valuable clues.

A report from as long ago as the year 565 records how Saint Columba, while travelling up to Inverness on a missionary journey to the Picts, rescued a man in danger on Loch Ness. The original account reports that "a strange beast rose from the water."

The geological history of Loch Ness suggests that it was at one time connected to the North Sea, and this would support the argument that members of the Plesiosaur group are reasonably strong claimants for being the Loch Ness Monster — if there is one at all. To add detail to the 565 account, it was said that Columba and his followers knew that a local swimmer had been fatally mauled by *something* big and dangerous in the loch. Despite this, one of Columba's followers had valiantly started swimming to retrieve a boat. Suddenly, a huge creature reared up out of the water and made toward the terrified swimmer. Some early accounts, which give the monster its Gaelic name of *Niseag*, describe it as resembling an enormous frog. This would link it with the vodyanoi of Finland.

Columba himself ran fearlessly into the water to save his companion, shouting sternly to the monster: "Go no farther! In the Name of God touch not thou that man!" Columba was a powerful man in mind and body — as well as a good and courageous one. Whether it was the saint's forceful voice, or some paranormal power of holiness surrounding him, the monster decided that on this occasion it had more than met its match and that discretion was definitely the better part of valour: it retreated ignominiously. Could the creature even have been a *thought-form*, like the Tibetan *tulpa*, that retreated when attacked by a powerful mind like Columba's?

The loch is about thirty-five kilometres long and 250 metres deep: a spacious enough home for the largest sea monster. Duncan McDonald, a diver, was working there in 1880 (albeit with the rather primitive equipment then available). As he carried out his salvage operations on a wrecked ship in the loch, he claimed that he had seen the monster swimming past him. In his report he paid particular note to the monster's eyes, saying that they were small, grey, and baleful. They gave him the impression that annoying or interfering with Nessie would not be prudent.

Fifty odd years after Duncan McDonald's encounter, George Spicer and his wife were driving along the south bank of Loch Ness when they saw a strange creature on land emerging from the bracken beside the road. The Spicers said that it appeared to have a long, undulating neck resembling an elephant's trunk. The head was disproportionately small, but big enough for the monster to hold an animal in its mouth. As the Spicers watched, whatever the thing was lumbered down the bank and into the loch, where it vanished below the water with a loud splash. In a later interview with a journalist, George said that it had made him think of an enormous snail with a long neck and small head.

During the 1930s, excitement over reports of Nessie reached fever pitch. Among hundreds of reported sightings at that time was one from an AA motorcycle patrolman. His description coincided closely with what George Spicer had reported. Hugh Gray, an engineer, actually managed to get a photograph of it — but although it was agreed by the scientific experts that the picture had not been tampered with, it was not sufficiently clear and distinct for the creature to be zoologically identified.

Alexander Campbell, a journalist, described his sighting in the summer of 1934. His cottage was situated beside the loch, and, as he left home one morning, he saw the creature rear up out of the water, looking remarkably like a prehistoric monster. He confirmed the descriptions of the long, serpentine neck given by other witnesses, and added that he had seen a flat tail, as well. Alexander said that where the neck and body joined there was a hump. He watched it sunbathing for some moments until the sound of a boat on the Caledonian Canal apparently unnerved it. Its sudden dive into deeper water produced a miniature tidal wave.

Saint Columba was by no means the only holy man to see the monster. Some fourteen centuries after Columba rescued the intrepid swimmer, Brother Richard Horan, a monk from St. Benedict's Abbey at Fort Augustus, also saw the creature. Richard said that it was in clear view for almost half an hour. Horan added that the head and neck were thrust out of the water at an angle of about forty-five degrees, and were silvery grey.

Just as a boat had disturbed the monster when Alexander Campbell saw it, so Brother Horan's view of it ended when a motorboat went past. At the sound of the engine, the monster sank back into the impenetrable darkness of the loch.

There have been so many reliable and sensibly reported sightings over so many years that it is not easy to dismiss Nessie as a figment of the imagination, an optical illusion, or a shrewd publicity stunt. Of the hundreds of reports, here are just a few of the most notable

1895: Several fishermen, timber workers, and a hotelier reported what they described as something "very big and horrible" surfacing not far from them in Loch Ness.

1903: Three witnesses in a rowboat tried very bravely to get closer to it but failed to narrow the distance between the creature and their boat. They reported the humped contour of what they saw.

1908: John Macleod reported seeing something more than twelve metres long with a body that he described as "eel-like and tapering." According to John's account it seemed to be floating on, or very close to, the surface. After a few moments, it moved away.

1923: Miller and MacGillivray had a good clear view of something in the loch and described its distinct hump.

1929: Mrs. Cummings and another witness saw a humped creature on the surface for a few moments. As they watched, it submerged.

1930: Ian Milne saw something inexplicable in the loch very early in the morning. He reported that it was moving fast — close to twenty knots — and he was sure he saw two or three of the characteristic humps along its back.

1943: Something at least ten metres long was observed submerged but clearly discernible just below the surface

MYSTERIES OF LAKES, SEAS, AND OCEANS

of the loch. It was very early in the morning and the witness was sure that he saw at least one large hump.

1947: The MacIver family and two or three other witnesses reported something very big and very strange that was moving fast across the loch.

1953: A group of timber cutters working beside the loch reported seeing the creature for two or three minutes.

1954: A fishing boat's echo-sounder detected something about twenty metres long at a depth of 170 metres.

1960: Torquil MacLeod and his wife reported seeing a creature while they were in the Invermorriston area. They had it in view for almost ten minutes as it sat on the opposite shore, and they described it as grey with skin like an elephant or hippopotamus. They also noted its paddle-shaped flippers.

[1960]: Tim Dinsdale took a very significant ciné-film of it in the same year. He gave up his profession as an aircraft engineer in order to devote all his time to investigating the creature.

1961: A large group of guests — nearly twenty of them — at a hotel overlooking the loch reported observing something more than ten metres long. It rose from the water and they had a clear view of it for five or six minutes. Those witnesses were convinced that they could clearly see the monster's humps — frequently reported during many previous sightings.

1962: Sir Peter Scott (1909–90), son of the famous polar explorer Robert Scott, was renowned for his high intelligence, his skills as an artist, his services to natural science — and his dry sense of humour. He helped to found the Loch Ness Phenomena Investigation Bureau, and named the creature being sought: *Nessiteras rhom-bopteryx*. That sounds like an excellent piece of scientific nomenclature, but it can be broken down into an anagram of the type that delights advanced crossword enthusiasts. The seemingly dignified, scientific Latin name which Sir Peter awarded to Nessie can be made to spell out the phrase *Monster hoax by Sir Peter S.*

Was it a deliberate anagram — or just a curious coincidence? Cryptographers and code-breaking professionals know just how easy it is for what seems like a clever anagram to be mere chance. No great mathematician from the depths of mathematical history ever decided to call a decimal point a decimal point simply because the anagram: *A decimal point = I'm a dot in place* existed. Sir Peter's naming of the monster might have been as accidental and innocent as the decimal point example. There are also a great many bluffs and counter-bluffs in the archives of investigations into anomalous phenomena: things that seemed inexplicable at first turn out to have simple, mundane explanations — but the next set of investigations shows that the so-called simple and rational explanations were themselves wrong — and there *is* an anomaly to be investigated after all! It might have appealed to Sir Peter's mischievous sense of humour to *pretend* that there was only a hoax in Loch Ness, not a mystery. As a dedicated conservationist, it might also have occurred to him that the best way to keep prospective monster-hunters away from the loch was to pretend that it was all a hoax.

1969: Four members of the Craven family watched a creature ten metres long surface, disturb the water significantly, and then sink down into the depths again.

1970: Dr. Robert Rines of the Academy of Applied Sciences in Belmont, Massachusetts, spent time investigating the loch and was convinced that the creature — or creatures — existed.

1971: Dinsdale's team reported something very mysterious and very much alive rearing up out of the loch.

1972: Former paratrooper Frank Searle investigated carefully and reported several significant sightings. He believes that there's a colony of at least a dozen of the strange creatures living in the loch.

1974: Henry Wilson and Andy Call described a creature twenty metres long with an equine head. They saw it surface and thresh the water for ten or fifteen minutes while they watched.

1975: On June 20, Dr. Rines's team took some very interesting and convincing pictures deep in the loch.

1996: Witness Bill Kinder described something odd rising up from the loch with two humps clearly visible.

2003: Witnesses on the Royal Scot train during the early afternoon saw something big and inexplicable moving at an estimated twenty-five knots along the loch. They also reported that the weather was calm at the time, so there was no wind to account for the movement of some casually floating, inanimate object.

Leaving Occam's Razor oiled, sharpened, and ready in its waterproof case for the sake of wider, more complex, and imaginative arguments, what speculative explanations *might* be available? The first possibility is the survival of something like a prehistoric plesiosaur: the general description of the plesiosaur included flippers, humps, a long neck and tail. The second theory comes within the sphere of phenomenalism. This is a philosophical theory that suggests that there are hard, scientific, material facts at one end of the spectrum of phenomena — things such as bricks, mortar, and Newton's Laws of Motion. At the other end are pure imaginings and fantasies, such as dreams of riding up cider waterfalls in canoes made of chocolate pulled by gigantic sugary dragonflies.

Phenomenologists hypothesize that of the hundreds of reports, between these two extremes there are some intermediate observations that are neither hard, provable fact, nor pure, subjective fantasy. Without necessarily including it in their theories, phenomenologists would entertain the ancillary possibility that things like the Loch Ness Monster, ghosts, apparitions, and phantoms might have a quasi-existence — perhaps gliding between time frames or probability tracks to impinge upon what we fondly call reality. This realm of speculation also includes tulpa-like thought forms.

There are other theorists who regard the Loch Ness monster as something paranormal, sinister, negative, and threatening — perhaps a primitive, elemental spirit-being, taking on quasi-physical appearances as and when it chooses.

There are also the mechanical theories — that the monster is really an artifact of some kind. According to these speculations, the more modern appearances may be due to tests of secret inventions of the Ministry of Defence — such as small submarines. The ancient appearances, if mechanical, would have to tiptoe into Von Daniken Land and incorporate theories about highly intelligent aliens from the stars, from Atlantis, or Lemuria, equipped with a technology that included submarines.

Interest in the loch is as fresh today as it ever was, and some is truly heartwarming. Lloyd Scott suffered from chronic myeloid leukemia until a life-saving bone marrow transplant put things right for him in 1989. Determined to help others in similar circumstances, Lloyd became a world record holder in a charity marathon, completing the London Marathon in an ancient diving suit with a copper helmet. His latest charity venture on behalf of children suffering from leukemia is to walk all around the edge of Loch Ness, on the narrow ledges a few feet underwater — in his famous antique copper-helmeted diving suit. The authors warmly congratulate him and wish him every success.

Almost as famous as the Loch Ness phenomenon is the account of the sea-serpent observed by Captain Peter M'Quhae and his crew aboard the frigate *Daedalus* on August 6, 1848. They were asea somewhere between the island of St. Helena (where Napoleon reputedly died — another mystery) and the Cape of Good Hope (notorious for its connection with *The Flying Dutchman*). It was five o'clock in the afternoon, and visibility was not

BOTTOMS UP!

Co-author Lionel wore a similar diving outfit to Lloyd Scott while filming an episode of *Fortean TV* on England's Channel 4. The director wanted him to get into a tank full of fish at the Great Yarmouth Sea Life Centre in Norfolk, England, and submerge, prior to coming up and introducing an item about a mysterious diver. The genuine antique diving suit supplied by a theatrical costume company had long since lost its original lead-soled boots, so when Lionel submerged, his feet shot upward. The big, copper helmet filled with water and held him upside-down. Fortunately, Alf, his stalwart guitarist, was also in the tank and fished him out again — none the worse for wear!

Co-author Lionel in RCMP officer's uniform while filming the Ogopogo episode for UK Channel 4, *Fortean TV*.

ideal: the weather was dull and rainy. A young midshipman reported that he had seen a "strange creature" moving toward the *Daedalus*'s starboard bow. Various shipmates — including the officer of the watch, the navigator, and the captain — responded to the midshipman's call. A total of seven experienced naval men were now watching the creature. Their reports clearly indicated *something* serpentine, estimated at more than thirty metres long and travelling at about twelve knots. With the aid of telescopes, they kept it in sight for nearly half an hour. Despite the poor visibility caused by the dull, damp weather, M'Quhae reckoned that he and his crew were able to see the monster reasonably well. He actually said that if the thing had been a person whom he knew, he would have been able to recognize him — the creature was as close and as clear as that! M'Quhae referred to the face and head as "distinctly snake-like." According to his account, the neck supporting this serpentine head was about forty centimetres in diameter, and the body went back a long way. The head was just above the water, and the underside of the neck was whitish-yellow. The rest of the creature, as M'Quhae and his team described it, was very dark brown, almost black.

The men of the *Daedalus* were somewhat puzzled by the creature's ability to maintain its speed and course without any apparent means of propulsion. They said that — as far as they were able to ascertain — it neither paddled with submerged flippers, nor undulated its lengthy body from side to side, as many marine serpents do when swimming.

The creature that M'Quhae and his men reported bore a striking resemblance to the sea-serpent described by Bishop Pontoppidan a century earlier in his book *A Natural History of Norway*. Pontoppidan had also described mer-folk as noted earlier. Media reports in 1848 were not necessarily accurate, and although the *Times* of October 10 reported that M'Quhae and his men had seen a beast with a huge mouth full of dangerous teeth, they did not appear to have reported anything about its dentition.

Although their accounts differed in certain details — as honest, independent accounts normally do — the witnesses agreed that the thing they had seen had not struck them as threatening or hostile to the *Daedalus* in any way. Neither had it seemed to be afraid of the ship. The general impression it gave them was that it was totally preoccupied with some purpose of its own — perhaps something as demanding as searching for a mate, or as simple as a quest for nourishment. M'Quhae made sketches of it, reproduced in the *Illustrated London News* on October 28 — after the *Times* had told the story on October 13.

Various theories were put forward as to what M'Quhae's monster might have been. It was suggested that it could have been a large species of seal, the *phoca proboscidea*, referred to as a "sea-elephant." But M'Quhae, who had seen one, was adamant that the creature observed from the *Daedalus* was very definitely not an elephant seal.

Brilliant professional underwater cinematographer Jonathan Bird encountered an oarfish (*Regalecus glesne*) in the Bahamas recently. Although this was by no means as long as the monster that M'Quhae and his team described, it was certainly similar to it. The specimen Jonathan saw was around fifteen metres long. The oarfish is very elongated and has yellow lures on the ends of its strange antennae. It swims in an upright position using its dorsal fin only — not its entire body: that also sounds like the movement of the weird creature that the men of the *Daedalus* reported.

A report from 1953 — about a century after the adventure of the *Daedalus* — came from a diver working in the South Pacific and attempting to establish a new depth record. He said that he was keeping a wary eye on a shark that was taking an unhealthy interest in him, and wondering just how far it would attempt to follow him down. His explorations took him to the edge of a vast submarine chasm vanishing down into awesome, unknown depths. He said that the water became markedly colder. The temperature drop was very significant and continued to become more pronounced. Clinging tightly to his ledge — to have dropped into the chasm would have been fatal — the diver saw a huge black shadowy shape rising very slowly toward him. About the size of football field, and dark brown in colour, it pulsated as it floated gradually higher and higher — convincing the diver that it was definitely a living creature of some type.

As it drew level with his ledge, he reported that the coldness became even bitterer. The strange mass drifted ever closer to the shark, which the diver felt was immobilized either by the cold or by pure terror. The outer edges of the sheet-like thing from the depths touched the motionless shark. It convulsed but made no attempt to resist or escape. Its weird attacker drew the doomed shark down into itself like an amoeba surrounding and digesting its prey. It then sank slowly back into the abyss. The diver who reported this episode added that he remained motionless on his perilous submarine ledge until the horrific thing from the abyss had vanished again into the depths.

Could whatever that thing was have been responsible for the tragic disappearance of several divers in that area in the late 1930s? *The Melbourne Leader* at that time reported that the Japanese captain of the *Yamta Maru* had gone down to salvage pearls from a wreck, and had given an urgent signal to his crew to haul him up fast. All that reached the surface was his helmet and lifeline: of the fearless captain there was no trace.

The same thing happened again in 1938. This time it was Masao Matsumo, another Japanese diver, who went down from the *Felton* and was never seen again. Like the skipper of the *Yamta Maru*, Masao gave the signal to be hauled up. His shipmates recovered only his empty helmet and a basket of shells. Fearlessly, his diving colleagues went down more than seventy metres looking for him — but Masao had vanished as completely as the ill-fated captain of the *Yamta Maru*.

There is a remote possibility that the weird, sheet-like, shark-killing creature seen in 1953 might have had some connection with another oddity reported in the *Daily Mail* on April 2, 2002. In this account it was stated that a huge dark blob — even bigger than the thing which allegedly came up from the chasm and disposed of the shark — was seen drifting toward Florida. Scientists put forward the theory that this particular "monster" was actually a huge cloud of algae. Scientific expeditions sent out to investigate noticed that other marine life seemed to be avoiding it assiduously. Observed from space satellites, it looked very dark, almost black, but when examined from the scientists' boat it was dark green. Marine chemist Dr. Richard Pierce explained that the algae cloud would remove oxygen from the water around it after dark, and marine life avoiding the strange, discoloured patch might be doing so because they sensed that the water in its vicinity was low in vital oxygen.

Of all the great sea monsters of myth, legend, and prehistory, the dreaded Kraken holds the most prominent place.

Something that was described as a Kraken-type monster was encountered by the crew of a French gunboat, the *Alecton*, on November 30, 1861. In fear they fired cannon shot into it and discharged various small arms, but nothing seemed to deter the creature. Next they harpooned it and attempted to get a line around it, but the rope slipped until it jammed against the dorsal fin. As the sailors tried to haul their strange catch aboard, the body of the monster disintegrated, leaving them with only a relatively small portion of tail section.

Arriving with their trophy at Tenerife, the captain contacted the French Consul, displayed the evidence, and made a full report. By December 30, this evidence reached the French Academy of Sciences, where Arthur Mangin, among other highly traditional and formal orthodox scientists, proceeded to ridicule the evidence provided by the *Alecton*'s curious catch:

"No wise person, especially the man of science, would permit stories of these extraordinary creatures into the catalogue."

With a few honourable exceptions, it was automatically assumed by the ultra-cautious, traditional, scientific elite of the mid-nineteenth century that reports of things that did not fit their schemata were deliberate lies, hoaxes, wild exaggerations, or hallucinations.

Erik Pontoppidan, Bishop of Bergen, who was an indefatigable chronicler of weird and wonderful aquatic life forms, described something Krakenesque in his *Natural History of Norway* (1752–53). The bishop believed his beast was two and a half kilometres around, with arms (or tentacles) long enough and strong enough to drag the biggest warship of the day straight to the bottom of the ocean.

He appears to have had something like a very large representative of the giant squid tribe in mind, and that certainly fits in well with an account from Dingle Bay in Ireland dating from 1673 — almost a century before Pontoppidan's book appeared. The Irish broadsheet describing the Dingle Bay monster said that it had been killed by James Steward "when it came up at him out of the sea." The picturesque language of the broadsheet was surprisingly accurate in its description of the creature as having eight long "horns" covered with hundreds of "buttons": very squid-like to the modern marine biologist.

Shortly after the Irish adventure in Dingle Bay, another Kraken of vast size ventured onto some rocks off the Norwegian coast, failed to free itself, and died there in 1680. Contemporary accounts said that the stench from its decaying carcass cleared the area for miles around more effectively than any fear of it while alive might have done.

Another Kraken spotter was the famous Hans Egede. Born on January 31, 1686, at Harrestad in Norway, Egede took a bachelor of theology degree at the University of Copenhagen in 1705, and was greatly influenced by the then popular religious movement known as Pietism. (It is necessary to understand Egede's character and faith in depth, in order to evaluate his evidence. He seems to have been a man of great intelligence and integrity, which makes him a highly reliable reporter.) The Pietists advocated intensive Bible study, and believed that priesthood was universal among Christian believers, which meant that the laity should have an equal share in Church government. Pietists also believed that Christian practice of goodness and kindness in everyday life was essential, and that instead of criticizing those with different beliefs, or with no beliefs at all,

THE BIG BOOK OF MYSTERIES

the Church should do all it could to help them and make them welcome. Pietists also wanted to reorganize the universities and give religion there a higher priority. In addition, they wanted to revolutionize preaching so that it concentrated on building people up and increasing their faith.

At the age of thirty-five, in 1721, Egede went to work in Greenland as a missionary, and stayed there for fifteen years. In 1734 he reported a "Kraken" seen in the Greenland area. Egede said that it was so vast that when it came up out of the water it reared up as high as the top of the mainmast and that it was of about the same girth as the ship — and several times longer. He described its broad "paws" and long, pointed snout. He said that the ragged, uneven skin of the huge body seemed to be covered in shells. Assuming Egede was making an accurate report, could these have been barnacles?

THE KRAKEN

Tennyson's famous poem captures the sea monster atmosphere associated with the Kraken perfectly:

Below the thunders of the upper deep;
Far far beneath in the abysmal sea,
His ancient, dreamless, uninvaded sleep
The Kraken sleepeth: faintest sunlights flee
About his shadowy sides: above him swell
Huge sponges of millennial growth and height;
And far away into the sickly light,
From many a wondrous grot and secret cell
Unnumber'd and enormous polypi
Winnow with giant fins the slumbering green.
There hath he lain for ages and will lie
Battening upon huge seaworms in his sleep
Until the latter fire shall heat the deep;
Then once by men and angels to be seen,
In roaring he shall rise and on the surface die.

Johan Streenstrup, a Danish researcher, found evidence going back to 1639 of a beached Kraken near Iceland. He lectured on his findings to the Society of Scandinavian Naturalists in 1847, and later backed up his archive evidence with parts of specimens washed up in Jutland. He gave his "Kraken" the scientific name *Architeuthis* which has stayed with it ever since. Recent scientific studies of *Architeuthis* describe it as having a probable maximum length of twenty metres with a body mass of approximately one tonne. They live at an average depth of around six hundred metres and their diet seems to be made up of fish and smaller squid. The eyes are among the largest found in any living creature — being up to thirty centimetres across. Such study of the brain as has been possible due to the very limited number of specimens available for examination is rather disconcerting: it appears to be very large and complex. The *Architeuthis*'s funnel is an amazing all-purpose organ that is capable of producing a powerful jet, expelling eggs, squirting defensive ink, breathing, and waste disposal!

Nondescript monsters — Krakens or otherwise — made several appearances along the eastern seaboard of Canada and the United States in the early years of the nineteenth century. In June of 1815, to cite just one widely publicized example, something more than thirty metres long and proudly displaying a series of the traditional undulating humps was seen ploughing its way southward through Gloucester Bay. Its head was described as equine.

Bostonian Sam Cabot saw a member of the same species — or the same one that had caused the disturbance in Gloucester Bay — when he was in Nahant in 1816. It also had a horse-like head and undulating humps, and Sam estimated that it was about thirty metres long. The following year another very confident expert witness had a high-quality telescope with him and said that the horse-headed marine creature he saw through it was definitely not a whale, nor an enormous member of the dolphin family. He was adamant that nothing he had ever seen among the giant cetaceans had an undulating back like the marine beast of Nahant.

Nova Scotia also had its fair share of eastern seaboard monster sightings during this period. One case involved two men from Peggy's Cove who were out fishing, John Bockner and his teacher friend James Wilson. They later reported their encounter with a sea-serpent in St. Margaret's Bay to the Reverend John Ambrose, who subsequently saw one for himself and contributed a scientific paper to the Nova Scotia Institute of Natural Sciences. Among Reverend Ambrose's accounts was an episode that took place in 1849 involving four fishermen, Joseph Holland, Jacob Keddy, and two of their colleagues. On South West Island on the west side of the entrance to St. Margaret's Bay, they observed something like a gigantic sea snake propelling itself through the water not far from the shore. They launched a boat to get a better view, and managed to get close to it without, apparently, being seen by it. The men who observed it said that it was eel-like. They were close enough to see that its huge body was covered in scales, each of which was about fifteen centimetres long by seven or eight centimetres wide. The longer part of the scales pointed along the length of the sea-serpent's body, which was black in colour. When the monster became aware of the observers' boat, it turned toward them and opened its huge jaws. The witnesses were close enough to see its great teeth all too distinctly, and decided to row as fast as they could toward shore.

After this narrow escape in 1849, there were many other sightings in St. Margaret's Bay. Some of the men who had observed at least one of the sea-serpents closely wondered whether there were two at least — perhaps a breeding pair.

Ten years later, in 1855, something in the sea off Green Harbour was described as "a hideous length of undulating terror" and more detailed accounts of it published in *Ballou's* magazine reported that it made a noise like escaping steam and moved through the water with a series of vertical curves. It was also credited with malevolent eyes protected by bony ridges, and with jaws full of dangerous looking teeth.

Another important Nova Scotia sighting was not recorded in the *Zoologist* magazine until 1847, although the events had actually taken place in 1833. Henry Ince was the ordnance storekeeper at Halifax, Nova Scotia, at the time. He recorded that on May 31 of that year he had been one of a party of five on a fishing trip in Mahone Bay, where intriguing Oak Island and its famous unsolved Money Pit mystery is also situated. The morning was cloudy, the wind in the south-southeast and rising. The other four onboard were Captain Sullivan, lieutenants Malcolm and MacLachlan from the Rifle Brigade, and Artillery Lieutenant Lyster. They saw what Henry Ince described as "a true and veritable sea-serpent," about thirty metres in length and undulating through the water.

Another episode occurred on October 26, 1873, when a "Kraken" in the guise of a giant squid attacked two sturdy Canadian fishermen in a small boat in Conception Bay — an area not noted for its depth of water. They were just on the north side of the Avalon Peninsula in

Newfoundland when the weird marine beast attacked them. Lesser men would have succumbed, but the powerful Canadians fought back courageously. They came away victorious and still very much alive — with a severed tentacle as a souvenir. They estimated that, including its tentacles, the beast had been a good fifteen metres long overall, with a three-metre body and a metre-long head.

Canadian lakes — like Loch Ness in Scotland — are often deep and mysterious, and have been the source of as many monster sightings as the seas and oceans. Geologists cite that what are now technically lakes may once have been connected to the sea, isolated from greater bodies of water by geological upheavals resulting from movements of the tectonic plates. Many of these very deep lakes lie between the Rockies and the Pacific, and Lake Okanagan, home of the Ogopogo — also known as Naitaka — is typical of them.

Modern interest in Ogopogo sightings dates from 1854 when a traveller was taking horses across Lake Okanagan. In his account of the attack by the aquatic monster, he said it was like being seized by a gigantic hand that was trying to pull him and his horses under the water. He was powerful and agile enough to fight his way out of the deadly grip of whatever lived in Lake Okanagan, but his horses fell victim to it. Some years later, another traveller, John McDougal, was crossing the lake with horses when he was attacked in a very similar manner. Once again the man survived but his horses were lost.

Another sighting was reported by a timber transporter named Postill in 1880. As he was constructing a timber raft, Postill said he was certain that whatever lived in the mysterious lake came up out of the depths and watched him working on the raft.

In that same year, another witness, Mrs. Allison from Sunnyside, saw something resembling a huge log floating in the lake — but it was travelling in the opposite direction from the prevailing wind and current.

One of the saddest and most sinister episodes recorded in the annals of Lake Okanagan is the unsolved disappearance of Henry Murdoch, a powerful swimmer who was practising for an upcoming marathon. He had planned to swim from the old Eldorado Hotel to the Maude Roxby Bird Sanctuary, a distance of some sixteen kilometres. His good and trusted friend John Ackland was rowing a pilot boat for him. As John took a few moments rest and bent forward out of the wind to light a cigarette, Henry vanished. Despite an intensive police search and two days of dragging the lake for his body he was never seen again. The water in that location was barely three metres deep and beautifully clear; yet Henry Murdoch had disappeared without a trace. It needs to be emphasized that he was a very strong swimmer and a professional lifeguard, so an accident was nearly impossible. Unless something very big and powerful had taken him, there was no way to account for his sudden disappearance. But how does that square with the water being clear and barely three metres deep at that point?

More recently, Ogopogo was described as resembling a telegraph pole with a sheep's head at one end. He was also said to have had a forked tail, only one-half of which came out of the water as he moved. The *Vernon Advertiser* from July 20, 1959, carried an interesting and well-authenticated account of an Ogopogo sighting by R.H. Millar. He had been cruising on the lake at about eight knots when he saw Ogopogo through his binoculars, about eighty metres away. He was surprised by its speed, as it was going twice as fast as the ship, and making about fifteen or sixteen knots. The snakelike head was only a few centimetres above the water, and Millar noted several undulating humps. He guessed — although he couldn't see them — that the monster had fins or paddles of some kind underneath.

More recent sightings from the Gellatly Road area, near the Gellatly Cemetery, suggest that Ogopogo is indeed real and lurking somewhere in the Okanagan Lake area. Very wisely, the Canadian authorities have declared Ogopogo to be a protected species under the Federal Law and Fisheries Act and the Wildlife Act.

In the early 1930s, when Nessie was hitting the world headlines following various reported sightings in Scotland, British Columbia newspaper editor Archie Willis christened a formidable Canadian sea monster *Cadborosaurus* — soon to be known as *Caddy*. The earliest reports of Caddy go back centuries and cover the sea area between Alaska and Oregon. Marine biologists and oceanographers have drawn up scientific criteria that points to something real and classifiable inhabiting those waters. Caddies seem to vary in length, with an average of around ten metres, and their bodies are serpentine — like gigantic eels. The head is variously described as resembling a horse or camel — definitely not snake-like or fish-like. The neck is long, and the body adjoining it is either humped or undulating — perhaps both.

There are powerful flippers, which must be highly effective as Caddies have been clocked at more than thirty knots when swimming on the surface.

The northwest Pacific coast, where Caddies are regularly sighted, lies close to an extremely deep submarine trench, an area where a creature of most any size could live undetected for millions of years. Is Caddy a survivor from the distant past, like the coelacanth? It seems highly likely. He also appears to have close relatives in Wales and in Cornwall, England.

A creature that was given the name Morgawr was reported off the Cornish coast in 1975. Morgawr was closely associated with the work of the famous Doc Shiels and his daughters, all of whom were at that time widely recognized and acknowledged as expert and knowledgeable practitioners of the "Old Religion."

The basic physical descriptions of Morgawr, the Cornish sea monster, are very similar to the descriptions of Nessie, Caddy, and other large aquatic beasts reported as broadly resembling plesiosaurs. There are, however, some strange and intriguing metaphysical questions raised by the apparent nexus between Old Religion practitioners and their monster-summoning spells on the one hand, and the reported sightings of monsters subsequent to those "magical works" on the other. In this connection, however, it is wise to remember the importance of the *post hoc ergo propter hoc* fallacy — "after this, therefore because of this."

Lyall Watson, whose scientific theorizing is of the highest, most rigorous, and most adventurous quality, has also wondered seriously about this possible connection. In his brilliant book *The Romeo Error* he argues that certain very gifted people can produce physical effects at a distance — purely by mental power. Watson also wonders whether magnetic flaws in specific locations may assist this process. He conjectures that dragons, elves, fairies, and UFOs may all exist, but that those who say these things are all in the mind might be right, too — because these strange tulpa-type phenomena *could* be produced at what Watson calls the "second or etheric" level.

The aberrant behaviour of these phenomena gives Watson cause to wonder whether they are subject to laws that differ from the laws and principles of the natural sciences as we currently understand them in this twenty-first century. When psychic or other anomalous phenomena behave in ways that support the theories of those who examine and explore them, Watson suggests that this indicates a degree of influence from the mind of the participant observer over the external phenomena themselves. He feels that if these two ideas could be studied seriously together, they would go some way toward explaining many phenomena that are currently regarded as anomalous.

There is a considerable body of evidence to suggest that Alexandra David-Neel's reported episode with a tulpa in Tibet was a perfectly genuine and objective experience. According to mystical Tibetan wisdom, a tulpa is an entity created by an act of imagination. A parallel may be drawn with the author, or script-writer, who "creates" a fictional character with words. Tulpas do not have to be written down — they are creatures of the mind. The technique of tulpa creation is a protracted one that requires very powerful concentration and visualization, but Alexandra was almost *too* successful. Her tulpa began as an entirely benign and innocuous, monk-like figure, plump and smiling. After a while other members of the party reported seeing him, too, but as time passed he became leaner and lost his benign smile. He had apparently managed to escape from Alexandra's conscious control and was only disposed of with great effort and difficulty.

There are researchers into the various sea monster phenomena who subscribe to the idea that Nessie, Caddy, and some of their strange companions may be akin to tulpas — quasi-solid thought forms with a kind of objectivity that can be influenced by group contemplation of the type involved in the experiments conducted by Doc Shiels, his daughters, and their colleagues. If the tulpa-creation theory can be applied to *some* sea and lake monsters, it would be one possible explanation for the success which Saint Columba had in rescuing the man being threatened by Nessie. The very powerful, sharply focused mind of the benign but formidable saint would have shattered a quasi-real thought-form like a sledge hammer going through an egg shell.

A PREHISTORIC FISH

The coelacanths, related to lungfishes and tetrapods, were believed to have been extinct since the end of the Cretaceous period. The first coelacanth known to modern science was discovered in 1938 when a young museum curator named Marjorie Courtenay-Latimer was invited down to the docks to examine a strange fish brought aboard a fishing trawler. She sent a sketch of the fish to experts, who identified it as a living coelacanth — a word meaning "hollow spine" in Greek. The coelacanths were previously known only from fossils, the most recent of which dated from the late Cretaceous period, 65 million years ago. Understandably, the discovery created a worldwide sensation and was referred to as the "biological find of the century," similar to finding a living dinosaur. Since 1938, coelacanths have been found in the waters off the coast of northeast, northwest, and southern Africa. The coelacanth has no real commercial value, apart from being coveted by museums and private collectors. As a food fish the coelacanth is almost worthless as its tissues exude oils that give the flesh a foul flavour. The continued survivability of the coelacanth may be at threat due to commercial deep-sea trawling. **An interesting fact:** Coelacanths have a tiny heart that looks like a straight tube and a brain that occupies only 1.5 percent of the braincase — the rest of the cavity is filled with fat!

5 SUBTERRANEAN MYSTERIES

The mysteries of labyrinths and mazes can be examined under seven broad main headings:

1. Those built for religious purposes, including the induction of altered states of consciousness and deep meditation.

2. The maze as a sacred place where a god or goddess may be found.

3. Gateways and vortices leading to other dimensions — tesseracts for example.

4. Places of imprisonment for people and spirit beings.

5. For defensive purposes against physical or psychic opponents.

6. The *Virgin-in-the-Maze* rituals as aspects of courtship and marriage practices.

7. The use of mazes and labyrinths as aptitude tests, or intelligence tests.

The induction of altered states of consciousness by using mazes and labyrinths seems to have been effected in two main ways: a small stone maze or labyrinth pattern is cut into a portable piece of stone such as a sheet of slate and kept at home by the user; or a maze pattern is carved into a large rock or cliff face, which the users then have to visit — perhaps at particular times such as the full moon, new moon, solstices, or equinoxes. Whether the stone is portable or fixed, the users seeking an altered state of consciousness close their eyes and trace the labyrinth pattern with their fingertips. This ritual can be accompanied by a low chanting or singing. Once the desired state of trance has been achieved, much depends upon the belief system of the particular labyrinth user. Some may think that they are in communication with the Cosmic Consciousness. Others believe that they are in touch with the spirits of dead ancestors or other psychic entities. Some users may simply feel that they are in contact with the vast powers stored in the depths of their own subconscious minds.

LABYRINTHS IN ART

Many artists have depicted labyrinths and mazes in their artwork. Some works include Piet Mondrian's *Dam and Ocean* (1915), Joan Miró's *Labyrinth* (1923), Pablo Picasso's *Minotauromachia* (1935), M.C. Escher's *Relativity* (1953), Jean Dubuffet's *Logological Cabinet* (1970), Richard Long's *Connemara Sculpture* (1971), Joe Tilson's *Earth Maze* (1975), Richard Fleischner's *Chain Link Maze* (1978), István Orosz's *Atlantis Anamorphosis* (2000), and Dmitry Rakov's *Labyrinth* (2003).

Rocky Valley is a unique and spectacular beauty spot near Tintagel in Cornwall. Carved into one of its steep sides is an ancient maze design that has defied the passage of time.

At the Boscastle Museum of Witchcraft, not far from Tintagel, is another stone that is closely connected with the Rocky Valley carving. This one is a sheet of slate forty-five centimetres long and fifteen centimetres wide carrying a typical labyrinth design very similar to the one at Rocky Valley. This fascinating old slate came from a field in Michaelstow, south of Boscastle. It had for many years done duty as a ritual object and been used by several local wise women. The stone was actually donated to the museum in the 1950s by the daughter of Kate "The Seagull" Turner, who had enjoyed a great reputation as a local wise woman during the first half of the twentieth century. Kate Turner had received it from Nan Wade, the Manx wise woman. Sarah Quiller from Ballaveare, Port Soderick, Isle of Man, had given it to Nan. But Sarah was far from being its maker; she had simply received it from an *older* wise woman. It appeared to have been handed down over many generations.

Carving of a labyrinth in Rocky Valley, near Tintagel, in Cornwall.

TROY STONES

A stone carved with a maze or labyrinth design is popularly known as a "Troy Stone," and is traditionally used to facilitate an altered state of consciousness. The myths and legends associated with the ancient city of Troy — and with the far older capital city of Atlantis — described the basic layout and plan of the city as seven concentric circles. If, as some researchers have suggested, Troy was modelled on Atlantis, then the maze carved onto a Troy Stone (traditionally credited with so many strange, magical powers) has very ancient and mysterious origins.

The old Egyptian labyrinth at Harawa, in the Fayum district of the Nile valley, built on the orders of Pharaoh Amenemhet four thousand years ago, may also have been constructed on this basic Troy pattern — but using the grand scale. The famous Cretan Labyrinth was said to have been modelled on the one at Harawa.

The labyrinth at Knossos on Crete.

Today, although very little remains of the original grandeur of the Harawa labyrinth, it was visited by Herodotus while it was still in pristine condition. The prolific ancient historian credited it with three thousand rooms and antechambers. Even allowing for the colourful exaggerations and occasional inaccuracies for which Herodotus is well known, he undoubtedly saw a very impressive structure: a huge complex that contained storage areas, burial chambers, shrines, and rooms for religious observances and initiations.

Much historical tradition lies behind the Troy Stones. The user would trace the labyrinth design with a finger-tip in both directions — to the centre and out again — and often sing or chant at the same time until a state of trance was reached.

In 1958 another famous old Troy Stone was deliberately destroyed on the instructions of the previous owner, who left orders to that effect in her will. It was duly smashed and the pieces hurled to the four winds.

Undoubtedly, among a small, surreptitious group of the initiated, some venerable old Troy Stones are secretly still in use today.

In Indian women's magic, something very like a Troy Stone, but called a "yantra," is used to help women in labour. One of their priests consecrates the yantra and tells the expectant mother to travel through it in her mind. This has the effect of providing her with an altered state of consciousness similar to the benefits of giving birth under mild hypnosis instead of anaesthetics. After making her mental journey to the centre of the miniature stone labyrinth, the young mother is told to find her own way out again — thus coming slowly and gently out of the mild analgesic trance. It is interesting to note in this connection that until comparatively recent times in England, the local wise woman was also the midwife.

In addition to its uses for altering the state of consciousness, the labyrinth's religious symbolism was connected with the traditional Seven Heavens. To start with, seven is regarded as a benevolently propitious and powerful magic number. The Babylonians believed in seven heavens, and according to their legend of Etemenanki, the biblical Tower of Babel, there were also seven labyrinthine layers below the tower — representing the seven concentric circles of hell, as in Dante's *Inferno* many centuries later.

The early Church was deeply involved with the idea of mazes and labyrinths. One of the oldest so far discovered is in Algeria, where walking the labyrinth became an important ritual for the early Christians. This one is laid out as a marble pavement, the idea being that the worshipper can tread its length without thinking about where to place his feet. The journey becomes monotonously rhythmic and tranquillizing so that the worshipper's mind can concentrate on immaterial things and the eternal verities.

THE NUMBER SEVEN

The number seven has significant meaning in many ancient traditions. The number seven was the Egyptian symbol of such ideas as perfection, effectiveness, and completeness. There are the Seven Hills of Rome, the Seven Hills of Constantinople, Seven Liberal Arts, Seven Sages of Greece, Seven Sages of the Bamboo Grove in China, and the Seven Wonders of the ancient world. In Christianity, God created the world in seven days; there are seven days of the feast of Passover; Seven Deadly Sins; Seven things that are detestable to the Lord (Proverbs 6:16–19), and Seven Pillars of the House of Wisdom (Proverbs 9:1). And the list goes on. Even the Canadian Oak Island legend discussed in this book maintains that the fabulous treasure deep below the island will not be recovered until seven men are dead.

The idea of a labyrinth representing the circuitous path of life itself, and of spiritual development, is interwoven with religious theory. The seeker after God and Truth has metaphorically — and *literally* in some old cathedrals like Chartres — to pursue a difficult and winding route. There was also a sense that by walking the labyrinth and giving money generously to the Church, the "pilgrim" could complete a religious journey without running all the grave risks of death, injury, and disease by making a real, physical pilgrimage to the danger-fraught Middle East.

The second mystery of the mazes and labyrinths was their role as a sacred place where a god or goddess might be found. Reaching from the everyday life of Earth to the Sphere of the Divine was no undertaking for the faint-hearted, or for those who lacked courage and stamina. The symbol of the sacred maze was a constant reminder to the worshipper that any worthwhile spiritual quest was an arduous undertaking. The gods did not choose to reveal themselves lightly. The mortal who sought them must prove himself, or herself, worthy of their Divine Favour. Mind, body, and spirit had to be committed totally to the quest.

DANGER IN THE MAZE

The maze was also a warning of danger. Some of its strange, convoluted pathways could lead to death and destruction. It offered a choice at every turn, an option at every branch of its ways. The right choice led to the heart of the labyrinth, to victory, to rich rewards and fulfilment. The wrong choice led to defeat, failure, and suffering.

The third set of theories is that mazes and labyrinths are gateways, entrances, portals, and vortices leading through hyperspace, opening into other dimensions, other times, or other probability tracks. Certainly the idea of the tesseract (a four-dimensional hypercube) in association with mazes and labyrinths is an intriguing one. A thirteenth-century Catalonian numerologist, who was also a mystic, was alleged either to have drawn a two-dimensional sketch of a tesseract, or, more likely, to have built a three-dimensional model of one. According to the account, he acquired an altered state of mind by meditating on it fixedly, and this significantly enhanced his psychic abilities. Modern scientific research into the link between tesseracts and psi-powers has suggested that contemplation of a tesseract by psychic sensitives and mediums may increase their powers.

A fourth group of theories concerning mazes and labyrinths suggests that they may have been designed either to imprison people or animals — or, more bizarrely, demons, genies, elemental spirits, or ghosts. According to this hypothesis, the design of the labyrinth worked like an old-fashioned wasp or slug trap: bait was placed inside (usually sugared water or sweet ale) and a funnel-shaped device led into it. The unsuspecting victim entered the trap and died (blissfully) wallowing in the bait! The maze (because of its religious associations) lured the lost earthbound soul — or the curious demon, elemental, or genie — inside, and, once trapped within the coils of the maze, the prisoner was unable to escape. This theory has some elements in common with the stories of King Solomon the Wise imprisoning evil spirits in brazen vessels, sealing them with his Great Seal and then hurling the brazen vessel into the sea where the occupant had to wait for Judgment Day. The labyrinth design was considered to be an effective psychic seal, though a genie who could perform all the mighty deeds that Aladdin's Slave of the Lamp performed likely wouldn't find it too difficult to get out of a maze!

One of the wilder speculations about the real purpose of the Oak Island Money Pit, Nova Scotia, was that the mysterious labyrinth below the shaft, reached via Borehole 10X, was not to guard a treasure but to keep something incredibly valuable but unimaginably dangerous safely imprisoned. This hypothesis takes account of the numerous layers of oak found within the original Money Pit two hundred years ago, and suggests that oak had magical as well as physical properties — being sacred to the wise and ancient Celtic Druids. The underwater television camera showed what looked like parts of a deep and complex labyrinth that was an artifact rather than a work of nature.

Ramifications of this hypothesis examine legendary and mythical beings like Ea, otherwise called Oannes, the Phoenician water deity. He was at one time a god of the Akkadians, to the north of Babylon, and his cult was absorbed from there. Records date him from as far back as 5000 B.C. The nineteenth-century archaeologist Paul Emil Botta found a carving of Oannes dating from almost three thousand years ago in the palace of Assyrian King Sargon II, at Khorsabad near Mosul (in northeastern Iraq).

The suggestion is that these strange amphibian beings with god-like powers were actually aliens from a distant world with an aquatic environment. The scenario then develops into a plot in which one of the aliens is held prisoner and kept alive in his labyrinthine submarine prison in return for technological secrets: a classic standoff situation. If the prisoner gives his captors all the information they want, there is no more need for them to keep so dangerous an entity alive. They won't kill him until they believe that they have all the advanced secrets of his alien technology. He won't give them that data because he still cherishes the hope of eventual escape. The Oannes legends have much in common with later mermaid legends — both hint at strange, intelligent beings that are adapted to life in the water.

The fifth set of theories concerning mazes and labyrinths relates to their possible uses as means of defence — against both physical and psychic foes.

ONE MERMAID LEGEND

When Mathy Trewhella of Zennor in Cornwall, England, disappeared, legend was that he had been abducted by a mermaid. Years after Mathy had gone missing, a sea captain came back with the story that while anchored off Pendower Cave, he had seen a mermaid who had begged him to weigh anchor as it was blocking the cave entrance, preventing Mathy and their children from getting out!

Secret defensive mazes and labyrinths in this category can also be invisible and conceptual — referring to a vital sequence, like the lines in a computer program. If a certain lever is not pulled, or a particular stone is not rotated, the lethal booby-trap will be activated. Those who know the secret order of this sequential labyrinth — similar in some ways to numbers or letters on a combination lock — will be able to enter safely: intruders will fall victim to the trap.

The sixth group of maze and labyrinth theories is connected with courtship rituals — older, more primitive and direct mating customs. There are numerous aspects of Scandinavian folklore and legend in which — more or less as a game — the most beautiful of the village girls stands in the centre of a maze while the village boys trace the difficult,

Oannes the fish-god of ancient Akkad.

A SAFE PATH

Hereward the Wake, the Anglo-Saxon hero of the East Anglian Fenlands in England, depended upon his secret knowledge of the safe paths through the dangerous marshes around the Isle of Ely not far from Cambridge and Huntingdon. While his heavily armoured Norman pursuers floundered and drowned in the swamps — like Pharaoh's charioteers crossing the Red Sea in pursuit of Moses and the Israelites — the agile Hereward ran boldly along firm, safe, secret ways that he had known since childhood.

circuitous pathways to reach her. In some versions, the girl represents the prisoner of a dragon, demon, or ogre, and the boys are running to her rescue — much as Perseus rescued the lovely Andromeda from the sacrificial rock and the savage teeth of the sea monster.

In Finland, certain mazes and labyrinths where these games are played are referred to as *Jungfrudanser*, meaning "the dances of the virgins." In a church at Sibbo, in the region of Nyland in Finland, there is a six-hundred-year-old painting that depicts a woman in the centre of a labyrinth.

The early Church connection with the girl-in-the-labyrinth theme may contain some oblique references to the temptations of Eve, the talking serpent, and the forbidden fruit of Genesis; the beautiful young Rahab who entertained her clients in the house on the labyrinthine walls of Jericho; Mary Magdalene, who was, perhaps, the same girl as Mary of Bethany; the woman whom Christ saved from the stoning party; and the "woman-who-was-a-sinner" who poured the precious ointment over Christ's feet. The labyrinth in that case could possibly refer to the symbolic maze of temptations, and the spiritual and mental struggles of the girls and their rescuers. Adam was with Eve, the Hebrew spies rescued the lovely Rahab, and Christ himself saved Mary Magdalene and the others.

From the village of Munsala near Vasa in Finland, as recently as the 1980s, an elderly inhabitant recalled how, as a young girl, she had actually participated in the girl-in-the-maze ritual. She said that the young people taking part kept it all very secret from their parents and guardians. In her account of the ceremony, the boy had to reach the girl without making any mistakes as he trod the convoluted pathway. If he was successful, he carried her out of the maze — and she then became his.

The seventh and final set of theories refers to mazes and labyrinths as aptitude tests. Ancient kings, emperors, and warlords needed two great qualities in their generals and statesmen: courage and intelligence. A brave commander is no asset if the enemy can out-think him. A brilliant commander is equally useless if he lacks the courage to get out on the field and put his first-rate strategy into action.

The legend of the world-famous Cretan Labyrinth at Knossos has this aptitude-test element. The courage required to tackle the vast and powerful bull-headed Minotaur made up one component of the test.

The Minotaur.

MODERN LABYRINTHS

In recent years, there has been a resurgence of interest in the labyrinth symbol. This has inspired a revival in labyrinth building, most notably in England at Willen Park, Milton Keynes, at Tapton Park, Chesterfield, and at Old Swedes Church in Wilmington, but also in North America — at Grace Cathedral in San Francisco, the Labyrinth in Shed 16 in the Old Port of Montreal, and at Trinity Square in Toronto.

The ingenuity needed to find a way out of the labyrinth again — if successful — was the second component. If Theseus had the strength and courage, it was Ariadne who had the intellectual power. Theseus was more than a match for the Minotaur in straight hand-to-horn combat, but it was Ariadne's powerful mind that devised a way out of the labyrinth by following the thread. Between them, therefore, they provided an ideal team and met all the requirements.

In less important aptitude testing situations, one of the main requirements was memory. Monastic life, the priesthood, the work of a storyteller, a Druid, a bard, or a minstrel: all required phenomenal powers of memory in the days when literacy was the jealously guarded privilege of the elite. To remember a maze, perhaps to remember it well enough to walk it blindfolded, or in the dark, was a fair indication that the candidate had a promising memory.

The power, persistence, and purpose of the ancient mazes and labyrinths may be assessed by considering how many of them still survive — and attract as much interest today as when they were first fashioned.

The maze at Hampton Court — which the authors first explored in 1956 — is probably the oldest hedge maze in England. It is unusual because it is based on a rudimentary trapezium pattern — perhaps signifying the plinth of a statue, suggesting that the royal owner of the maze deserved to be raised on such a platform.

Other fascinating mazes can be found in the Parish Church of St. Mary Redcliffe in Bristol, the village green at Hilton in Cambridgeshire, Saffron Walden in Essex, Mizmaze Hill in Breamore in Hampshire, Tor Hill in Glastonbury in Somerset, in the ruined church of Rathmore in Meath in Ireland, and at Caerleon in South Wales.

SECRETS OF THE CATACOMBS

There are a number of strange theories connected with the ancient Roman catacombs to the effect that they may be *more* than simple resting places for the dead. Only the *fossores* were allowed to work there. They were an exclusive guild, like a secret society, which had special knowledge of exactly how the work should be done, and precisely how the labyrinthine catacombs should be dug out of the tufaceous earth below the city of Rome. The fossores made a number of *lucemaria* throughout the catacombs — openings that allowed a little light and air to enter. What strange secrets did the fossores guard? What else came and went through the lucemaria?

6 MYSTERIOUS PHANTOM SHIPS

Many of us will already know the broad outline of the legend of the *Flying Dutchman* through Wagner's superb opera *Der fliegende Holländer* (1843) and Coleridge's *Rime of the Ancient Mariner* (1798). One version of the story has a hero (or anti-hero) named as Captain Falkenberg, doomed to sail the North Sea forever, playing an interminable dice game with Satan. In Coleridge's version, Death and Life-in-Death arrive on a strange ghost ship and play dice for the Ancient Mariner.

Was this the ship of Coleridge's strange vision?

THE ANCIENT MARINER SEES THE GHOST SHIP

And those her ribs through which the Sun
Did peer, as through a grate?
And is that Woman all her crew?
Is that a DEATH? and are there two?
Is DEATH that woman's mate?

Her lips were red, her looks were free,
Her locks were yellow as gold:
Her skin was as white as leprosy,
The Night-mare LIFE-IN-DEATH was she,
Who thicks man's blood with cold.

The naked hulk alongside came,
And the twain were casting dice;
"The game is done! I've won! I've won!"
Quoth she, and whistles thrice.

Like all enduring myths and legends, there are numerous versions of the *Flying Dutchman* narrative, all of which repay careful study and research. One of the oldest may even have Norse roots. There is an account in the saga of Stote, a fearless Viking who dared to steal a precious ring from the gods themselves. When the outraged Norse gods caught up with him, he finished up as a skeleton enrobed in flames and sitting on the mast of a huge black Viking longship.

The title *The Flying Dutchman* actually refers to the Dutch skipper — rather than to the vessel itself. His name is usually rendered as Falkenberg but he also becomes Hendrik van der Decken, Van der Decken, Vandecker, Van Demen, Van Demien, Van Strachan, Van Straaten, and several similar allied spellings. When stirring adventure writers like Captain Philip Marryat create an exciting fictional version of the story, names may change.

Whatever the skipper's name implies, most versions of the tale are centred on the challenging, storm-bedevilled water off the Cape of Good Hope. The period is late seventeenth or early eighteenth century, and the skipper was a man to be reckoned with — if not a man to be admired or emulated. Determination and an unbreakable will can be great virtues: they can also be doom-laden harbingers of disaster. In Van der Decken's case, they were definitely the latter.

Pandora and the Flying Dutchman was a 1950s film version of the legend, starred James Mason and Ava Gardner. A German TV/film version, *Der fliegende Holländer*, appeared in 1986.

One popular version of the tragedy says that he was obsessive, fanatical — and roaring drunk on top of his potentially lethal, psychological defects. Van der Decken was trying to round the Cape of Good Hope in the teeth of a force ten storm-wind that put the ship, passengers, and crew in mortal danger. The passengers pleaded: the crew eventually mutinied. Van der Decken refused to alter course. Formidable man that he was — no Captain Bligh of the *Bounty* to be overpowered by Fletcher Christian's determined mutineers — Van der Decken shot the leader of the mutineers in cold blood and tossed his body casually overboard like so much insubstantial garbage. Throughout his battle with the elements, the mighty Dutchman sang bawdy songs and cursed both God and Satan with reckless impartiality.

A shadowy figure — like Nemesis of ancient Greek tradition — appeared on the deck and reprimanded Van der Decken for his fanaticism

Viking runes.

and his murderous response to the mutineers. The wild Dutchman laughed, cursed, and threatened to shoot the mysterious newcomer. In some versions his pistol failed to work, in others the heavy shot passed harmlessly through his insubstantial, paranormal visitor, or the pistol exploded in his hand. Following his unsuccessful attempt to shoot the mysterious entity, it spoke again. Van der Decken was roundly cursed: his food would be hot iron, his drink would be as bitter as gall, and he was condemned to sail the seven seas forever — with hideous animated corpses for his crew. In a slightly different version of this account, Van der Decken was allowed to retain the unfortunate cabin boy for company. The lad was to be transformed into a hideous creature with the jaws of a tiger, the horns of a stag, and the skin of a dogfish. "Damn you!" roared Van der Decken. "Let it be so then. I don't care. I'm not afraid of you! Do your worst, and then to Hell with you!"

Part of the Dutchman's curse was that he would bring death and disaster to all other ships his ghostly vessel encountered: food onboard some of the ships that met his would instantly become corrupted and

WHAT'S IN A NAME?

Washington Irving (1855) called his fictional Flying Dutchman Ramhout van Dam. The linguistic root of *decken* — the significant part of the legendary skipper's name — may contain some cryptic clues to the story. *Decken* can mean to cover something, to put a roof over it, to set a table, or spread a cloth over it ready for presenting a meal, but it can also mean to disguise, to camouflage, to conceal or hide something. In the sense that animal breeders use the word *cover* when referring to horses at stud, *decken* can also have sexual connotations meaning mating or copulating — and another version of Van der Decken's story involves alleged adultery and brutal sexual jealousy as tragic and as violent as Othello's. *Die decke* used as a noun can refer to a bedcover such as a quilt or blanket — raising the adultery perspective again. It can also mean a box or casing — even a ceiling. It may also refer to a geological layer or stratum, a bed of clay or rock. Yet another meaning is "tegument" — the skin or hide of some living creature.

start to decay; other ships that he met would be wrecked by rocks or storms; some would spring inexplicable, unstaunchable leaks and go down to Davy Jones's Locker with all hands.

There was another mysterious sea captain, a genuine historical character this time, named Bernard Fokke, who was such a superb seaman that nautical rivals attributed his ship's great speed and his exceptional navigational skills to a deal he'd done with the devil. Captain Fokke actually disappeared at sea, and his jealous rivals nodded sagely with a knowing wink and a look that said "I-told-you-so" — convinced that Satan had come to claim his part of the bargain.

Over the centuries, witnesses who have claimed to have seen the Flying Dutchman — and survived in spite of him and his notorious curse — have described him as gaunt and wild-eyed, but strangely reformed and penitent, crouched bareheaded over the ship's bucking wheel and praying for forgiveness. Others claim to have laid eyes on his living-dead, skeletal-zombie crew, swarming around in the rigging as they battle with torn sails and the awesome power of a supernatural wind that constantly plagues their ship.

In the Othello-type version of the legend, Van der Decken was insanely, groundlessly jealous of his beautiful young wife, and after a protracted and dangerous voyage he came home obsessed by the delusion that she had been unfaithful to him. He murdered her and was sentenced to death accordingly. As he lay in the condemned cell, awaiting execution, some strange supernatural power intervened, put the guards into a trance-like sleep, and magically opened all the prison doors and gates. Van der Decken reached the harbour where his loyal crew were waiting for him and the Dutchman sailed away into legend. The insanely jealous skipper's punishment for murdering his innocent young wife was to sail the oceans until he met a woman who would love him enough to give her life for him voluntarily.

In a third version, Van der Decken plays dice with the devil — betting his soul, his ship, and his crew against eternal life, eternal youth, and infinite wealth. Needless to say, throwing two ivory cubes against an opponent who has the power to control them isn't a good idea: predictably, Van der Decken lost!

Sightings of the *Flying Dutchman* have been made by many reliable witnesses over the centuries. A report from a British ship in the Cape of Good Hope area in the 1830s described the *Flying Dutchman* sailing toward them on a collision course. The seamen did not realize that it was a phantom until it suddenly vanished just seconds before what looked like an imminent and fatal collision.

The *Flying Dutchman*.

The most famous and probably the best authenticated sighting of the *Flying Dutchman* took place on July 11, 1881. The future King George V of England was then a sixteen-year-old midshipman in the Royal Navy, serving aboard HMS *Inconstant*. The young prince wrote:

At 4 a.m. the *Flying Dutchman* crossed our bows. She emitted a strange phosphorescent light as of a phantom ship all aglow, in the midst of which light the mast, spars and sails of a brig 200 yards distant stood out in strong relief as she came up on the port bow, where also the Officer of the Watch from the bridge saw her, as did the quarter-deck midshipman, who was sent forward at once to the forecastle, but on arriving there no vestige nor any sign whatever of any material ship was to be seen even near or right away to the horizon, the night being clear and the sea calm.

The information comes from a book by John H. Dalton entitled *The Cruise of Her Majesties* [sic] *Ship Baccante*. The future George V and his brother, the ill-starred Eddie, Duke of Clarence, who was a suspect in the Jack the Ripper murders, were both aboard the *Inconstant* because the *Baccante* had had problems with her rudder. Two other vessels were with HMS *Inconstant* at the time: the *Tourmaline*, and the *Cleopatra*. Numerous witnesses from both ships also saw the phantom and verified the prince's report.

As the legend emphasizes, to see the *Flying Dutchman* was considered to be the worst kind of bad luck because the doomed vessel was allegedly carrying a fatal curse. In considering curses in general — on both land and sea — it is important to remember that once an event, or a phenomenon, is *alleged* to be cursed, any tragedy that happens in association with it will be attributed to the curse, regardless of whether there is any statistically significant correlation.

After the future king George V and a dozen or so of his shipmates had witnessed the *Flying Dutchman*, the sailor who had first seen the strange apparition was killed by a fall from the mast, and the admiral died shortly afterward. Ripper suspect Eddie, Duke of Clarence, died young in the tragic "flu" epidemic of 1892.

Of course, there is absolutely no way of proving causality, or of establishing any link with the *Dutchman*'s appearance: neither is there any way of disproving causality. Some curses may indeed be self-fulfilling prophecies: rendered nervous and uncertain by thinking about the supposed curse, victims may have become victims by failing to concentrate and to pay proper attention to dangerous machinery or hazardous road

SELF-FULFILLING PROPHECIES

When co-author Lionel was serving as Deputy Head in a very large comprehensive high school, an unfortunate young student with hitherto unsuspected psychiatric problems was suffering from the delusion that he was accompanied by a malevolent Egyptian mummy — invisible to all but him. He terrified several older students by telling them that under instructions from the ghostly mummy he had cursed them. His technique was to wait for an accident to happen, and then claim that his curse was responsible. Lionel gathered the frightened students together with the sadly deluded mummy-keeper, asked the boy where the mummy was standing, struck the empty air in that vicinity and said: "Come on! Do something! I think you're ugly and stupid! Now, if you have any mysterious powers, why not bring a bolt of lightning down on me? These people are innocent: I'm the hard man who just hit you and insulted you! Show us what you can do, bandage-boy!"

Needless to say, nothing happened. The lad with the psychiatric problems was taken for mental hospital treatment, and the formerly frightened students started to laugh. Lionel later reported the incident to the Head, whose revealingly anxious comment was, "Whatever you do, don't have an accident on the way home!" That attitude goes some way toward illustrating the vulnerability of the human mind when confronted with supposed curses!

conditions. There is nothing more likely than mental distraction to render a person more vulnerable to potential accidents. An appropriate degree of concentration and sharp mental focus, combined with a confident, relaxed attitude, is a very effective shield against accidents.

The mental powers of *expectation* (which we can all generate to a greater or lesser extent) also seem able to affect our environment positively or negatively. The happy and well-balanced individual, who enjoys first-class health, dynamic energy, and the superhuman stamina of a trans-Canadian steam locomotive, goes into every situation expecting to win, to succeed, to conquer, and to triumph. That powerful, positive expectation effectively reinforces the likelihood of success. The sad, tense, depressed, unhappy, negative person, low in strength, energy, and stamina, and suffering from indeterminate chronic, psychosomatic illnesses, dreads the future and expects misery and failure. Again, those expectations are likely to be fulfilled.

Another world-famous witness to the *Dutchman* was Grand Admiral Karl Dönitz of Germany. Born on September 16, 1891, at Grünai-bei-Berlin, Dönitz was the creator of Germany's Second World War submarine fleet — in direct contravention of the Versailles Treaty, which absolutely forbade Germany to have a submarine fleet after the First World War. In 1936, Dönitz became its commander. In 1943 he replaced Admiral Erich Raeder as commander-in-chief of the German Navy. By 1945, with the Nazi war machine in tatters, Dönitz was made head of the North German Civil and Military Command. Hitler's last political order appointed Dönitz as his successor. Dönitz was sentenced to ten years imprisonment by the International Military Tribunal at Nüremberg in 1946, was released in 1956. He died in Aumühle on December 22, 1980, just a few months short of his ninetieth birthday.

The report concerning the Dönitz sighting of the *Flying Dutchman* related to a German Naval Tour of Duty "somewhere east of Suez" — a very long way from the Dutchman's traditional haunts near the Cape of Good Hope. Believers in Van der Decken's prowess might have argued that the indomitable *Dutchman* had finally rounded the Cape, beaten the devil, and sailed in triumph up Africa's eastern seaboard, past Madagascar, Mozambique, Tanzania, Kenya, and Somalia, before entering the Gulf of Aden and proceeding up into the Red Sea. Was Dönitz's vessel anywhere near the Mediterranean end of the Suez Canal at the time of the reported sighting?

It was the Emperor Napoleon who first looked at the problem of connecting the Mediterranean to the Red Sea at a relatively recent date. Round about 1800, his engineers reported (incorrectly!) that the sea levels were different by at least ten metres, and too much land would be flooded if a direct canal was constructed. Despite the engineers' pessimism and miscalculation, Ferdinand de Lesseps, former French Consul in Cairo, had the canal finished by 1867, and it was officially opened — very lavishly — on November 17, 1869, by the Egyptian Khediv Ismail.

THE EARLIEST CANALS

The *Dutchman* legend goes back to the seventeenth century, or even earlier, and, interestingly, ways of creating a water link between the Mediterranean and the Red Sea go back to ancient times. The earliest canals linked the Red Sea to the Nile, and used the river to reach the Mediterranean. Pharaohs Necho and Thutmosis III have both been credited with creating the very first link, but it was the Persian Darius I who gave orders for the canal to be completed. In his day, the canals were in two parts: one connected the Great Bitter Lake to the Gulf of Suez; the other completed the link by going to the Nile Delta and thus out into the Mediterranean. The canal worked regularly and effectively during the time of the Ptolemies, but decayed and fell into disrepair and disuse after their era. In Roman times it was refurbished while Trajan was emperor, and centuries later the great Arabian ruler Ibn-al-Aas restored it again.

It seems a trifle anachronistic for a seventeenth-century ghost ship to use a canal that wasn't destined to be completed for another two centuries!

On the other hand there are reports of ghost ships to which land presents no obstacles. The phantom vessel *Goblin* has been reported many times off the coast of Porthcurno Cove, not far from St. Leven in Cornwall. Witnesses usually describe her as a black, square rigged vessel that steers toward the coast as they watch her. However, the *Goblin* does not stop when she reaches the land but glides on over it for a fair distance before simply vanishing.

Ghost ships that fly over land, or glide just above it, are linked to the old sailors' legends of the *Ship of the Dead*. This is a strange vessel that calls to collect the souls of retired seamen who die ashore. It's a legend that may be as old as the Norse belief in the Valkyries — goddesses who chose the best Viking warriors and then flew with them to Valhalla after they had died fighting boldly on the battlefield.

Legends like that of the *Palatine* and the infamous *Palatine* light illustrate the complications and difficulties encountered when tracing the various versions of phantom ship stories back to their origins. The poet John Greenleaf Whittier (1807–92) wrote a poem called "The Palatine" in which the ship of that name was wrecked on the rocks by Block Island (in Rhode Island, U.S.A.).

The actual tragic history behind the story of the wreck as Whittier's famous poem described it seems to have referred to another vessel, the *Princess Augusta*. The passengers aboard the ship were Germans from the area known in those days as the Palatinates — hence the confusion over the name *Palatine*. Another contribution to the historical doubt and uncertainty is the existence on Block Island of a simple granite monument bearing the inscription PALATINE GRAVES —1738. This stands on private property near the house of Simon Ray on the west side of the island.

It seems likely that the name *Palatine* referred to the people who died in the tragedy rather than to their ship. The wreck of the *Princess Augusta* seems to have occurred in 1738 and not in 1752, which is frequently given as the date on which the *Palatine* met her tragic end. The immigrants aboard *Princess Augusta* were hoping to reach Philadelphia, with a view to joining the Pennsylvanian Deutsch (a German-speaking community already established there). The name "Deutsch" apparently misled some researchers into thinking that the immigrants were Dutch, and at least one otherwise reliable and factual account said that the doomed passengers of the *Princess Augusta* had set sail from Holland, not Germany.

Several accounts agree that there were many troubles and difficulties for the passengers. One version suggests that as the ship neared New England there was a dispute among the officers as to exactly where they were. The captain — said in some versions to be a savage bully, an inveterate alcoholic, and a greedy exploiter of the helpless passengers — was thrown overboard by the angry officers and crew. They then robbed the passengers and raped the women before escaping from the *Princess Augusta* in the only lifeboats, thus effectively condemning the remaining passengers to death. If this version that includes the rape is true, it would account for the later detail of the woman who emerged from hiding only to die in the flames.

The helpless, abandoned ship drifted onto the rocks by Block Island. To their credit, local fishermen rescued as many of the passengers as they could see, helped themselves to anything of value that the crew had not already stolen, and then set light to the sinking wreck as it drifted off the rocks — presumably floated off by the rising tide. As the blazing wreckage

THE BLAZING GHOST SHIP

This extract from Whittier's poem "The Palatine" details the blazing ghost ship *Palatine*, which so many witnesses were certain they had seen:

> For still, on many a moonless night,
> From Kingston Head and from Montauk light
> The spectre kindles and burns in sight.
> Now low and dim, now clear and higher,
> Leaps up the terrible Ghost of Fire,
> Then, slowly, sinking, the flames expire.
> And the wise Sound skippers though skies be fine,
> Reef their sails when they see the sign
> Of the blazing wreck of the *Palatine*.

drifted out to sea on its last voyage, a terrified woman passenger (who had been hiding in the hold to escape the rapists) ran up onto the blazing deck, screaming desperately for help — but by then it was too late for the Block Island fishermen to reach her.

In 1882, an accurate and factual report of the sighting of the blazing Block Island ghost ship was given by a Long Island fishing-boat owner. It actually appeared in *The Scientific American* magazine. At that time, the menhaden were plentiful. These fish were an unusually oily species of herring, and their excessive oiliness is an important feature of the explanation offered in this 1882 account.

The mate was unwilling to sail off Montauk Point because he claimed that he had seen mysterious glowing ships moving very late at night, although there was no discernible wind, and conditions were dead calm. The skipper and the owner both ignored the mate's protests and they eventually anchored in Gardiner's Bay. In the middle of the night, the terrified mate shook the owner awake and pointed to a big schooner bearing down on them at a speed of at least ten knots — *although there was a dead calm*. They tried desperately to take evasive action — impossible when there was no wind for their sails — and prepared to jump overboard. At the last second the schooner simply vanished, just as the *Flying Dutchman* had done in the Cape of Good Hope area fifty years earlier when it seemed a collision with the British ship there was inevitable. By the time the skipper joined them there was nothing to see.

A week later they were fishing in the same area when the mysterious phantom light appeared again — like a strangely glowing sailing ship. The owner boldly ordered his skipper to set sail in pursuit of the ghost ship — and to lower the seine net as they went. (A seine net, based on a French term, is a type of net that is used vertically with floats at the top and weights below. A fisherman, or a fishing boat, using such a net is referred to as a "seiner.") They netted an amazing haul of menhaden as they pursued what seemed to be the glowing phantom ship.

The hypothesis seeking to explain the "ghost-ship" in rational and scientific terms put forward in the 1882 article suggested that it was the huge shoal of menhaden that was responsible for the weird glow that gave the impression of a luminous ghostly vessel. As the shoal moved, it was suggested, the excessive oil exuded from the fish produced the same kind of glow that is described as Will o' the Wisp on land. It also seemed possible that the glow effect mirrored the fishing boat, or reflected and distorted the image of any other boat in the vicinity. The fact that the "ghost ship" was able to move when there was no wind *could* be explained as the swift movement of a gigantic shoal of oily fish swimming through the water. As theories go, it's both interesting and ingenious — but it still leaves many unexplained phantom ships sailing the seven seas.

One of the most famous ghost ships, reportedly seen near Britain at fifty-year intervals, is the *Lady Lovibond*, which was reputedly involved in one of the hundreds of marine tragedies associated with the hazardous Goodwin Sands.

The Goodwin Sands are traditionally associated with the powerful Anglo-Saxon Earl Godwin, son of Wulfnoth, supporter of Danish king Cnut who became king of England in 1016. Cnut gave Wessex, one of the four great English Earldoms, to Godwin, and in 1019, while accompanying Cnut on a visit to Denmark, Godwin married Gytha, sister of Ulf, the most powerful of the Danish earls. Their children included the future King Harold.

Traditionally, part of Godwin's vast estates once included a beautiful and fertile island named Lomea, off the coast of Kent, where the Goodwin Sands drift around so treacherously today. One of the several infamous

"Great Storms" of the type recorded in the *Anglo-Saxon Chronicle* seems to have destroyed Lomea in the eleventh century — changing it into the Goodwins. Earl Godwin was blamed for failing to maintain Lomea's sea defences, according to the legend, but geological drilling on the Goodwins seems to indicate that only decayed marine matter exists between the layers of shifting sand above the chalk base, and most professional geologists think it unlikely that there was an island there in the first place.

The outline of the *Lady Lovibond* legend records that on February 13, 1748, the ship was on its way from London to Oporto in Portugal carrying its newlywed skipper, Simon Peel, his lovely young bride, Annetta, and many of their wedding guests. This was in spite of the old sailors' superstition that it was unlucky to have a woman onboard. The mate, however, had also been in love with the beautiful Mrs. Peel. In a fit of insane jealousy (shades of Van der Decken) because of her marriage to Simon, the mate murdered Captain Peel and steered the *Lady Lovibond* onto the fatal Goodwin Sands, where she was totally wrecked, leaving no survivors.

Witnesses over the centuries have claimed not only to have seen the ship's ghostly outline, but to have heard the happy voices of the celebrating guests immediately before the phantom vessel ran onto the Goodwins. On February 13, 1798, the skipper of the *Edenbridge* made a log entry to the effect that he had almost collided with a schooner, a three-master, which was sailing straight for the Goodwins. In 1848, the lifeboat crew from the town of Deal went to the rescue of a schooner that seemed to be in distress on the notorious Sands. When they reached the spot where they had last seen it, however, there was no trace of any vessel at all. In 1898, the ship was seen again, and there were other reports of sightings in 1948 and 1998.

The legend of another ghost ship that re-enacts a centuries-old tragedy begins with the violent blood feud between the de Warrennes and the Pevenseys. In outline, the Fourth Earl de Warrenne met Lord Pevensey in mortal combat at Lewes Castle and was about to kill him when Lady de Warrenne prayed to St. Nicholas (whose belt was a sacred relic in the care of the de Warrennes). Miraculously, her husband reversed the fortunes of the mortal combat and killed Lord Pevensey. The triumphant de Warrennes then vowed that St. Nicholas's belt would be taken to Byzantium and placed on Saint Mary the Virgin's Shrine there — before their infant son was old enough to marry. Years passed and the vow remained unfulfilled. Beautiful young Lady Edona was betrothed to the de Warrennes' son Manfred, now in his twentieth year. The de Warrennes recalled their vow and sent Manfred

THE MYSTERY OF THE SS VIOLET

Another inexplicable spectre ship of the Goodwins was the SS *Violet*, an old cross-channel paddle steamer that met its end on the treacherous Sands during a heavy blizzard in the second half of the nineteenth century. In 1939, witnesses saw an old paddle steamer run onto the Goodwins, and called out the first available lifeboat, which came from Ramsgate. They searched for an hour but found nothing. If it was the ghost of the *Violet*, it had vanished back into the mysterious limbo from which it had so strangely emerged.

off to Byzantium with the precious belt. A year later, so the legend of the Lewes ghost ship runs, the family was watching and waiting eagerly as young Lord Manfred's ship approached. Suddenly, it struck a rock, tilted on its side and sank with all hands. Lady Edona collapsed and died on the spot where she had so eagerly awaited her lover. Every year, on the anniversary of her death, and Lord Manfred's, the marine tragedy is re-enacted, and the ghostly ship collides with the rock once more, keels over, and vanishes.

A very colourful ghost ship legend originates from the authors' home county of Norfolk, and concerns a traditional Norfolk wherry called *Mayfly*, a large cargo sailing boat intended for use on the Norfolk Broads and rivers. The skipper's name is variously rendered as Blood Stephenson, or Blood Richardson. He seems to have shared several of Van der Decken's character defects — and added a few of his own.

The story begins with an apparently imbecilic banker named Dormey from Beccles entrusting the fearsome and amoral Blood with a huge amount of cash and his beautiful young virgin daughter Millicent, who was to go along to enjoy the scenery. Instead of taking the girl and the banker's cash safely to their destination in Yarmouth, Blood set out into the North Sea, heading for Holland (another link with Van der Decken?). Not welcoming his powerful, lecherous advances, the banker's daughter screamed and struggled like the virtuous heroine of a three-volume Victorian romance. At this point, Bert, the plucky little cabin boy, emerged from belowdecks and did his best to rescue her. Quite how a tiny teenaged lad and the banker's young daughter managed to fight off the gigantic, rock-hard Blood has never been realistically explained, but there was supposedly a terrific struggle in which the girl was killed and Blood fatally injured. Bert managed to escape the scene of all this carnage on the blood-drenched wherry by launching the *Mayfly*'s dinghy. He floated about helplessly in the North Sea for hours, and then saw a vessel approaching. Thinking he was about to be rescued, he cheered loudly and waved — only to discover that it was the *Mayfly* with the ghosts of the screaming girl and the maniacal skipper running around the blood-soaked decks. Not surprisingly, Bert stayed cowering in his little dinghy until the *Mayfly* vanished. Every June 24, it is said, the ghostly *Mayfly* reappears, trying, like the *Flying Dutchman*, to find her way to port.

The story in that highly colourful and not very historical form seems to have originated with an East Anglian raconteur named Bill Soloman, who had an irrepressible sense of humour and a vivid imagination. There is, however, much more to it than merely entertaining fiction, or vividly creative exaggeration. Bill himself is the first to acknowledge that he did not create the story from scratch — there was a much older, more sinister version of the *Mayfly* tragedy before Bill embellished it for the benefit of a broadcaster who was interviewing him in the 1950s.

In sad, realistic contrast to the melodramatic tale of Blood and his wherry is the grimly factual account of the loss of the *Pamir*, a beautiful four-masted sailing ship capable of carrying over four thousand square metres of sail. In September 1957, a few hundred kilometres from the Azores, she was hit by Hurricane Carrie and sank. A fearless radio man, doing his vital duty to the last, gave out her position on the last distress call he was able to transmit. Ignoring the danger to their own ship, the gallant officers and men of the U.S. freighter *Saxon* raced to the *Pamir*'s last reported position and picked up six survivors: eighty of the *Pamir*'s ship's company were lost.

In 1961, the spectral *Pamir* was sighted by the *Esmereld*. She was reportedly seen again near the Virgin Islands. She was also seen on later occasions by Norwegian and German witnesses, and by shrewd observers aboard the *Eagle*, a ship manned by the U.S. Coast Guard — highly trained professionals, and not easy men to deceive!

When rational, reliable, objective witnesses provide convincing evidence for the existence of *something* — however unlikely that something seems to be — their reports deserve careful and thoughtful attention. Phenomena variously described as "ghost ships" — of which the *Flying Dutchman* is a prime example — come into this category. The heart of Fortean philosophy is the principle that nothing is so obvious and so apparently well-fortified by "common sense" that it should be exempt from interrogation: neither is anything so bizarre or improbable that it can be dismissed as ridiculous and never given serious examination.

The phenomenon broadly categorized as phantom vessels or ghost ships can be examined from several perspectives. First is the scientific angle on mirages.

A mirage can be defined as a refraction phenomenon. Refraction means that rays of light have been bent — turned through an angle from their original direction. When a ray of light enters a denser medium, it turns *toward* the normal ray — the normal ray in optical science being defined as a ray which enters the surface at an angle of ninety degrees. When the ray of light leaves a denser medium for a less dense medium, it refracts *away* from the normal ray. For example, when light leaves air and enters water, it bends toward the normal ninety-degree ray. When it leaves water and enters air, it bends away from the normal ninety-degree ray. A long-handled spoon standing in a glass of water illustrates the basic principle of refraction due to light moving through transparent media with different densities. Mirages are seen when the image of some distant object (for example, a ship at sea or a pool of water on land) appears a long way from its real, spatial position. This apparent displacement happens because of atmospheric density variations close to the surface. Mirages frequently look as if they're distorted, upside-down, wavering, and shimmering. This has given them their association over many centuries with magic, fairy lore, divine intervention, or the malicious work of demons and evil spirits. Psychology plays a part here: observation is carried out with the mind as much as with the eyes. But mirages are not illusions, and can be photographed.

There are two main categories of mirage. The variety that appears in arid deserts and is popular with novelists and adventure-story writers is technically referred to as an *inferior* mirage, most frequently seen today as pools of water across a highway. Inferior mirages almost invariably appear over land. The *superior* mirage is seen over expanses of water, snow, or ice. The scientific, meteorological terms *inferior* and *superior* are not qualitative in this context. An inferior mirage appears in a position which is *lower* than the real position of the material object which it represents, and a superior mirage appears at a site which is *higher* than the object it mimics.

In a nutshell, mirages occur when rays of light generated by, or reflected from, some material, physical source are refracted (bent) as they pass through air layers that have different densities. So a real oasis — a pool of water surrounded by shady fruit trees — can appear many kilometres away and tantalize thirsty travellers in a sun-baked desert. A real, solid East Indiaman with all sails set, battling her way through a savage gale a hundred kilometres away, could appear to be speeding toward another tall ship — barely fifty metres away — on an apparently disastrous collision course — and then vanish like a phantom at sunrise.

If mirages explain some of the famous and persistent ghost ship sightings, what of the others? Many modern physicists are far from skeptical about the possibilities of irregularities in *time*. The Norfolk Broads — especially Wroxham Broad — have curious data associated with them, which might be explicable in terms of time-slips. Several reliable witnesses have reported going back to Roman times when they were in the vicinity of Wroxham Broad. Two staid and respectable Victorian schoolteachers who had a strange experience in the gardens at Versailles over a century ago may have experienced a time-slip. There are innumerable other reports of anomalous phenomena which *might* be accounted for by some sort of time-malfunction. Do ghost ships like the *Dutchman* sail across centuries as well as seas and oceans?

PSYCHIC RECORDINGS?

Another theory that experienced researchers into the paranormal would advance is that some strange sightings of ghost ships — and other spectral phenomena — are replays. If sound and vision can be recorded so easily and deliberately onto tapes and discs, what if nature has her own rather more spasmodic recording techniques? What if emotional energy is just as effective as electrical energy in creating such natural recordings? The terror of doomed passengers and crew would constitute a formidable barrage of emotional energy. Could that energy have etched its data onto the very rocks where the ship was wrecked? Or onto other rocks far below the surface? Could that grim data of death be read, even centuries later, by observers with sufficiently intuitive and sensitive minds?

Dimensional gateways, and links with those strange quasi-real "worlds of if" — the so-called probability tracks — present the open-minded researcher with other real and serious possibilities. If event A had happened instead of event B, if decision C had been made instead of decision D in the past, the present might now be very different. If other dimensions exist, if probability tracks exist, then things from those other dimensions' tracks — including what appear to be phantom ships — may be able to glide from their realm into ours.

It is, of course, undeniable that ghosts — even those with the theatricality of Hamlet's murdered father or Scrooge's old pal Jacob Marley — might be surviving, intelligent entities who have travelled from the spirit world to ours with their own particular purposes to fulfil. Is Van der Decken just such a psychic being — giving warnings, unloading his guilt, and trying to find peace?

There are as many possible solutions to the riddle of the ghost ship reports as there are square kilometres of salt water over which those controversial phantom vessels may wend their enigmatic way.

7 TEMPLAR SECRETS

There are awesome unsolved mysteries attached to the great and noble Order of Guardians and Protectors who were known for part of their long and honourable history as the Templars.

THE FOUR TEMPLAR MYSTERIES

The first of the mysteries is the enigma of their true origins and purposes. The second is the precise nature of the eldritch, arcane secrets they protected long ago, and still protect today. The third is their system of code-making and code-breaking: they were, and still are, expert semiologists and cryptographers. The fourth Templar mystery is the riddle of what happened to them after the treacherous and unprovoked attack launched against them by the odious and cowardly Philip le Bel in 1307.

An overall hypothesis encompasses all four of the great, unsolved Templar mysteries. The original hidden Order of Guardians and Protectors is so old that its beginnings are lost in the intriguing mists of prehistory, myth, and legend.

The secrets of the Order's ancient origins may be lost, but its purposes are not. It exists to guard, to protect, and to preserve — perhaps one day, in time of great need, to attempt to reactivate something of immense importance to the future of the whole human race.

Trying to solve the mysteries of Templar codes is like searching for the Rosetta Stone — something that will provide vital clues to ancient, hitherto indecipherable secrets.

Our research over the years has led us to examine the strange Yarmouth Stone in Nova Scotia and the curious symbols on the unusual slab of porphyry found in the Oak Island Money Pit in Mahone Bay, Nova Scotia. We've examined Norse runes and Egyptian hieroglyphs, as well as the mysterious unknown alphabet inscribed by person or persons unknown found in Glozel (near Vichy, France) in 1924 by fourteen-year-old Emile Fradin, whom we interviewed in 1975. We have also studied the enigmatic symbols on the extraordinary Phaistos Disc from Crete.

One Templar mystery is the strangest and most significant of them all. By miracles of courage, endurance, and an ingenuity to rival Ulysses, hardy groups of the indomitable Templars defied Philip's mindless henchman and made their way to freedom and safety — some by land, some by sea. Wherever these dauntless adventurers travelled — and some almost certainly reached the New World nearly two centuries before Columbus — they took their Templar spirit and their Templar secrets with them.

As well as being superb warrior-priests, these medieval Templars were exceptional architects and builders. Their skill in designing and constructing fortresses was admired and acknowledged by the world. Clues to where they went to get beyond the range of the petulant and aggressive Philip IV and his successors may be detected in characteristic Templar architectural features in buildings dating from 1307 — the period that may be termed the start of the Templar Dispersion.

As well as this Dispersion that took many Templars to safety beyond the reach of Philip's henchmen, there were other, secret ways in which ingenious Templars went underground — in a figurative as well as a literal sense. Discretion, as the proverb reminds us, is the ally of valour, not an alternative to it, or a substitute for it. An experienced craftsman working quietly and discreetly as an expert armourer for some local warlord would be too valuable to be questioned about his past.

Although the line grew thin at times between 1307 and our own twenty-first century, it never broke. The indomitable Templars are as much a part of modern life as they were of medieval life.

Renewed twenty-first-century interest in the Templars and their mysterious, ancient secrets suggests that it would be helpful to begin any detailed study of them with a synopsis of who and what the Knights Templar were — and are!

When nine knights arrived in Jerusalem in 1118 they ostensibly took on the role of protecting pilgrims from bandits. The king made them welcome and provided them with accommodation in what were then called Solomon's Stables, below Temple Mount. What they *really* did — apart from protecting pilgrims — is central to the great Templar mystery.

With help and protection from the immensely influential Bernard of Clairvaux, the Templar Order was recognized by the Vatican and known formally as The Poor Knights of Christ and the Temple of Solomon. It was a tremendous advantage to the Templar Order to be answerable to the Pope and to no one else, and to pay no taxes to any secular ruler or local Church Official.

The Templars bravery in battle was deservedly legendary. Their motto was "First to attack and last to retreat." Their enemies rightly feared their military prowess and unyielding ferocity. They were skilled architects and builders as well as supreme warriors, and their fleet was also widely renowned.

Betrayed by the evil and treacherous Philip le Bel (Philip IV of France), the Templar strongholds were attacked simultaneously on Friday October 13, 1307, and almost wiped out. But a significant minority of them, nevertheless, escaped to carry on with their vital, secret work. The Templar fleet was never captured, and it is highly probable that significant numbers of resolute and indomitable survivors reached Scotland, the Scottish Islands, and the New World.

It is difficult, if not impossible, to estimate worldwide Templar numerical strength in the twenty-first century. There are many different groups of Templars today — some are Masonic, others are not. Browsing Templar websites with a good search engine will give some idea of their diversity and numerical strength. Undoubtedly, there are a great many more Templar groups who value their secrecy and privacy and, accordingly, prefer *not* to register their activities on the Internet. A conservative estimate would put Templar membership today at several thousand worldwide.

In addition to the many Templar commanderies and priories, there are also several Templar churches that are usually wide open and inclusive, theologically broad, liberal, and very welcoming. Membership of several of these modern Templar churches is open to anyone of any denomination. Templar church members and clergy retain their own original church membership while *adding* their Templar church membership to it. In this way, those Templar churches that accept dual memberships of this kind are working toward unification of the Church at large and doing what they can to overcome denominational boundaries.

A great many Templars today are deeply involved in charitable work, and contribute substantially to those in need — much as their forebears protected pilgrims in medieval times.

Mysteries are inseparable from human curiosity. Questions are as natural to us as breathing. When they can't be readily answered, or when they're argued over and then answered in strikingly different ways, they graduate to the realm of unsolved mysteries — and intrigue us more than ever.

The more important the question, the greater the mystery that surrounds it: cosmology is one of these major areas of uncertainty. Is the universe finite or infinite? Is there an "outside" to it? If so, what *is* outside? Has it always been here? Will it always be here? Did it have a beginning? Was it created, and, if so, who — or what — created it? Again, if it was created, how was it created? How does it operate? Did what we think of as the natural laws of physics, chemistry, and biology just appear on their own as the thing developed and evolved — or were the rules of the game laid down by the Maker when he created the board and the players?

The original Hebrew name for the book now known as Genesis in the Bible was *Bereshith*, meaning "in the beginning." It's an intriguingly interwoven collection of narratives from at least four very ancient sources, and it sets out — within the limited terminology of its own culture period — to answer a few of those philosophical, cosmological questions. The subtext below its symbolic stories and etiological myths hints that there are some people — priests, prophets, princes, and patriarchs — who know a lot more than others and who understand certain very important ancient secrets.

Oral traditions predated written accounts by thousands of years, and although richly coloured by mythology and restricted by the educational and cultural limitations of their time, such oral traditions richly repay serious study today. What clearly and consistently emerges from studying these ancient traditions, and from the early written records such as Bereshith, is that there were strong, well-informed guardians, guides, protectors, and leaders of their people who seem to have had access to knowledge and power sources that were not generally available.

Adherents of the great world faiths would argue that such leaders were appointed and inspired by their God (or by their gods and goddesses).

Darwinian neurologists and psychologists would suggest that they had special, but perfectly natural and explicable, abilities that came from genetic modifications and mutations leading to superior brain and body function. There were — and are — mathematical, musical, and artistic prodigies everywhere who outperform the rest of us in their special fields: Leonardo da Vinci, Beethoven, Mozart, Einstein, Trachtenberg, and Hawking are cases in point. The late and greatly admired grand-slam golfer Bobby Jones (1902–71) was an outstanding performer in his fields. His brilliant legal mind was as magnificent as his skill on the golf course: in ancient times, such a man — perhaps a uniquely gifted swordsman and statesman — would have been a natural leader and guardian of his people.

Other theories put forward to explain the charisma and superhuman qualities of some of these ancient "Guardians of Humanity" have included the idea that they were either extraterrestrials themselves, or the result of interbreeding between extraterrestrials and human beings. In this context, Bereshith (Genesis, chapter 6, verses 1–4) poses the question inescapably:

> The sons of God saw the daughters of men that they were fair and took them wives of all that they chose.... The Neph'i lim [giants?] were in the earth in those days.... When the sons of God came in unto the daughters of men and they bore children to them, the same were the mighty men which were of old, men of renown.

The account does not by any means exclude a simple and direct religious interpretation: the beings described as "sons of God" could be understood simply as angelic entities, or other benign, heavenly lifeforms. They might (in accordance with Occam's Razor!) simply have been humanoid extraterrestrials with mental and physical abilities greater than those usually found among terrestrial humanoids at that time. Or they could have been Atlanteans or Lemurians from one of those legendary lost or submerged civilizations with a high level of culture, technology, and academic prowess.

Apart from the references in Bereshith that hint strongly at the historical existence of superhuman heroes, such as Nimrod, "the mighty hunter" of the *Bereshith* account, many other ancient texts describe the epic adventures of heroic figures possessing attributes beyond those of "normal" *Homo sapiens*. Among the most famous of these records is *The Epic of Gilgamesh*.

WILLIAM OF OCCAM AND HIS RAZOR

William of Occam was a medieval philosopher who created a logical instrument for cutting out unnecessary complications: "One should not increase, beyond what is necessary, the number of entities required to explain anything." In theory, Occam's Razor shaves away "unnecessary" things and makes it easier to reach logical conclusions. Although admittedly helpful on occasions, it's frequently a hindrance in a universe that's almost incomprehensibly complicated!

The story of Gilgamesh is believed by many experts to be at least six thousand years old — possibly much older. It tells the story of the semi-divine Sumerian king Gilgamesh of Uruk, his friendship with the powerful wildman Enkidu, their joint conquest of the terrifying Guardian of the Forest, Humbaba, Enkidu's death, and Gilgamesh's inconsolable grief for his lost friend. Throughout the epic, Gilgamesh is seen as the defender and protector of his Sumerian people. He has numerous superhuman powers together with great wisdom, and his word is law throughout his empire. In the broadest and most general sense, Gilgamesh can be understood as a Templar-type Guardian and Protector of something very powerful and deeply secret. Following his training by Gilgamesh, so too can Enkidu. It is almost as if Gilgamesh can be viewed as a prototype Grand Master, with Enkidu as his trusted assistant and knightly-bodyguard.

Selecting a sample of just nine such ancient and mysterious guardian-heroes provides a curious symbolic link with the nine traditional founders of their twelfth-century resurgence under the guise of Templarism. Who are these nine entities?

If the father-god figures of Odin, Jupiter, and Zeus are regarded as one being — known by different names in different cultures at different periods of time — and the war-gods Thor and Mars are also seen as one being, that accounts for two of the nine. If we add another Norse god such as Ull (also called Ulir and Oller), plus Nimrod, Gilgamesh, and Enkidu from the ancient Middle East, the total reaches six. The mysterious but very powerful Enlil of Babylonia is a strong candidate for one of the three remaining places, alongside Hermes Trismegistus — Hermes the Thrice

Blessed — also known as Thoth, the awesomely wise and powerful scribe to the gods of Egypt, and controller of the famous Emerald Tablets. Last, but not least, comes the mysterious Melchizedek: the man "without father or mother — with neither beginning of life nor end of days." He appears in early sacred writings as the friend and benefactor of the great patriarch Abraham, who came from the ancient city of Ur.

The nine great beings listed are merely a sample of the many divine and semi-divine figures, half-remembered through the mists of time and imperfectly recorded down the millennia that followed. But they provide a pointer to the central hypothesis at the heart of all real Templarism: ancient Protectors and Guardians existed long ago, and were involved in some type of warfare — like a cosmic chess game — a game demanding the highest intelligence, and indomitable courage: something like a war between Good and Evil, or between Order and Chaos. They possessed what seemed to their contemporaries to be superhuman powers. They understood awesome mysteries and secrets. They held keys to forbidden knowledge. As the centuries went by their arcane riddles were passed to others, to secret societies and hidden organizations — including the nine mysterious knights who searched below the ruins of what they believed to be part of Solomon's Temple in Jerusalem.

It is essential to make the initial jump of several millennia — from the ancient patriarchs and pantheons to the knightly adventurers in

WAS GILGAMESH A PRE-TEMPLAR GUARDIAN?

Gilgamesh's writings are believed to contain many strange secrets that could relate to the mysterious origins of the secret order of Guardians and Guides who were popularly known as Templars in the twelfth century. How does *The Epic of Gilgamesh* begin?

"Great is thy worthiness, O Gilgamesh, Prince of Kulab. You are the one who knows all things. You are the Emperor who understands all the countries of the world. You are the wisest of the wise. You know and understand all mysterious and secret things. You are he who knows about the World before the Flood…. You are the great architect and builder…. No man alive can rival what you have built…. Seven Sages laid its foundations."

twelfth-century Jerusalem — in order to establish the connections between those ancient origins and what is popularly known today as Templarism. Now some of the intriguing gaps in those long millennia can be bridged.

Where had those first ancient heroes come from, and where had they acquired their secret knowledge and powers? They're worth looking at in more detail. The first is:

At least, that's what Bereshith calls him — the biblical Abram, later Abraham. He was from Ur of the Chaldees according to the Genesis account, and was the son of Terah, a descendant of Noah via his son Shem. With other members of his family, including his nephew Lot, Abraham

THE NINE FIRST JERUSALEM TEMPLARS

Who were these nine original Templar Knights? And what was their *real* reason for being in Jerusalem in the twelfth century?

First came Hugh (or Hugues) de Payen. Hugh had been in the service of another Hugh, Hugh de Champagne, and our Templar Hugh de Payen was also related through marriage to the St. Clairs of Roslin. This is particularly significant in the light of the massive importance of Roslin (various later spellings exist) Chapel in Scotland and the meaning of the site it occupies.

André de Montbard was the uncle of Bernard of Clairvaux and was also in the service of Hugh de Champagne. Next came Geoffroi de St. Omer, one of the stalwart sons of Hugh de St. Omer, and Payen de Montdidier, who was closely connected with the ruling house of Flanders, as was Achambaud de St. Amand. The other knights were Geoffroi Bisol, Gondemare, Rosal, and Godfroi.

moved from Ur to Haran, a renowned trading centre in the valley of the River Euphrates. Terah died there, and, according to the biblical account, Abraham felt a divine call to move on to a new land where God promised that he would become the father of nations and be a universal blessing.

The salacious episode involving Sarah (who was Abraham's half-sister as well as his wife) and their contemporary Pharaoh is a strange one. Famine had more or less forced Abraham's nomads to seek food in Egypt, where, because of her great beauty, Sarah was likely to be acquired as an addition to Pharaoh's harem. It may have occurred to the politically astute Abraham that the inconvenience of a husband was unlikely to deter an all-powerful Pharaoh with a keen eye for beautiful additions to his harem. His loyal guards could dispose of such an inconvenience swiftly and permanently, so that Pharaoh would be able to take on the unencumbered widow! Abraham,

THE ROYAL GAME OF UR

The famous Royal Game of Ur, also known as the Game of Twenty Squares, was similar to chess in some ways, although very different in others. Two boards discovered in the Royal Tomb of Ur in Iraq date from the First Dynasty of Ur, before 2600 B.C., likely making it the oldest board game equipment ever found. The game is still played in Iraq to this day. There are many links between this ancient game from Ur, chess, and Templar codes.

Board used in playing the Royal Game of Ur.

therefore, prudently decided to tell Pharaoh that Sarah was his *sister* — which was not entirely untrue! This Egyptian episode has raised doubts in the minds of some speculative historians about whether Abraham and Sarah were actually Egyptian in origin, rather than Chaldeans from Ur. It has even been suggested by adventurous researchers and historians that Abraham and Sarah were originally from India — and were far more powerful and mysterious than the straightforward biblical accounts suggest.

A completely different — and equally probable — version of the Sarah and Pharaoh episode suggests that, far from attempting to deceive the Egyptian ruler about his real relationship with Sarah, and meekly handing her over to Pharaoh, Abraham commanded so formidable a force of armed retainers that when Pharaoh *abducted* Sarah, her husband demanded her swift, safe return — or else Pharaoh would bitterly regret it!

Confronted by the might of several hundred Chaldean warriors, Pharaoh swiftly handed the lady back. But what if Abraham had fearless and skillful *Indian* soldiers at his command, as well as his Chaldean warriors? The Jewish scholar Flavius Josephus, who wrote prodigiously during the first century of the Christian era, quoted Aristotle as saying, "The Jews are descended from great Indian Philosophers; they are called Calani in the Indian language." Clearchus of Soli, who was a disciple of Aristotle, wrote, "The philosophers are called in India Calanians and in Syria Jews. The name of their capital, Jerusalem, is very difficult to pronounce."

There is also evidence that Megasthenes was sent to India by Seleucus Nicator of Syria in the third century B.C. He reported back to the effect that the Jews had originated as a highly cultured Indian tribe known as the *Kalani*. Much later, in the nineteenth century, Dr. Martin Haug, distinguished author of *The Sacred Language, Writings, and Religions of the Parsis*, argued that the Magi had referred to their own religion as Kesh-i-Ibrahim, claiming that all their religious wisdom had come from him, and that he had brought their scriptures from heaven.

Voltaire, writing in the eighteenth century, believed that Abraham was closely connected with Brahman priests who had left India. He supported his arguments by pointing out that Chaldean Ur, traditionally associated with the Abramic Patriarchs, lay near the Persian border on the road from India to the Middle East. What other mysterious shades of meaning are associated with the original word *Chaldean*?

Ancient cuneiform characters.

In these ancient cuneiform characters, the root word *cal* or *gal* is combined with another root word, *du*, and has the combined sense of "one who does great things" — a Chaldean, therefore, was "one with the power to do great things." If Abram and Sarai were Chaldeans — with great and mysterious power — where had they *really* come from in the beginning? The general conclusion of these researchers is that the link between the Chaldean Abram and Sarai (later Abraham and Sarah) and Indian religious history seems to be more than coincidental. Some theorists have actually argued that the Indian god Brahma and his consort Sarai-svati are the same people as Abram and Sarai.

Another ancient Indian temple.

There are other intriguing etymological theories surrounding the name of Abram. These focus on the *ram* syllable, leaving the *ab/ap* prefix as the Kasmiri word for father. In Hindu religion, the god Ram, known as Lord Ram, is an incarnation of Vishnu. It seems especially appropriate to identify him with the Chaldean Patriarch Abram because Ram was regarded as the personification of all that is good, ethical, and virtuous. Ram never lied. He was always respectful, kind, and gentle with the old and the wise, no matter how frail their age had made them. He himself was never ill, and he never aged. He had the gift of eloquent and persuasive speech. He was omniscient, knowing especially the deepest and most secret thoughts of all whom he encountered. He was also described as an invincible warrior and the most courageous spirit on Earth.

It may also be significant that when Abraham was about to sacrifice his son Isaac, he realized his mistake and sacrificed instead a ram that was entangled in a thicket. The symbolism of the ram needs to be taken into careful consideration when taking into account this particular biblical episode, which played a major part in Abraham's life.

Ram.

The exciting Mexican author and researcher Tomas Doreste, writing in *Moises y los Extraterrestres*, ventures more widely than the Bereshith account, and argues for a close and highly significant connection between Abram and Melchizedek. What if the name Melchizedek is derived from the Indian name Melik-Sadaksina? Traditionally, he was the son of a renowned Kassite (or Cassite) king, and the second part of his name *Sadaksina* can be traced through both Sanskrit and Kashmiri root words to mean "someone who has supernatural powers." Does this also tie in with Zadok, the priest who anointed the great and wise King Solomon? Was the name Zadok really a variation of Sadak? The possession of super-human powers also ties in closely with the cuneiform *Galdu*, as described earlier: the ancient root words describing a Chaldean astrologer, wise man, or magus.

This name, *Zadok*, or *Sadak*, provides another intriguing link with the nine twelfth-century Guardian Guides who surfaced as Knights Templar and dug for an unknown *something* under what they believed had once been part of Solomon's palace. Was that mysterious object they were searching for connected with a wise and mysterious Chaldean, or an equally wise and mysterious Sadak from India, alias Zadok, Solomon's very powerful priest?

If Thoth and Melchizedek were actually one and the same superhuman entity, the strange legend of Sarah in the cave is particularly significant. According to various ancient myths and legends, Noah had access to the miraculous Emerald Tablets on which all the greatest secrets of "magic" (lost science/forgotten technology?) were inscribed. Having survived the flood, he hid the precious artifact in a secret cave at Hebron. One version of the story relates that Sarah found it there along with what, at first, looked like the incredibly well-preserved corpse of Hermes Trismegistus. He was, apparently, not dead — just in a state of suspended animation. When she took the arcane Emerald Tablets from his hand, he stirred and spoke to her. Understandably, Sarah fled from the cave.

One account says that she took two tablets with her and that they eventually became the mystical *Urim* and *Thummim* with which the oldest and most knowledgeable Hebrew priests determined the Divine Will. Another account says that she dropped them as she escaped the cave. Yet another chapter of the history of the Emerald Tablets — and a particularly interesting one in terms of the line of ancient Guardians — is that they came eventually into the hands of Alexander the Great when he explored the mysterious Hebron cave where Hermes lay sleeping. There are some researchers who would attribute Alexander's meteoric success to the knowledge that he gained from reading the Emerald Tablets.

So we draw these strands together to pursue the hypothesis that there was a nexus between the early stories of the Hindu gods and the adventures of the widely travelled Chaldean hero Abraham, as recorded in Bereshith and elsewhere. This theory spreads the potent secret knowledge (which its hypothetical ancient Guardians such as Abraham and Melchizedek supposedly protected) much farther afield. Might it also shed some unusual light on Alexander the Great's exploits many centuries later — especially his conquest of Persia and his progress to India? Did the brilliant and humane Macedonian Emperor have access to ancient secrets that were for him — in his time — the key to world power?

Head of Alexander.

TEMPLARS IN CANADA AND THE UNITED STATES

There is undoubtedly strong Templar influence in Canada and the United States. Much as the work of Christopher Columbus may rightly be acknowledged and appreciated, there is a vast reservoir of evidence suggesting that he was by no means the first European or Mediterranean traveller to cross the Atlantic successfully.

One such piece of evidence is the mysterious Old Stone Mill in Newport, Rhode Island. It stands in Touro Park, off Bellevue Avenue, and its ancient stones are the centre of many controversial theories. Its architectural style has been described by some experts in the field as medieval Scandinavian: its basic shape is cylindrical, and it stands on eight columns with arches between them. It was there before Newport was founded in 1639. It could just as well have been Templar as Norse.

Research carried out by mathematician, scientist, and researcher Dr. Youssef Mroueh suggests that Muslims reached the Americas before Columbus. He cites an episode that took place during the reign of Caliph Abdul-Rahman III at the end of the tenth century, when it was claimed that African Muslims sailed fearlessly into what was referred to then as "the sea of fog and darkness," and returned with treasure from what they described as "a curious land."

The Muslim stronghold of Granada fell to the Christian forces shortly before history noted the voyage of Columbus and the inauguration of the Spanish Inquisition. The Inquisition caused many non-Christians to leave, to try to get away from their persecutors as far and as fast as they could. By 1539, the staunchly Catholic Charles V of Spain had passed a decree prohibiting Muslims from going to the West Indies, which were then under his control. Despite the royal order, it seems that some succeeded in getting there, and travelling on from there to the Americas.

Working much earlier, the Muslim historian and geographer Al-Masudi (871–957) gave an account of Ibn Aswad's voyage to some huge unknown landmass across the Atlantic during the reign of Caliph Ibn-Mohammad, who ruled Spain from 888 to 912. Ibn Aswad came back loaded with treasure.

Another historian named Al-Gutiyya recorded how a navigator named Ibn Farrukh, who came from Granada, visited the Canary Islands during the reign of the Spanish Caliph Hisham II (976 to 1009). The renowned Harvard historian, Leo Weiner, author of *Africa and the Discovery of America* (1920), gave his opinion that Muslims from West Africa had reached Canada and North America, where they were trading with the Iroquois and Algonquin nations — and intermarrying with them.

Another weighty reference comes from Al-Idrisi's work dating from the eleventh century. He records how an expedition sailed from North Africa into the Atlantic and eventually reached an island that was well-cultivated by its people, who soon provided an Arabic interpreter to converse with the sailors. Reportedly another man, Al-Mazandarani, set out from Morocco and reached one of the Caribbean islands toward the end of the thirteenth century.

Not *all* Templar interactions with Muslims in the Middle East were hostile military ones. The Templars and other medieval Europeans learnt a considerable amount about medicine, science, mathematics, geography, navigation, and astronomy from their contact with wise and cultured Arabians. There can be little doubt that part of the Templars' knowledge and some Templar secrets came from their contact with the well-educated Arabians.

Was it from these early Muslim navigators that the Templars acquired their knowledge of what lay beyond the "sea of fog and darkness," so that when their fleet escaped from Philip le Bel they had a serviceable idea of where to go and how to navigate their way across the vast Atlantic? Did they pass some of that important information to Henry Sinclair the navigator, and his friends, the Zeno brothers from Venice?

There is also evidence that Columbus was informed by the residents of Haiti that black navigators had already visited their island. The Haitians showed Columbus spears that these earlier visitors had left behind. These were tipped with a metal referred to by the Haitians as *guanine*, which was a mixture of gold, silver, and copper, and was thought to be an alloy of the type made by craftsmen in their workshops in Bata, Mbini, and Mongomo in Equatorial Guinea on the West Coast of Africa.

There are other significant connections between pre-Columbian voyages and the Mandinka people of West Africa, made internationally famous by the widely acclaimed book and television series *Roots*, which traced the origins of the hero Kunta Kinte to his Mandinkan origins in the village of Juffreh in Gambia, West Africa. What is especially interesting about the Mandinka is that they became an independent nation and then started to expand their empire and culture during the thirteenth century. Did Mandinkan explorers and navigators make contact with the Templar fleet? Did they share their knowledge?

The Mandinka navigators are believed to have ventured as far as America before Columbus, and to have explored much of the interior by using rivers and waterways. The states of Utah, Colorado, New Mexico, and Arizona all meet uniquely at Four Corners, where some of the most spectacular and interesting ruins in the world are located. Well over a thousand years old, they are thought to be mainly the work of the Ancestral Puebloan people, but when knowledge of the early Mandinka navigators and explorers is added to what the Four Corners' ruins reveal, the story becomes more complex. According to ancient Muslim records, there are symbols carved in a cave at Four Corners that can be translated as "the elephants are unwell and behaving badly." If the Mandinkan Atlantic expedition one thousand years ago was massive enough to transport elephants, it would have been of some serious historical consequence. Barry Fell has produced important — if challenging — supporting evidence for pre-Columbian visitors of that kind.

Professor Howard Barraclough "Barry" Fell was one of the outstanding — if controversial — geniuses of the twentieth century, ranking alongside Einstein, Tesla, and Hawking in intellectual power. Born in England in 1917, Barry Fell had a very distinguished academic career, ending with a professorship at Harvard. He also served with gallantry and distinction during the Second World War.

In his book *Saga America* (1920) Professor Fell provided evidence based on various old American texts, diagrams, and charts that suggested that schools had existed there in pre-Columbian times, and that those schools had taught in the old Kufic scripts of North African Arabic. Traces of them were found at Mesa Verde, Colorado, and Mimbres Valley in New Mexico. According to Fell's research, subjects taught in these ancient schools included mathematics, astronomy, geography, and navigation.

Other interesting evidence of Templar visits to pre-Columbian America consists of the Knight's Carving in Westford, Massachusetts. Who is the Knight commemorated by this strange old stone? Many expert historians, archaeologists, and researchers believe that he was Sir James Gunn, who was believed to have been a Templar and a close friend of Henry Sinclair.

ROAD TRIP

To investigate the strange Knight's Carving in Westford, Masachusetts, first-hand, drive along highway I-495 and turn off it at exit 32, which is the Boston Road leading toward the centre of Westford. Turn right into Lincoln Street just before reaching Westford Common. Lincoln Street leads onto Main Street and the Roudenbush Community Centre. Take a left into Depot Street, and the carving of the knight is about fifty metres from Abbot School.

Gunn was in the party travelling inland from the New England coast to investigate smoke they had seen in the distance; he died on the journey, and was buried there. To remember a noble, loyal, and gallant comrade, his friends carved the Knight's Stone in his honour and worked the Gunn family coat of arms into his shield. The sword has a break in it — which symbolizes the death of a knight. The Westford library contains a stone that dates from roughly the same period and shows a fourteenth-century ship, the number *184*, and an arrow. Was it meant to tell other members of the Sinclair–Zeno expedition which way the explorers had gone, or to advise them of the location of the campsite?

Then there are the challenging discoveries of Roman, Berber, Phoenician, and Egyptian artifacts in the Canary Islands, which provide evidence of trade between Europe and Africa and the Canaries from roughly 500 B.C. to A.D. 500. If there were maritime traders from Europe and Africa in the Canaries, the probability that one or more of their ships went from the Canaries to the Americas — either by design or accident — is high.

Another stubborn little piece of evidence from this period is the famous Roman terra cotta head with features that don't seem to be typically Amerindian. It can be seen by researchers today in Mexico City, displayed in the National Museum of Archaeology's Ceramics Hall.

The three-centimetre head was discovered in the Toluca Valley near Tecaxic-Calixtlahuaca. It seems to have been some sort of interment offering put in place in the tomb or grave during the twelfth or thirteenth century. The little Roman head was accompanied by seashells. Did they indicate that it had been brought in from over the sea? The style, design, and facial features all strongly suggest that the head is Roman and may belong to the second century.

Returning to Nova Scotia, the authors visited the Yarmouth Museum and made a close and careful inspection of the so-called Yarmouth Stone, otherwise known to scholars and historians as the Runic Stone, or the Fletcher Stone, after Dr. Richard Fletcher, who claimed that he had discovered it in 1812.

Patricia with Eric J. Ruff and the Yarmouth Stone.

Fletcher's family averred that he was a highly intelligent man, but with a mischievous sense of humour to match his intellect. The possibility of a hoax, therefore, has to be taken into consideration. On the other hand, the stone weighs in the region of two hundred kilograms and was found in a place where Norse maritime adventurers might have decided to leave a permanent record of their visit for posterity. Runic experts have been divided on the subject for nearly two centuries. One said that the runes meant "The son of Harko spoke to the men." Another runic expert translated it as "Leif to Eric raises this monument." Does this indicate that the Viking hero Leif Erickson visited Yarmouth, Nova Scotia?

Other experts, including Professor Magnus Oleson of Oslo, have said that in their opinion the marks are not a genuine runic inscription at all, and have no meaning as such.

The most intriguing possibility of all is that they are not runes at all but secret Masons' marks of the kind that would be understood by members of the Craft, and which can be seen, discreetly placed, in Roslyn Chapel.

Yet another possibility is that whoever carved the mysterious Nova Scotian Yarmouth Stone was familiar with the strange Glozel alphabet, discovered near Vichy, in central France, in 1924. Despite the accusations of fraud and hoax levelled against the Fradin family who discovered the curious Glozel Tablets, the tablets and artifacts found with them stood up well to thermo-luminescent dating tests: the youngest of them being at least five hundred years old, while some date back for several millennia.

Could the enigmatic underground chamber at Glozel where the tablets were found have been the hiding place of a group of refugee Templars some time after 1307? Did some or all of the medieval Templar group from Glozel ultimately join up with Henry Sinclair, or with a vessel belonging to the lost Templar fleet, and so make their way across the Atlantic? If the letters on the Yarmouth Stone are a message in the cryptic Glozellian alphabet, were they intended for later Templar expeditions?

Is it remotely possible that they were intended to indicate that the main party were busy on Oak Island in Mahone Bay, Nova Scotia,

Yarmouth Stone													
Glozel Alphabet													
Morlet's Numbering	4	16	15	31	24	65	41	32	15	16	14	24	43	1

Comparison of Glozel Script and Yarmouth Stone Script: Morlet's Numbering System.

creating the artificial beach, the great coffer dam that made their work possible, and their death-trap flood tunnels designed to protect whatever mysterious treasure they concealed in the Money Pit?

Widespread as it is, the evidence is still not conclusive. But there are mysterious ruins, strange monuments, curious inscribed stones, and other odd, ancient artifacts throughout the Americas that, when taken together, give credence to the possibility that not only the Norse adventurers, but Henry Sinclair, the Zeno brothers, the Templars, Ibn Aswad, and the early Mandinkan mariners also crossed the Atlantic long before Columbus.

What if all these heroic voyages were not random, or haphazard, but were part of some grand design of the ancient pre-Templar Guardians? Is it possible that, one way or the other, these Guardians were trying to establish something extremely important, or to hide something extremely important, on the western side of the Atlantic Ocean — for them, the ill-famed "sea of fog and darkness"?

8 ARTHURIAN MYSTERIES

In a strange old Welsh document known as the *Gododdin of Aneurin*, which goes back to the sixth century or earlier, there is a reference to a hero who fought well "although he was no Arthur." It would be tantamount to complimenting a great athlete on his or her excellent performance today by saying he or she did well "although it wasn't quite up to Superman's standard." We all understand that Superman is a fictional character, but that doesn't prevent us from using his performance as a yardstick for others. Was the writer of *Gododdin* comparing his admired warrior to a fictional Arthur or to a historical character, or even to someone who had a foot in both worlds? In a Hollywood epic about King David, the old king is asked by a wide-eyed boy whether Goliath was really as big as people said he was, to which David replied, "I think he grows a little every year." Arthur, although real enough, may have gradually increased in stature in much the same way as that Hollywood Goliath. But allowing that Aneurin, the *Gododdin* author, was talking about an historical Arthur, whose prowess on many a battlefield was still recalled with awe a century or two later, who was he?

Gildas, a monk who wrote during the sixth century, recounts a great battle at Mount Badon, which apparently halted the westward thrust of the Saxon invaders for several years. Gildas himself doesn't mention Arthur by name in connection with the Badon victory, but the Welsh Annals do, and, although they were a few centuries later than Gildas, they do not hesitate to link Arthur with that great victory over the Saxons. These Welsh Annals also contain a sombre reference to the "strife of Camlann in which both Arthur and Medraut perished."

So the search for Camlann may start the quest for similar-sounding Camelot, and Medraut would seem to be Arthur's fatal kinsman Mordred, born — according to some accounts — of an incestuous relationship with Arthur's evil and treacherous kinswoman, the enchantress Morgana.

Another interesting early source of Arthurian information is Nennius, who was busy translating old Welsh stories into Latin during the early ninth century. In Nennius's *History of the Britons* Arthur was involved in at least a dozen great conflicts of which Badon was only one. Nennius also refers to Arthur as a sort of warlord or field marshall rather than a king, using the Latin phrase *dux bellorum*.

A romantic adventure poem, *The Spoils of Annwn*, which appeared in the 900s, has Arthur performing all kinds of strange, magical, heroic deeds, as well as winning ordinary battles against mortal foes. Giants are slain. Dragons and monsters are dealt with. Witches and wizards are overcome.

The quest motif features here, as well: Arthur, like the classical warrior heroes centuries before him, goes to The Land of the Dead to search for the magic cauldron. Is this, perhaps, a foreshadowing of all the Christianized Holy Grail stories which accumulated later around Arthur and the knights of Camelot? Gwalchmai (Galahad?) and Llenlleawc (Lancelot?) also feature in these earliest Welsh versions of Arthur's adventures. The beautiful but unhappy Gwenhwyfar (Guinevere?), Arthur's wife, also features prominently in these early tales. After these first fragmentary, semi-mythical records had played their pioneering part, the medieval writers began to dominate the Arthurian scenario.

In 1125, William of Malmesbury, an early historian, wanted as complete an account of Arthur's life, exploits, and death as possible. He got one from Geoffrey of Monmouth's *History of the Kings of Britain* in 1135. Geoffrey possessed a vivid imagination, a fine sense of narrative, and a curiously muddy reservoir of miscellaneous data in which myths, legends, folk tales, and oral traditions were partially dissolved, while a few historical facts bobbed about rather uncertainly on its brackish surface.

In 1155, Robert Wace made a free translation of Geoffrey's work into French, and added a few nice touches of his own. Robert de Borron wrote *Merlin* in the early thirteenth century and introduced the sword-in-the-stone theme. French author Chretien de Troyes embroidered the tales still more delicately, and Sir Thomas Malory drew down the medieval curtain in the fifteenth century with his tragic *Morte d'Arthur*, set in Glastonbury and featuring the return of Arthur's magic blade Excalibur to the Lady of the Lake.

Excalibur.

What then was this medieval legend of Arthur, Merlin, Guinevere, and the knights at its fullest extent? As Merlin is usually regarded as the agent by whom Arthur reached the throne via the sword in the stone, it is with Merlin's legend that the story really begins.

In the Arthurian Merlin legend, King Constans, who drove Hengist from Britain, died, leaving three sons: Constantine, Uther, and Pendragon. Constantine, the eldest, succeeded his father and appointed Vortigern as his chief minister. Hengist invaded again; Vortigern betrayed Constantine, and the young king was slain. Vortigern then took the throne despite the existence of the dead Constantine's younger brothers.

Vortigern, aware that his throne was precarious, prudently decided to build a fortress on Salisbury Plain. Each morning, however, according to the legend, the masons found that the walls they had built the day before had collapsed during the night. Wise men, soothsayers, and astrologers were duly consulted. They told Vortigern that the walls would continue falling until the ground had been sprinkled with the blood of a child without a human father.

At this point in the story there is a dynamic confrontation between the wise and powerful St. Blaise and Satan himself. Satan was plotting to introduce his offspring via a pious and innocent virgin who came regularly to St. Blaise, her confessor. Because she told him her every thought and action, Blaise was able to frustrate the Satanic incarnation plot. The pregnant girl was locked in a tower until the baby was born. The unfailingly vigilant Blaise then beat Satan's minions to it, rushing in before they could and baptizing the babe, and naming him Merlin, thus delivering him from becoming a satanic agent. Although Christian baptism — especially by a saint — saved the child and neutralized what would otherwise have been the satanic aspect of Merlin's character, he still retained various superhuman powers because of his parentage. After all, according to Christian tradition, Satan, or Lucifer, had once been a bright and holy angel.

As a child of five Merlin met some of Vortigern's men, who he knew were looking for him, and fearlessly accompanied them to the usurping king's palace. On the way, they passed a youth buying shoes. Merlin laughed. Vortigern's men asked what he was laughing about. Merlin said that the unfortunate young man's purchase was a waste as he would die that day — and he did. Vortigern's men were impressed. He gave them several more grim examples of his prophetic powers before they reached Vortigern's throne room.

Once in the king's presence, Merlin told him boldly that the wise men had deliberately misled him about the reason for the walls' collapsing, as they were jealous of Merlin's greater wisdom and powers, and wanted the king to kill him. Vortigern asked what the real reason for the collapse was. Merlin explained that a white and a red dragon were fighting to the death belowground. Their mortal combat was renewed each night, and that was what threw the walls down. Vortigern gave orders that the beasts must be found and stopped.

Everyone duly assembled to watch the fight as soon as the dragons were uncovered. After an earth-shattering contest, the white dragon won the battle, but then, seeing all the king's warriors assembled, it shuffled away as though afraid and was never seen again. The walls of Vortigern's fortress on Salisbury Plain could now be built.

THE INFANT MERLIN SAVES HIS MOTHER

Legend has it that Merlin's beautiful and innocent young mother was due to be condemned to death for bearing Satan's child, but that same miraculous child started talking at two or three days old and told her that he would save her. When the trial began, he sat upright in her arms and argued the case for her innocence so effectively that she was acquitted.

Merlin made another prophecy: the dragons, he declared, were symbols of the struggle between the usurping Vortigern and the sons of King Constans, who would soon land in Britain with a great army and defeat Vortigern. They did, and the usurper was burnt to death in his newly completed castle on Salisbury Plain.

Merlin was now appointed adviser and chief minister to Uther and Pendragon. Hengist was preparing another attack with his vast Saxon army, and Merlin prophesied that Uther and Pendragon would win, but that one of them would die fighting for Britain. His words came true when Pendragon died in the battle in which Hengist was defeated yet again. Uther, to honour his brother, added Pendragon's name to his own, and asked Merlin to construct a fitting monument to the dead king.

Merlin complied with the king's wishes by bringing from Ireland in a single night the stones with which he erected Stonehenge.

Merlin's legend next involves him with the round table. He went to Carlisle (then known as Carduel) and constructed a magnificent castle for Uther Pendragon. A superb round table became its main feature. Merlin said that this circular table was made in the tradition of a similar one which had once been the property of Joseph of Arimathea, who had once had a following like Uther Pendragon's knights.

When the table was completed and ready for guests to feast at, the medieval equivalent of a house warming party was held at Carduel, to which all the knights and nobles with their wives were invited. The most beautiful woman in the land was Yguerne, wife of Gorlois, the ruler of Tintagel in Cornwall. Tragically, Uther Pendragon fell passionately in love with Yguerne and Gorlois couldn't help but notice. The situation was grimly parallel to David and Bathsheba in the Old Testament, when Bathsheba's loyal and loving husband, Uriah, was murdered on David's orders so that David could have Bathsheba. Gorlois stormed out of Carduel, locked Yguerne in the formidable sea-girt fortress of Tintagel and went to war against Uther Pendragon.

The hapless Gorlois, however, was killed in battle next day, and Uther Pendragon lost no time in marrying the beautiful Yguerne. When Arthur was born, he was generally regarded as the posthumous child of Gorlois, and was given to Merlin to raise. The magician entrusted him to the care of Sir Hector and he grew up to all intents and purposes as the younger brother of Hector's son Kay.

When Uther Pendragon finally died, there was apparently no heir. Only Merlin knew the truth, and he bided his time, prophesying that in due course the true king would be revealed by magic.

Arthur duly became king through the sword-in-the-stone miracle, and Merlin, showing no apparent signs of age — like the equally mysterious Count of Saint-Germain — became King Arthur's loyal and trusted adviser and chief minister, as he had once been to Uther Pendragon.

UTHER AND YGUERNE

The legendary Merlin was always Uther Pendragon's man through thick and thin, irrespective of the ethics of the situation. He changed Uther into the likeness of Gorlois — who was away fighting Pendragon's men elsewhere on the battlefield — and changed himself and his companion, Ulfin, into facsimiles of two of Gorlois's squires. Then the three of them presented themselves at Tintagel, where the completely unsuspecting Yguerne opened the gates to admit them. Uther's night of passion in the guise of Gorlois left Yguerne pregnant with Arthur, who was always understandably thought to be Gorlois's son.

It was due to Merlin — in this version of the legend — that Arthur was always successful in battle, overcoming twelve kings and acquiring an international reputation rivalling Charlemagne or Ghengis Khan.

Merlin's ability as a shape-shifter also features prominently in his legend. On one occasion he was supposed to have turned into a stag and delivered a challenge from Arthur to Oberon's father.

Apart from the great funeral monument at Stonehenge, which he allegedly raised magically to honour the dead Pendragon, Merlin had a great reputation as an architect and builder. He built Camelot for Arthur, and designed and created several magical fountains.

There is also a connection between Merlin and the Grail, or rather one of the earlier, pre-Christian drinking vessels or cauldrons which became blurred together in the Holy Grail legends. He is given credit in one of the stories for making a drinking vessel which could detect character. When an evil or treacherous person attempted to drink from Merlin's Cup, it always overflowed. His other magical artifacts included Arthur's impenetrable armour, and a magic mirror that reflected whatever the user asked to see. Tolkien has a similar one in *Lord of the Rings*, which Galadriel uses. The Wicked Queen in *Snow White* has another.

Just as Arthur had problems with Guinevere and Uther Pendragon had difficulties with Yguerne, so Merlin's life was overshadowed by his relationship with his beautiful mistress, Vivian, the Lady of the Lake. Anxious to learn all his magical secrets, Vivian followed him everywhere, and finally, having stolen the spell from him, she imprisoned him forever in a hawthorn bush deep in the forest of Broceliande in Brittany. There are many Breton legends of how Merlin's voice can still be heard shouting for help there.

Curious, but relatively recent carvings in the Forest of Tay in Scotland may be artists' impressions of this tree-entrapment magic: one could represent the prisoner's wide-open, silently screaming mouth, and another shows a fierce dragon desperately attempting to claw his way out of the encircling wood.

Another version of the legend, which shows Vivian in a better light, relates how she imprisoned him in an underground palace to protect him, a palace to which she alone could gain access. How does this square with the legendary idea that Merlin, like Arthur and the knights, lies sleeping somewhere, waiting to be called? Legends of sleeping knights in a hidden chamber below Roslyn Castle in Scotland, or in a secret tomb beneath its neighbouring chapel, also echo the legend of a Merlin who waits there while the centuries roll past.

There can be little doubt that those great friends and formidable scholars J.R.R. Tolkien and C.S. Lewis had professional access over the years to some very curious old manuscripts, some of which undoubtedly influenced their brilliant writings. Every now and then the judicious Lewis and Tolkien reader comes across tantalizing hints of things in their work that seem to owe more to myth and legend than to pure, imaginative fiction. One such glimpse relates to Merlin. In *That Hideous Strength*, which completes Lewis's science-fiction trilogy, the forces of evil discover Merlin lying in suspended animation in a secret tomb not far from what sounds remarkably like Durham University — Lewis actually disguises the fictional university in his story, but its scenic resemblance to the real Durham is striking. When revived, Merlin brings about the downfall of the evil forces that disturbed his long rest.

Most interesting of all in this connection is Lewis's suggestion that the Merlin of Arthurian legend is one of the last of Tolkien's ancient Men of the West. If, as some scholars have suggested, Tolkien's entire mythology of Middle Earth, with its wizards, elves, dwarfs, orcs, ents, and strange semi-human races is not based solely on the professor's brilliant imagination but on certain ancient manuscripts that came his way, then the strong possibility exists that his powerful and long-lived Men of the West may have had some basis in fact.

Is Lewis's tantalizing reference to Merlin a carefully disguised clue, just as his "imaginary" university bears an uncanny resemblance to Durham? Biblical references to patriarchs who enjoyed great longevity abound. Were they also, in some way, an echo of Tolkien's Men of the West and Lewis's Merlin?

Some of the strangest Arthurian evidence is to be found in the Pictish stones of Meigle, in Scotland. When we closely examined and photographed these recently, it became apparent that the strange old designs on them were open to various conflicting interpretations.

One explanation of the indistinct figure surrounded by stylized lions or wolves is that it represents the death of the unfaithful Guinevere. This version of the story was told to us by a local expert in Meigle. During a period of imprisonment, Guinevere had agreed to sleep with the warden of the Castle where she was being held to ransom, in return for not being passed around the rest of his castle garrison. When Arthur's men finally stormed the castle, he unsympathetically ordered her to be thrown to the wolves for accepting the warden's offer with such alacrity, when most of us would have found it perfectly understandable given the alternative.

Another traditional interpretation of this particular carving was that it represented Daniel in the lions' den, and the beasts surrounding the central figure were powerless to cause harm.

This same ancient Pictish stone at Meigle also contains carvings of a centaur, warriors on horseback, and a child. Other stones in the same collection depict mysterious aquatic beasts and strange unidentifiable crypto-zoological creatures.

A more elaborate and detailed version of the sword-in-the-stone phenomenon that started Arthur's reign concerns an assembly of British nobles at St. Stephen's Church in London on Christmas Day. After Mass had been celebrated, a large stone appeared mysteriously in the churchyard. Above the stone was an anvil, and in the anvil the magic sword was lodged. An inscription declared that only the man who was able to withdraw the sword was the rightful king.

King Arthur.

It has been suggested by some researchers that the whole sword-and-stone episode was historically factual, but that there was a trick to withdrawing the sword. One of the jewels on the hilt was cunningly attached to a system of thin levers and a gear or two inside the blade. Part of the way down the slot in the anvil was a recess into which a bolt sprang from the side of the blade. This bolt, like a mortise lock, slid into its secret socket deep inside the anvil and kept the sword in place. The theory goes on to suggest that Merlin had either engineered the whole thing himself, or had it constructed to his design by a skillful armourer or blacksmith. There were fifth- and sixth-century artisans who would have been capable of carrying out such work.

According to one version of the legend, Arthur handed the sword to his adopted brother, Kay, Hector's son, to use in the tournament. Sir Hector, who had brought up Arthur on Merlin's instructions, saw this happen and recognized the blade as the one from the anvil of destiny on the stone. The whole company was summoned and Arthur replaced the sword and then withdrew it again. He was then warmly acclaimed as the rightful king.

This honeymoon period of ready and joyful acceptance at the start of Arthur's reign was short-lived, however. Dark rumours began to spread. Some now said that he was *not* the pre-wedlock son of Uther Pendragon and the voluptuous Yguerne — as Merlin had declared him to be after the episode with the sword in the stone — but that he had been cast up as a miraculous babe from the depth of the Atlantic on the crest of a huge ninth wave, and had landed at Merlin's feet.

This mysterious sea-babe aspect of the Arthurian story links in with the donation of the sword Excalibur from the equally mysterious and aquatic Lady of the Lake. If he was a strange aquatic child, was she his real mother — guarding the magical blade for him until he came of age to use it?

It also ties in with the strange history of King Mérovée, founder of the early French Merovingian Dynasty, and sometimes referred to as "Mérovée the Twice Born."

According to this legend, his mother, while already pregnant with him, was swimming in the Mediterranean when she was either raped or seduced by an intelligent aquatic being referred to as a Quinotaur. In some inexplicable way, part of the Quinotaur's genetic material was infused with that of the embryonic Mérovée. From this, according to legend, came the magical powers associated with the Merovingian Dynasty, often referred to as the Thaumaturgical Kings.

SECRETS OF THE DOGON

The remarkable Dogon people of Bandiagara in Africa have a puzzling ancient tradition that includes frequent references to a race of highly intelligent — and technologically advanced — amphibian extraterrestrials that they call *Nommos*, which means "associated with water" in the Dogon language. Their tradition asserts that the Nommos landed somewhere northeast of Bandiagara, and looked like a fish-anthropoid hybrid. Like the Oannes of the ancient Babylonian records, and the Sumerian Enki, these amphibian demigods of the Dogon tradition acted as helpers and teachers to the terrestrial people whom they visited.

The third century B.C. Chaldean priest and astronomer Berosu, described *something* that rose from the Erythraean Sea to teach and heal the Babylonians: "The entire body of the creature resembled a fish, but had a second head below its fish's head. It also had feet attached to its fish's tail."

If only a small fraction of these amphibian super-being legends is taken at face value, the possibility exists that benign, water-dependent extraterrestrials were visiting the Earth in those same romantic Dark Ages from which Arthur and Merlin sprang. If Arthur, like Mérovée, had unusual genetic material, some of the traditional Arthurian stories are open to interesting reinterpretations. Was the submerged Lost Land of Lyonesse somewhere off the rugged Cornish peninsula, west of Gorlois and Yguerne's Tintagel? Was it merely the terrestrial human, Uther Pendragon, whom Merlin contrived to bring to the beautiful Yguerne's bed that night? Or did the wily old magician have other stronger and stranger masters than Uther living beneath the waves?

This area of conjecture raises the old and unanswerable question of which legends cloak the truth, and which myths mask the hidden facts. Folklore and mythology have proved time and time again to be more than fiction and fable. There is almost always an intense fire behind their smoke. The stronger and more persistent the mythology and legend the more interesting that true, historical fire turns out to be. The final, irrefutable evidence vindicating the historical reality of both Arthur and Merlin has yet to be discovered: when that evidence is unearthed it may reveal a greater mystery than anything in the medieval legends.

ARTHURIAN LEGEND IN LITERATURE

There have been hundreds of books written about the legend of Camelot and King Arthur. Here are a few of the most famous:

- *The Lady of Shalott* (Alfred, Lord Tennyson)
- *Idylls of the King* (Alfred, Lord Tennyson)
- *A Connecticut Yankee in King Arthur's Court* (Mark Twain)
- *That Hideous Strength* (C.S. Lewis)
- *The Acts of King Arthur and His Noble Knights* (John Steinbeck)

Arthurian Legend on Film

- *A Connecticut Yankee in King Arthur's Court* (1949)
- *Camelot* (1960)
- *The Sword in the Stone* (1963)
- *Monty Python and the Holy Grail* (1975)
- *Excalibur* (1981)
- *First Knight* (1995)
- *King Arthur* (2004)

9 Masonic Secrets

The greater a thing is, and the more important it is, the harder it is to describe, to define, and to analyze. To attempt to answer the basic questions about Freemasonry is almost as deep and wide an undertaking as asking what life itself is, what our universe is, and what our place within it is as members of the human race.

A march of ten thousand kilometres begins with the first step, and the first step in understanding the mysteries of Freemasonry is to consider it as a fraternal organization, a worldwide brotherhood. But it is a brotherhood that is not exclusively gender-specific: the best Freemasonry includes a sisterhood, as well.

Freemasonry can also be thought of as a family, with the kind of bonds between its members that exist in the best, the most loving, the most loyal, and the most mutually supportive extended families.

Just as an ideal family is held together by certain shared ideas and ideals, so is Freemasonry. Freemasons from every walk of life, from every nation, and from every ethnic group share an extremely high moral code and excellent ethical principles. They also share profound metaphysical, theological, and philosophical beliefs. Freemasonry places great stress on the word *free*. There is great tolerance and understanding within its codes of belief. Masons generally accept the existence of a Supreme Being, and see the structural, practical aspects of architectural masonry as reflecting the creative and sustaining work of that Supreme Being. Nevertheless, an honest, open, objective, unbiased, and inquiring mind is the surest mark of a real Freemason. Freemasonry welcomes the traditional owl design as a symbol of wisdom.

Freemasonry is also definable as an *esoteric* art, and just as every profession has its own special secrets, so there are aspects of Masonry that are carefully protected. Barristers, medical practitioners, and computer wizards all tend to have their own specific internal professional knowledge that is usually kept within the group: Freemasonry has its parallel secrets.

Part of this esoteric knowledge stems from the Masonic initiatory system; understandably, there are various degrees within Masonry, as more and more of the ethics and metaphysics of the craft are revealed to the members one stage at a time. Those who understand the language of Masonry will readily describe these gradually unfolding mysteries as "a system of morality veiled in allegory and illustrated by symbols."

Prehistoric proto-Masonic carving of an owl.

All individuals and organizations — religious, social, or political — need to have aims and objectives, and Freemasonry is no exception to this rule. Each Masonic lodge may vary slightly in the way that it phrases its aims and objectives, but every Mason and every lodge would agree about the central aims and objectives:

1. To practise, encourage, and advocate honesty, integrity, friendship, and charity as aspects of the individual's personal life, and his or her social life.

2. To serve and be loyal to one's own religious faith, but to acknowledge and respect different faiths, and to accord them equal value. In the same way, where there are duties and responsibilities to a Mason's home community, he or she aims to comply with those communal duties and demands — insofar as they are in perfect harmony with the good of the wider community.

3. Freemasons aim to do all in their power to show the world that in business and in private life — as well as in their personal relationships — they and the Masonic society they represent — are upright, fair, and honest.

4. Freemasons aim to be team players, to enjoy the company of other Masons, to participate in Masonic fellowship, and work as members of the worldwide Masonic team.

5. Another important objective is to do everything possible to make good people even better and more valuable to society. Masons believe in developing themselves as individuals — and in trying to improve the outside world through education, social interaction, and discussion.

6. Masons recognize the importance of time — our most precious commodity. They seek to balance leisure with work, religious thought with practical service to others.

7. Masons regard human beings as having mental, spiritual, and physical gifts, and Freemasonry teaches its
   members how to make the best use of all of them.

8. Christ taught his disciples the Parable of the Talents:
   Masons follow the teachings of that parable. They seek
   to use whatever talents God has given them for the
   benefit of their families, friends, and neighbours. They
   aim to do this through their private life, as well as their
   business and professional work.

9. Freemasons aim to be totally honest and forthcoming
   about their membership of the organization — especially
   if there is any risk that a conflict of interest may arise.

10. Despite what is often wrongly thought about the
    way that members of the Craft may seek to help one
    another, real Freemasons never use their membership
    to promote their own interests.

These then are the laudable and unobjectionable surface definitions
and the declared aims and objectives of Freemasonry. But there is much,
much more, and although it is equally laudable and unobjectionable, it
goes far deeper and raises enormous questions.

There can be no full and proper understanding of the mysteries and
secrets of Freemasonry without very deep and thorough research into its
earliest history — and that enigmatic history goes back a great deal farther
than is generally understood.

The real beginnings of Masonry in its most archaic forms are lost in
the mists of time. To understand its true nature and purpose, those mists
must be penetrated.

The good and wise King Solomon of Israel is credited with being a
leading Freemason three thousand years ago, and the architecture of his
amazing temple in Jerusalem contained many Masonic symbols.

According to the history of Freemasonry, the temple was the work
of three very great and talented men. The first was King Solomon the
wise; the second was Hiram, the sensible and statesmanlike king of
Tyre; and the third was Hiram Abiff, an artisan with the same level

THE DEEPEST MASONIC SECRETS

When he was a young newcomer to Freemasonry, co-author Lionel was talking confidentially to a far older and much more experienced high-ranking Mason. They had recently been participating together in a Masonic service in their temple, when, referring back to the nature and purpose of that particular service, the wise old man said, "There has to be much more to it than this. It wouldn't have flourished, prospered, and survived as it has unless there were deeper secrets than these."

Lionel has pondered that wise man's words for more than thirty years. There are intriguing truths and mysteries at the back of them. The real secrets of Freemasonry are far older and more profound than anything that takes place at a lodge meeting in a Masonic temple.

King Solomon's Temple.

of skill as the great Bezalel, the craftsman whom Moses praised fulsomely. The third member of the triumvirate was the son of a widow, something of great importance in Masonic tradition. Hiram Abiff was brutally murdered when he courageously refused to reveal the secrets of the Craft.

Among the many fascinating riddles of Solomon's Temple is the mysterious human shape of its floorplan. Some specialist historians and expert archaeologists even suggest that the temple was deliberately laid out to represent not one but *three* human figures. The floorplan has to be read in conjunction with the temple furnishings in order to reveal these secret proto-Masonic designs.

One school of thought proposed that the three humanoid outlines are meant to represent Jacob, father of the twelve sons who became leaders of the Israelite tribes; the current high priest; and *something* very strange and esoteric, *something* that ties in with the myths and legends of the terrifying golem, *something* that at least one daringly unconventional historian has referred to as a "metal messiah."

This metal messiah theory suggests we envisage that the figure consists of a golden head and thorax, arms of silver terminating in brazen fingers, and a pelvis and legs made of bronze. The Holy of Holies is the golden head, the priests' cells along each side are silver arms, and the ten brazen lavers (the vessels in which the officiating priests washed) formed the fingers, five at the end of each arm. In 2 Chronicles 4:6, the precise details of these finger-like lavers are provided, while in 3:17 of the same book there are detailed descriptions of the two pillars known as Jachin and Boaz. These are fitted into the metal messiah theory as comprising the legs of the huge human figure.

But what did Solomon the Wise *intend* this metallic figure to represent? Was he passing on some strange ancient proto-Masonic wisdom about the mysterious appearance of the original guides and guardians of the human race?

There is a possibility that the metal messiah temple design theory may be associated with the old Hebrew golem traditions. Numerous myths and legends are linked to the animated clay monster known as the golem, but the one that is of particular significance to Masonic historians concerns Rabbi Bezalel, or Bezaleel. His name is significant because of his famous forerunner, the great craftsman who worked with Moses during the Exodus. This original Mosaic Bezalel was a strong candidate for high proto-Masonic rank, and it seems reasonable to assume that Rabbi Bezalel, who lived in Europe during the sixteenth century, had been so named because of his important Masonic connections.

Rabbi Bezalel's wife gave birth to their son, Judah Arya, during Passover in 1579 (Jewish Year 5273), and his father prophesied that he would be a potent force for good and would be instrumental in bringing an end to the mindless anti-Semitic persecution of the time. The talented boy grew up benefiting from his father's proto-Masonic wisdom and depth of secret ancient knowledge, and became a rabbi himself, first in Posen in Poland, and later in Prague. When the persecution of the Jews in Prague reached an intolerable level, it was said that Bezalel's wise and skillful son used his mystical powers to create a golem that defended them from their enemies.

Is it possible that the story of the Golem of Prague is more than myth and legend? Is there a mysterious connection between that golem legend and the metal messiah theory of the Jerusalem Temple? There is a persistent historical seventeenth-century tradition that when things were particularly bad for the Jewish community in Prague, someone or some*thing* mysterious and powerful delivered them. If the Golem of Prague is set aside as myth and legend, who or what intervened on behalf of the persecuted Jews of Prague?

If the oldest proto-Masonic thinking contains vestigial truth about the extraterrestrial origin of the first proto-Masonic guides and guardians of humanity, then a being of paranormal powers operating benignly in seventeenth-century Prague is not impossible. What if the learned son of Rabbi Bezalel did not *create* something abnormally powerful to defend his people, but rather *summoned* it?

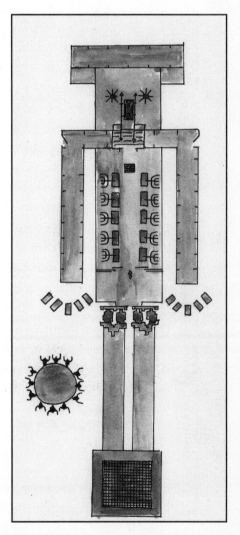

Floorplan of Solomon's Temple.

THE GOLEM

In Jewish tradition, the golem is most widely known as an artificial creature created by magic, often to serve its creator. The word *golem* appears only once in the Bible (Psalms 139:16). In Hebrew, *golem* means "shapeless mass." The Talmud uses the word as "unformed" or "imperfect," and according to Talmudic legend, Adam is called "golem," meaning "body without a soul" (Sanhedrin 38b), for the first twelve hours of his existence.

Tradition maintains that the first record of a Freemason in Canada was in 1634 — even before the nation was known as Canada. Viscount Canada, Lord Alexander, was the son of the first Earl of Stirling in Scotland. Lord Alexander was Master of Works for King Charles I, and was responsible for leading a band of Scots who settled along the banks of the St. Lawrence River during the first half of the seventeenth century.

Viscount Canada was recorded as being a member of Edinburgh Lodge Number One, who met in St. Mary's Chapel in that city. It must be remembered in connection with this very old and honourable Scottish lodge that it was situated very close to Roslyn Chapel — filled with Masonic mysteries. This venerable Edinburgh lodge has records dating as far back as 1599, and there is some evidence that it existed more than a century earlier than that.

Annapolis Royal in Nova Scotia was named after the British Queen Anne (1665–1714) and passed its historic name to Annapolis County in August 1759. In 1738 it had the distinction of being home to the first Canadian lodge.

On October 25, 1854, a very efficient and gallant Canadian soldier, Lieutenant Alexander Dunn, who was also a Freemason, took part in the Charge of the Light Brigade during the Crimean War. Brother Alexander was responsible for saving the lives of two of his equally heroic companions and was awarded the Victoria Cross, which he richly deserved. He was the first Canadian to have been recognized in that way.

Four years after Alexander's unselfish gallantry at Balaclava, Amor de Cosmos, who was a newspaper proprietor in Victoria, British Columbia, advertised for interested local Freemasons to start a lodge there. He was a very good and capable man who demonstrated Masonic ethics and morals throughout his life — and was destined to become the second premier of British Columbia. The following year was a sad one — but it nevertheless created a landmark in Canadian Masonic history. Brother Samuel Hazeltine was a government inspector with special responsibility for steamboats: he died following an accident and was buried with full Masonic honours, the first to have been honoured thusly in Canada.

In 1860, just one year after Brother Samuel's death, Victoria Lodge Number 1085 was formally constituted. Two years later, Brother Thomas Harris was elected as the first mayor of Victoria. When the Dominion of Canada was formally established on July 1, 1867, Brother Sir John A. Macdonald became Canada's first prime minister. Canadian Freemasons have made tremendous contributions to their great nation over the years.

Other famous Canadian Freemasons include Brother Henry Josiah DeForest, artist, and Brother Charles Mair (1838–1927), poet and dramatist who wrote *Tecumseh*. This is a singularly interesting and significant work in which the magical tradition of the strange-looking, carnivorous fluted red pitcher plant is recalled — the pure-hearted who drink from it are said to find both forgetfulness and endless, enchanting dreams of love and romance. Brother Oscar Emmanuel Peterson, the outstanding jazz pianist who was born on August 15, 1925, in Montreal, Quebec, was also listed as a very distinguished member of the Craft in the annals of the Grand Lodge of British Columbia and the Yukon.

Another great and good Canadian Freemason was Brother Joseph-François Perrault (1753–1844), who was known as the Father of Education. A member of the House of Assembly from 1796 until 1800, he abandoned politics and directed his energies toward education. He and his associates in the Canadian education societies devoted themselves to providing education for the poor, and went as far as providing free footwear for necessitous children so that they could walk to school in cold weather. He launched schools for both boys and girls, and inaugurated agricultural educational establishments as well as academic ones. Here, indeed, was a man to admire and follow, a Brother who practised the highest standards of Masonic ethics, morality, and charity.

FAMOUS FREEMASONS

The following individuals are said to have been members of the Masonic Order:

> Gene Autry (actor)
> "Buzz" Aldrin (astronaut)
> William "Bud" Abbott (of Abbott and Costello fame)
> William "Count" Basie (jazz musician)
> Irving Berlin (composer)
> Ernest Borgnine (actor)
> Robert Burns (Scottish poet)
> Marc Chagall (artist)
> Winston Churchill (British prime minister)
> Jack Dempsey (boxer)
> Sir Arthur Conan Doyle (author)
> Clark Gable (actor)
> Wolfgang Amadeus Mozart (composer)
> Arnold Palmer (golfer)
> Paul Revere (hero of the American Revolution)
> Peter Sellers (actor)
> Mark Twain (author)
> Oscar Wilde (author)

Among outstanding Masonic sportsmen were Brother Tim Horton, the hockey star, and Brother Fred "Cyclone" Taylor (1884–1979), who played professional ice hockey for the Ottawa Senators, Vancouver Millionaires, and Vancouver Maroons.

Benign and honest leaders of business and commerce also make great contributions to society. They manufacture quality products at fair prices, and provide worthwhile jobs at fair wages. Two such noble Masonic contributors were Brother Eddy of the Eddy Match Company and Brother John Molson, the founder of Molson Breweries.

As well as being outstanding captains of industry, Freemasons also serve as statesmen. Brother William Grenville Davis and Brother Stuart Miller both served with distinction as premiers of Ontario.

In order to understand the work and importance of worldwide Masonry today, it is necessary to read the profound results of the inspired and dedicated research carried out by Brother Dr. Robert Lomas and Brother Christopher Knight in *The Hiram Key*. An equally important volume is Brother Dr. Robert Lomas's brilliant work *The Invisible College*. What Brother Robert has highlighted is that The Royal Society, founded in 1644 thanks to the tireless work of Brother Sir Robert Moray, succeeded in bringing together former royalists and former parliamentarians after the bitterness and tragedy of the British Civil War. Seventeenth-century Freemasonry was the bridge that enabled the founders of The Royal Society to put the quest for scientific truth above personal grief and political differences.

In so doing, Freemasonry has made possible innumerable scientific advances of the type that are still being made exponentially in our own century. Scientific advances throughout the world today owe more to Brother Sir Robert Moray's work in 1644 than is understood and realized today. One of the greatest Masonic secrets is Masonic modesty. The movement succeeds in doing so much that benefits society — the mystery is that so little of that good work is known and acknowledged. As an example of this, it is undoubtedly true that Brother Lomas has been indirectly instrumental in saving a great many lives. His wide scientific skills include statistics and information systems, some which have been placed at the disposal of the fire brigade in England, to which he is a national consultant/adviser. Brother Lomas and his team at Bradford University created the first computer-based training simulators for firefighters, and practise on those simulators has fine-tuned the skills of many.

A very interesting and informative Masonic book was published, *circa* 1795, written by William Preston, a Past Master of the Lodge of Antiquity. It was entitled *Illustrations of Masonry*, and again Brother Robert Lomas has performed a great service by co-transcribing it with Geraint Lomas. In the introduction to the book, Brother Preston quotes a definition of Freemasonry from *Arnold's Dutch Dictionary*. Arnold says that Freemasonry is a moral order, created by virtuous men, designed to remind us of sublime truths along with innocent social pleasures. Freemasonry, he says, is founded on liberality, brotherly love, and charity.

It is with that definition in mind that we survey Masonry worldwide. We have already looked at the Masonic situation in Canada, Europe, and the United States: we turn now to Africa.

The Cape of Good Hope was opened up in the eighteenth century by the Dutch East India Company to provide fresh food for trading vessels making their way to the East Indies. Many skippers were Freemasons, and it was only natural that Brother Abraham van der Weijde should be appointed as Deputy Grand Master Abroad for the G.E.N. (Grand East of the Netherlands), with full authority to found lodges in Africa. On September 1, 1772, the Lodge de Goede Hoop was duly ratified, and is now Lodge Number One on the register of the Grand Lodge of South Africa. When Nazism almost destroyed the Craft in occupied Europe, it was the strength of the South African Grand Lodge that helped to revive the G.E.N, under whose aegis it had originally come into existence. Freemasonry flourishes in South Africa today, and does much to aid society there. On April 22, 1961, the Grand Lodge of Southern Africa was formed, with Colonel Colin Graham Botha as its first Grand Master.

An examination of Freemasonry in Argentina highlights the work of Brother General José Francisco de San Martin (1778–1850). Regarded as one of the prime liberators of Spanish South America, Brother José was a national hero of Argentina. His father was a Spanish official in Yapeyú, in the province of Corrientes, then one of Spain's colonies. Brother José was trained as a soldier in the Military Academy of Madrid, and commissioned in 1793. By 1808, he had risen to the rank of lieutenant colonel. In 1812, he left the Spanish army and returned to Argentina to fight for the revolutionaries who wanted freedom from Spanish rule. He was massively successful, and it can be argued that he was one of the most significant liberators of modern South America. His love of liberty and independence were typically Masonic, and he was an honest and honourable man as well as an outstandingly able one. Both he and Simon Bolivar were Freemasons.

The deepest secrets of Freemasonry are truly global secrets.

FREEMASON BOLIVAR OF BOLIVIA

There is a very real sense in which Freemasonry enabled Simon Bolivar to cope with the tragedies that shrouded his short life. Born in 1783, he died of tuberculosis in 1830, when he was only forty-seven. His parents died when young Simon was only nine years old, and the maternal grandfather who took care of him also died shortly afterward. An uncle then took care of him in Madrid, where Simon met and married the lovely Maria Teresa Rodriguez in 1802. He returned with her to Venezuela, where she died of yellow fever in 1803. He became a Freemason in Cadiz, and joined the Scottish Rite in 1807. He was later to found the Order and Liberty Lodge Number 2 in Peru. After his victories in the Wars of Liberation, Bolivia was named after him.

10 SECRET SOCIETIES

Working for the sake of argument on the assumption that ancient pre-Templar Guardians actually existed and employed strange knowledge and superhuman powers, it seems probable that the Templars were not their only terrestrial instruments. Many contemporary secret societies and hidden, closed orders claim to have Templar connections, and to share at least some of the arcane secrets that the ancient Guardians later entrusted to the medieval Templars. The Rosicrucians are prominent in this category of "other secret societies."

ROSICRUCIANS

Round about 1610 there appeared a strange pamphlet entitled *Farma Fraternitas RC*. The RC initials stood for *Rosae Crucis*. Several similar pamphlets appeared shortly afterward. The gist of what they had to say was that a Rosicrucian Brotherhood had been founded by a high-ranking German aristocrat named Christian Rosenkreuz, who had lived from 1378–1484. It was said that Rosenkreuz had at one time been a monk, and that he had travelled extensively, including visits to Fez, Jerusalem, and Damascus. During these journeys in the Middle East, he had learnt much from the Arabian friends he had made there, and some of their secret knowledge that he had acquired was described as "magic."

It was said that early Rosicrucian teaching was opposed to formal Roman Catholicism and papal authority, and that seventeenth-century Rosicrucian pamphlets also apparently upheld a form of theosophy. Theosophy may be described as a body of belief contending that all religion worthy of the name represents humanity's various attempts to reach "the Divine" — whatever *that* Ultimate Mystery may eventually turn out to be.

The *Concise Oxford Dictionary* defines *theosophy* in part as "any of various philosophies professing to achieve a knowledge of God by spiritual ecstasy, direct intuition." Modern theosophy — which is not a million light years from the ideas ascribed to Rosenkreuz — has seven main features:

Its first principle is that consciousness is both universal and individual. Theosophists believe that nature and the entire natural order are directed and guided by laws and principles. Nothing is haphazard. Nothing happens by pure, random chance. Theosophists also suggest that *everything* experiences consciousness.

Their second premise is that human beings are potentially immortal, but their eternal aspect is part of a "higher self." The individual personality and normal self-awareness, which we call the individual or the character, is unaware of the undying "higher self." Immortality, in Theosophy, is dependent upon uniting the "lower" human self with the "higher" spiritual self.

The third principle relates to that part of the human entity which is the centre of desires and wishes.

Karma is their fourth basic idea, but their version of Karma seems to approach Gnostic dualism of the kind known to the Cathars of the Languedoc (whose secrets most likely passed to the Templars during the thirteenth century). Spirit is seen as good, and matter is regarded as bad. One seems to turn into the other — then back again. This part of their teachings suggests that Universal Destiny consists of progressing through as many as seven distinct stages.

Fifth, there is a belief in universal brotherhood and sisterhood, because everything — and everyone — came from the same divine source. The word *monad* is used in this context by theosophists, who believe that all things are really "monads." A number of dictionaries define *monad* in its philosophical sense as "one of the simplest individual entities of which the universe is made up, according to Leibniz." In its Greek aspect of being an ultimate, indivisible unit, monad is derived from *monas, monados.* The mysterious mathematical codes and ciphers

STAGES OF REINCARNATION

The word *reincarnation* comes from Latin, meaning "entering the flesh again." Reincarnation is seen as something universal: a human being may once have been a rock, then an insect, a fish, an amphibian, and a mammal, before attaining human form. The idea of reincarnation is a central belief in the majority of Indian religions, such as Hinduism, Jainism, and Sikhism. The concept of rebirth in Buddhism is also often referred to as reincarnation.

of men like Euler and Bernoulli may well have contributed to *The Da Vinci Code* and the enigmas it conceals. It is particularly significant at this stage to remember that Pythagoras — one of the earliest fathers of mathematics — also referred to the monad. In his view it was the unity from which all numbers and multiplicity flow. In his *Metaphysics*, Aristotle called the monad the principle (Greek *arche*) of number. To him it was without quantity, and was unchangeable and indivisible.

The neo-Platonists used monad to signify what they called "The One": the Christian Platonist writer Synesius of Cyrene, who lived from 370 until A.D. 414, described God as "The Monad of Monads." If Leibniz got it right in his struggle to bridge the intellectual chasm between Descartes' teaching that matter is inert and Spinoza's pantheistic monism, then Leibniz's monads may well provide useful insights into the real nature of the ancient pre-Templar Guardians. Other philosophers have certainly considered monads to be indivisible centres of force, but have not always gone along with Leibniz's wider view that such monads can also have the distinctive qualities of representation and perception.

The sixth principle of theosophy is often called *evolution* — but it is evolution seen from a particular and special perspective. Theosophical evolution incorporates progress in ethics and morality, goodness and concern for other people's welfare, philosophy, science, religion, and the arts. Theosophists see this kind of evolution as helping humanity to approach the Divine.

Their seventh and final principle is numerological: the mathematical codes return! This final idea is known to theosophists as the *Septenary*.

their universe is understandable in terms of the mysterious number seven. To summarize this theosophical Septenary concept, the monad is seen as having seven distinct bodies: physical, vital, desiring, mental, causal, intuitional, and, finally, ineffable.

Although it was alleged by the early-seventeenth-century Rosicrucians that the alchemical production of gold was a relatively simple and straightforward process, Rosenkreuz apparently aspired to go far beyond the advantages of mere material wealth: he wanted his followers and co-workers — sometimes referred to as the "Invisibles" — to concentrate on theological and philosophical principles and to study the deep secrets of nature in order to benefit humanity. That sounds remarkably close to the aspirations of the ancient pre-Templar Guardians.

There is a significant amount of material that is morally and philosophically commendable among Rosicrucian teachings, and much of it coincides with the ethics of leaders like Alexander and Charlemagne as examined in earlier chapters. The question arises persistently: were these shared moral precepts an indication that the ancient pre-Templar Guardians were working with several different secret groups like the Rosicrucians, as well as with the medieval Templars of Jerusalem?

More speculative and less accessible to researchers than Rosicrucianism is the so-called *Prieuré de Sion* — rendered as the "Priory of Sion" in English, sometimes with the variant spelling *Zion*. Theories range from

THE MYSTERIES OF ROSENKREUZ'S TOMB

An interesting old book called *The Secret Societies of All Ages and Countries* appeared in 1875, and was revised and reissued in 1896. Its author, Charles William Heckethorn, reported on various claims made by early supporters of the group that came to be known as Rosicrucians. These claims included the discovery and reopening of Rosenkreuz's mysterious tomb in 1604 — 120 years after his death. This arcane tomb was alleged to have contained many strange things, including lamps that were either still burning or had been so cleverly constructed by the ancient alchemists that they lit themselves as soon as fresh oxygen entered the chamber.

its being merely a harmless but elaborate hoax to its being one of the most ancient, powerful, and sinister secret societies in the world. In 1956, Article IIIc of what purported to be the Statutes of the Priory of Sion maintained that the organization took its name from Mount Sion — not the one in the Middle East, but the one that was close to the little French town of Annemasse near the Swiss border, where Pierre Plantard and André Bonhomme lived at that time. The official registration was made by them in the sub-prefecture of Saint-Julien-en-Genevoise on May 7, 1956. Plantard's critics would argue that he was an impostor rather than a genuine Merovingian descendant — but that is an issue between him and them. Certainly claims were made — perhaps implicitly, rather than explicitly — that he was a claimant to the throne of France, and perhaps of Europe as well, via his Merovingian ancestors. In their world-famous *Holy Blood, Holy Grail*, Baigent, Lincoln, and Leigh made much of *The Secret Files of Henry Lobineau*, variously described by its detractors as a pseudo-historical document. This, together with Plantard's own assertions, led to the hypothesis that The Priory of Sion dated back at least to the time of the medieval Templars of Jerusalem, that it was one of the powers behind the Templars, that it wanted to re-establish a Merovingian monarchy in Europe, and that the Merovingians were deserving of this because they included the descendants of Jesus and Mary Magdalen.

Considering the slow but resolute progress of those federalist Europeanizers, who seem to be working toward a European Superstate rather than a simple, but commercially useful, Common Market, a perceptive political observer might wonder whether the Priory's dream of a new version of the Holy Roman Empire, perhaps restyled "The Holy European Empire," could really be on track. If it genuinely aimed at worldwide peace, prosperity, and justice — rather than domination, control, and exploitation — it might, perhaps, have some commendable qualities! It might also be part of what the ancient and mysterious pre-Templar Guardians are steering toward!

One of the most contentious aspects of the Priory — if it exists as anything other than an elaborate hoax — is its supposed list of Grand Masters, who are not universally recognized by Priorists, some of whom support different versions of its history. Plantard maintained that the Priory had been founded in 1681 at Rennes-le-Château (*where else?*) — and Dan Brown's use of the idea in his bestselling *Da Vinci Code* has done a great deal to revive interest in it.

Just for the record, and on the outside chance that there's a glimmer of reality behind the smoke surrounding the myths and legends concerning the Priory, the list of alleged Grand Masters included Bertrand de Blanchefort (1156–69), Jean de Saint-Clair (1351–66), Leonardo da Vinci (1510–19), Nostradamus (1556–66), Louis de Nevers (1575–95), Isaac Newton (1691–1727), Victor Hugo (1844–85), Claude Debussy (1885–1918), Jean Cocteau (1918–63), and Pierre Plantard (1963–81).

Both Plantard and the Priory claimed that their motto was *Et in Arcadia Ego*. Wherever the real truth about the arcane and diffuse Templar secrets may lie concealed, it is always remarkable how the various quests for it are circular in nature — they inevitably curve back to Rennes-le-Château, to Poussin's paintings, and to that curious Latin text, *Et in Arcadia ego*.

The easiest way in may be via Adam Weishaupt's life and work. Weishaupt, who was born in 1748, simply referred to himself as Brother Spartacus. The Abbé Barruel spoke of him as a devil, while Jefferson regarded him merely as a harmless philanthropist. An accusation so vehement that it is close to being a paradoxical compliment came from John Robinson, one-time professor of natural philosophy at Scotland's Edinburgh University. He described Weishaupt as "the profoundest

Poussin's *Et in Arcadia ego* version 1.

THE ILLUMINATI

One of the earliest uses of the term, which is based on the Greek root from which the English word *illumination* is derived, was in connection with baptized Christians in the early church — they had "received illumination," or "seen the light." The Alumbrados, who were religious mystics in sixteenth-century Spain, were also called Illuminati, as were the followers of Adam Weishaupt — who seemed to have gone in an entirely different direction and aimed to replace religion with rationalism.

conspirator that ever existed." Robinson sent a copy of his book *Proofs of a Conspiracy* to George Washington on the subject of Weishaupt and the Illuminati. Washington replied that he knew about them, and that some of them were already in America.

The background of the real, historical Spartacus is helpful insofar as it illustrates what Weishaupt would have thought of as his brand of idealism. The defiant hero after whom Weishaupt named himself was a Thracian who had once served as an auxiliary in the Roman Army in Macedonia. He deserted, but was recaptured and sold into slavery. From there he became a trainee gladiator at Batiatus in Capua. He led a breakout from the gladiator school involving almost one hundred fellow trainees in 73 B.C. They attracted thousands of runaway slaves as followers. After many battles, Spartacus and his men were finally defeated, and the Roman authorities enacted a bloody and terrible vengeance. Nevertheless, the name of Spartacus became synonymous with a fight for freedom and equality — and has been so for many centuries.

During his mid-eighteenth-century upbringing, Weishaupt lived in Ingolstadt in Bavaria, where he learned Czech, Italian, Latin, Greek, and Hebrew. He would have had the ideal background knowledge to compile the strange secret parchments that were allegedly found in Rennes-le-Château, and which purportedly led Saunière to his enigmatic treasure.

Weishaupt's parents had originally been Jewish but had converted to Roman Catholicism. Despite the powerful persuasion of his Jesuit teachers, Weishaupt avoided the role of overseas missionary that they recommended for him, and instead became professor of canon law at Ingolstadt University. His high intelligence, linguistic skills, and access to the university's library of interesting old documents brought him into contact with the occult, and he focused in particular on the mysteries of the Great Pyramid of Giza.

THE GREAT PYRAMID OF GIZA

The Great Pyramid of Giza is a unique structure — counted among the Seven Wonders of the Ancient World — and it points to what is best described as the celestial North Pole with an accuracy that modern science would be challenged to equal. If its alignment is genuinely deliberate, and not merely a remarkable coincidence, the builders of the pyramid were impressive technologists and astronomers — men and women in the same league as Pythagoras, da Vinci, and Newton. It's a quantitative masterpiece as well as a qualitative one. There are roughly two and a half million limestone blocks in the Great Pyramid.

Investigators and researchers from various scientific disciplines have put forward several different theories about the age of the Great Pyramid. One accurate and ingenious hypothesis put forward by Dr. Kate Spence, an expert Egyptologist from Cambridge University, points out that Polaris (the Pole Star), which is a very useful guide to the Earth's North Pole today, wasn't in its present position from the standpoint of earthly observers when the pyramids were allegedly being built. Instead, the ancient Egyptian astronomers would have had access to *two* stars, Kochab and Mizar, which together enabled north to be fixed accurately. The positions of Kochab and Mizar in 2467 B.C. would have been particularly helpful to Egyptian astronomers, and this could well have been around the time when the Great Pyramid of Giza was being constructed.

There is other intriguing evidence, however, that leads different researchers to suggest a far older date for the Great Pyramid: 10 000 B.C., or even farther back, perhaps. That suggestion would link up with the legends of Atlantis and Lemuria, and would point yet again to the influence of the ancient pre-Templar Guardians.

The Arabian historian, philosopher, scientist, and mathematician, Abu Raihan Al Biruni, who lived from 973–1048, was of the opinion that the ancient pyramids had watermarks on them at one time that indicated a flood of unprecedented proportions in that area in the distant past. Such a flood — possibly the same as the one described in Genesis, and in the Mesopotamian account that has a hero named Utnapishtim playing Noah's role — actually seems to have occurred around 10 000 B.C. Al Biruni's evidence is well worth considering. He ranks alongside da Vinci as a great all-round scholar and a profound thinker. Was Al Biruni one of the Ancient Guardians, or just one of their very able human supporters?

So what did Weishaupt find in the Great Pyramid? Where did his occult research lead him? He certainly had a close friend and collaborator named Franz Kolmer, who had lived in Alexandria and visited Giza on several occasions. The society that they founded together — unless it was actually a much older and more mysterious group into which they were initiated — had five major principles: the abolition of hereditary monarchies; the end of private property and legacies; getting rid of nationalism and the patriotism that accompanied it; the end of marriage and family life; and the abolition of religion — of *all* religion!

Although the term *Cognoscenti* may refer in general usage simply to "those who know," to connoisseurs and experts in various fields such as

MYSTERIOUS LIGHTNING STRIKE

The Illuminati's progress came to a dramatic end when lightning killed one of their couriers — a sort of eighteenth-century James Bond type. Police found coded messages from Weishaupt sewn into the dead messenger's clothes. After that particular balloon went up, Weishaupt spent the rest of his life in exile in Gotha in Thuringia, now part of modern Germany. Even here there are strange links that seem more than coincidental: Princess Basina (mother of Mérovée the Twice Born) came from Thuringia. It was also in Thuringia that Tannhauser had a whale of a time with the local version of Venus-Aphrodite, known in German folklore as Frau Hulda, in her subterranean love-palace deep in the Hörselberg.

music, drama, wine tasting, cuisine, and art, it may also have a very special "secret sense" and relate to an actual undercover organization like the Illuminati.

In this connection, the remarkable Johannes Vermeer van Delft (1632–75) has been suspected of belonging to a secret society — many of whom were also artists — whose members were referred to as *cognoscenti*. Very little is known about Vermeer's life — and he may have taken care that it was kept as secret as possible. His remarkable paintings are thought by some of the art experts who are intrigued by the apparent geometry of Poussin's paintings and their connections with the Rennes-le-Château mystery to be based on the same — or very similar "Grail geometry."

In these enigmatic canvases, some simple object, such as the shepherd's staff in Poussin's *Shepherds of Arcadia*, can apparently be used as an indicator line that leads on to a complex geometrical construction. In Vermeer's case, one very significant painting is his *Little Street*, where the gutter — unusually prominent in his composition as a whole — may be the key-line for a Grail-geometry construction. On occasion, when his work has been X-rayed, there are hints of figures that have been painted out. They may mean nothing more than that a talented painter changed his composition as a better idea occurred to him — on the other hand, they may be highly significant.

Just as Templar codes were frequently associated with the Knight's Tour on chessboards, so checkered floors have considerable significance in other contexts. It is, therefore, interesting to observe that the tiles which the woman is apparently cleaning in Vermeer's *Little Street* are arranged as a checkerboard. The checkerboard patterns in the Church of St. Mary Magdalen in Rennes-le-Château may also be meaningful in this context.

Another very powerful and well-concealed secret society seems to have been in the hands of Francis Bacon: one of the most mysterious characters in sixteenth- and seventeenth-century history. Born in 1561, he supposedly died in 1626 following a bout of pneumonia. Bacon's keen interest in all branches of science and philosophy — as well as his great literary achievements — had led him to experiment with food preservation using snow and ice. The details of the episode that was said to have led to his death are his experiment with a chicken. In bitterly cold weather, with snow falling heavily, Bacon ordered his coachman to stop so that he could gather up a quantity of snow to pack around the chicken he had just bought from a nearby butcher and poulterer. Exposure to the severe weather gave him a chill, which developed allegedly fatal complications.

There are researchers, however, who tell a different story of the end of Bacon's life. For reasons of his own, and those of the secret society in which he is believed to have played a prominent part, Bacon's recovery from the pneumonia was kept secret and he was smuggled out of Britain. There was

Sir Francis Bacon.

THE BIG BOOK OF MYSTERIES

a mock funeral, and it would have been characteristic of Bacon's generosity and gentle humour to have sent the body of an unknown pauper into a dignified resting place in St. Michael's Church in Gorhambury, where Bacon's family had their home. That *someone* was buried in Bacon's coffin can be argued from an episode in which Dr. King of St. Alban's allegedly disturbed Bacon's skull during the interment of Sir Thomas Meautys, Bacon's loyal old friend and secretary who had expressed a wish to lie near his former employer. King had attended Meautys during his last illness in 1649. More disturbances were to follow some thirty years later. According to John Aubrey's account in *Brief Lives*, Sir Harbottle Grimston, who was Master of the Rolls in 1681, ordered Bacon's coffin to be moved in order to make space for his own!

BACON'S SECRET LIFE?

If accounts of Bacon's mock funeral are true, where did Sir Francis go in 1626? The evidence points to his having enjoyed a long and happy life in Germany under another name, where he was well cared for and protected by powerful and influential members of his secret society.

A reasonable case can also be made that Francis Bacon was the illegitimate son of Queen Elizabeth I — not by Dudley, Earl of Leicester, the rather effete and unpleasant murder suspect in the death of his young wife, Amy Robsart, and the man who is sometimes *said* to have been Elizabeth's lover, but by the dashing, bold, and fearless Sir Francis Drake, who would have been much more attractive than Dudley in the queen's eyes, even though he was a few years younger than Elizabeth.

There was a very delicate religio-political balance in England at the time. If Elizabeth had produced an illegitimate son, her Protestant throne would have been in peril. Francis Bacon's ostensible parents, Sir Nicholas and Lady Bacon, were enthusiastic Protestants and were totally loyal and dedicated to Queen Elizabeth. It might just have been possible for Lady Bacon to have spread the word that she was pregnant in advance of the birth of Elizabeth's son. Elizabeth is known to have visited the Bacon family at Gorhambury. Was it on one such visit that the all-important baby-switch was made?

Between the mysteries of Francis Bacon's birth and death came the mysteries of his secret society, and the codes they used.

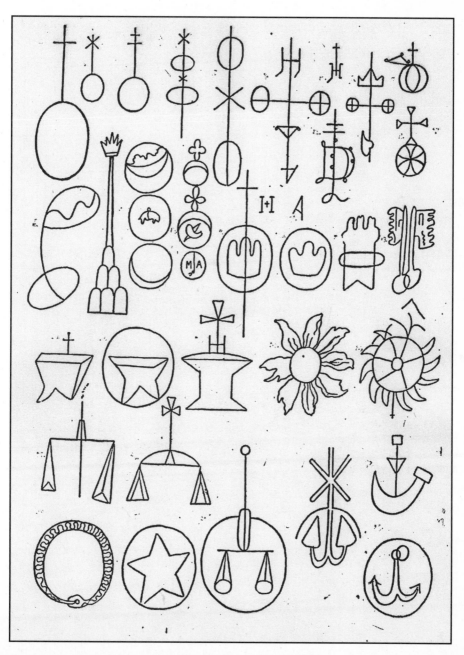

Some examples of Bacon's mysterious watermark codes.

RENNES-LE-CHÂTEAU AND THE BLOODLINE MYSTERY

Acentury ago, an impoverished French priest apparently discovered an amazing secret which made him immensely rich. Rennes-le-Château is a tiny hilltop village in southwestern France, resting among the foothills of the Pyrenees. Today, there are a few shops and restaurants; a small museum; the ruined Château Hautpoul, owned by Monsieur Fatin, the sculptor, and his sister; the mysterious old Church of St. Mary Magdalene, where many lost secrets could still lie buried; a gaunt watchtower with a steel door; and the stately Villa Bethania — once owned by Bérenger Saunière and his housekeeper, Marie Dénarnaud.

Rennes-le-Château poses three challenging questions. First, *where* did Bérenger and Marie find the money to do all that they did in the village between 1885 and 1917, when Saunière died in what were alleged to be

The ruined Château Hautpoul at Rennes-le-Château.

sinister circumstances? A second and greater riddle is the unknown *source* of whatever mysterious wealth they uncovered. The third and greatest question is *where is it now?*

There are at least ten major theories concerning the origins of Saunière's sudden wealth. Some researchers believe that it can all be accounted for by anonymous donations, by selling masses, and simply by collecting money from grateful visitors, pilgrims, and local parishioners.

But when every last account book has been audited and every legal record of Saunière's spirited battles with the querulous and obsessively bureaucratic Bishop Beauséjour has been scrutinized, there still appears to be a significant credibility gap. To put the counter-argument at its most basic, Saunière seems to have spent a lot more money than the supposed gifts and paid masses could ever have brought in.

So if that first basic common sense "explanation" of Saunière's wealth and conspicuous spending isn't quite adequate, what else might account for his undeniably conspicuous spending power? Ever since New Testament times, the opponents of Christianity have tried — so far with singular lack of success — to discredit Christ's resurrection. Two thousand years ago, the high priest and his minions even attempted to bribe the Roman guards to testify that Christ's disciples had stolen his body from the rock tomb while they, the soldiers, were sleeping on duty.

This ancient and badly decayed red herring has been revived, disguised, camouflaged, and otherwise hidden under a veneer of contemporary pseudo-science, then exported with alacrity to Rennes-le-Château.

There are several quaint variants of this completely untenable hypothesis, but in essence it proposes that Jesus was secretly married to Mary Magdalene, and eventually fled with her and their children to the south of France, where their descendants became part of the Merovingian Dynasty. It is alleged that Christ either recovered after the crucifixion, or allowed someone else to die in his place — Simon of Cyrene being the favourite candidate for this altruistic but unenviable role. It is then further proposed that two millennia later Saunière found some damning anti-resurrection "evidence" hidden in or near Rennes. Proponents of this idea seem to be suggesting that it was Christ's mummified body (neatly labelled, of course, and duly signed and verified as authentic by a conscientious first-century Frankish government embalmer.) How about Christ's birth, wedding, and death certificates — while they're at it — witnessed by Peter, James, and John, of course, and then countersigned by the local Rabbi and a respectable Roman notary public?

The theory then goes on to suggest that Saunière promptly used whatever he'd found to blackmail the Church. The whole idea goes down faster than the *Titanic* once it collides with the inconvenient iceberg of fact. The historical evidence then dismantles even the sunken wreckage. If the disciples and the early Church had had the slightest doubt about whether Jesus really was who he said he was, and that he had, in fact, risen from the dead, they would never have faced persecution and death for their faith. A brave man or woman is willing to die for the truth, or a greatly loved person. Nobody knowingly dies for a lie.

Then there is the *personality* of Jesus himself: it shines radiantly but realistically through all the contemporary accounts in the Gospels, the Acts, and the Epistles. This totally unselfish and dedicated God-Man had immense courage and the highest moral principles. He would never have quit. He would never have let someone else die in his place while he escaped ignominiously to France.

It is historically possible (and perhaps likely) that Mary Magdalene, Mary of Bethany, and "the woman who was a sinner" (who anointed Christ's feet with perfume and tears, and then dried them with her hair) were really one and the same person — and that *that* woman was married to Jesus. She might also have been "the woman taken in adultery" and brought to Jesus by his enemies to see whether he would condone the ancient Mosaic Law about stoning her to death, or choose instead to obey the current Roman Law which prohibited the death penalty except with Roman permission. It was an impossible situation for him. Either answer was a decisive socio-political loser. Yet how much worse for him if it had been *his own deeply loved wife* whom his enemies claimed they had just caught in the act, and cynically brought to him for judgment?

Christ's intensely busy public mission would have left him little or no time to be a loving and attentive homemaker, husband, and father — which is the strongest argument (and the only acceptable one) for his never having married. But what if it had been his beloved wife, Mary Magdalene, alias Mary of Bethany, who was now in the hands of these hostile, hypocritical puritans, and waiting at his feet for life or death judgment?

Just suppose for an instant that her understandable human feelings of loneliness and neglect had led her into an almost fatally disastrous adulterous relationship. Christ's total understanding and ready forgiveness — his skill in turning her would-be executioners aside with the unforgettable "Let him who is without sin cast the first stone at her" — all these factors would make poignant sense of her subsequent anointing of his feet, and her grateful tears. And again, if they *had* been married, was it at Christ's earlier instigation — his thoughtful provision for his family's future — that she later took their children to the relative safety of southwestern France following his crucifixion and resurrection? After all, Mary *was* the first person to see him alive again in the garden. Was that genuinely miraculous reassurance and earthly farewell a special, unique privilege for a loving wife?

Another moment's reflection raises several deep questions about the *nature* of this supposed "Saunière-blackmailed-the-Church" evidence that the boldly adventurous village priest was thought to have found.

It would have been incredibly easy for the opponents of Christianity to proclaim that almost any crucified male body of approximately the right height and age was the body of Jesus. If Saunière had merely turned up some imperfectly preserved mortal remains *purporting* to be Christ's, it would constitute no proof at all. Insurance investigators' records contain numerous records of fraudulent claims based on the criminals' hope that the body in question would prove unidentifiable. Saunière could not have found incontrovertible "proof" that Christ's resurrection never took place simply because *no such proof could* exist.

The obnoxious Bishop Beauséjour and his superiors had their faults — but they weren't fools. It would have been much easier and cheaper for the Church authorities to challenge Saunière's hopelessly insubstantial claims than to submit to his blackmail. On the scale of probabilities, it is infinitely more likely that the mummified body of Donald Duck will be discovered at Rennes rather than that the body of Jesus is hidden there.

That Saunière was a blackmailer is yet another theory put forward from time to time. Some researchers suggest that he betrayed the Seal of the Confessional and made certain wealthy — but indiscreet — penitents pay exorbitantly for their past misdemeanours. Admittedly, it's a possibility, but it doesn't fit with what we know of Saunière's character after twenty years of research. The profile is all wrong.

Saunière emerges as a bold, extravagant, ambitious, and resolute man. He was physically and mentally powerful, independent, unafraid, and unconventional. If sufficiently provoked or threatened, he might well have killed an opponent on the spur of the moment — just as Moses "smote" the Egyptian taskmaster who was ill-treating a Hebrew slave.

Saunière was also romantic and red-blooded: he could easily have succumbed to the attractions of his nubile young housekeeper, Marie

Dénarnaud, or indulged in a passionate fling with the glamorous and sophisticated opera star Emma Calvé, as some researchers have suggested. But Saunière's characteristic sins would have been those impetuous and understandable sins of the flesh — not the mean, cruel, calculating, and premeditated sins of a heartless, professional blackmailer.

A far stronger possibility is that Bérenger found either a treasure — or some strange, ancient secret that made it possible for him to *create* wealth.

The mysterious Tomb of Arques (now demolished) once stood very close to Rennes-le-Château. It seems to be the same tomb as the one painted by Poussin in his *Shepherds of Arcadia*. Was Poussin making a secret, coded reference to the treasure of Rennes? He used the mysterious code phrase *Et in Arcadia ego* as the inscription on the tomb in his painting. Was Poussin saying that the mysterious treasure of Rennes lay in or near the Tomb of Arques?

Co-authors Lionel and Patricia examining the Tomb of Arques.

THE VISIGOTHS AT RENNES

Although only a tiny hilltop village today, there is viable evidence that Rennes was once a significant Visigothic citadel, defended by a garrison of two thousand men. There are plenty of possible sources for such a treasure. The Visigoths sacked Rome in 410. Where better to hide the cream of their precious Roman spoils than in their own easily defended citadel of Rennes?

The Templars had strongholds in the area near Rennes, and when their gallant Order was decimated by the odious King Philip le Bel in 1307, it is possible, even probable, that some Templar treasure would have been hidden in or near Rennes — perhaps even in or under Saunière's ancient Church of St. Mary Magdalene.

The almost impregnable Cathar fortress of Montségur was overrun by the Catholic Crusaders in 1244, but, just before the final disaster overwhelmed the defenders, four of their best mountaineers descended the precipitous crag below the fortress, carrying with them "the treasures of their faith" — described in the Latin records of the Inquisition as "*pecuniam infinitam*" — literally "infinite or unlimited money." Did those same fearless and fanatical mountaineers conceal their priceless secret somewhere in the vicinity of Rennes? Was that what Saunière found six centuries later?

There were Roman gold mines near Rennes, and strange medieval legends — with at least *some* factual basis — told of parties of workmen labouring for *something* in part of the subterranean limestone labyrinth near the village.

There is also the persistent and semi-historical legend of the unfortunate shepherd boy Ignace Paris. Searching for a lost sheep, Ignace climbed down after it into a crevice in the limestone and found a tunnel. He followed the tunnel and discovered a cave where armoured skeletons lay around great chests filled with gold coins. Hardly believing his good fortune, Ignace put as much gold as he could carry into his robes and went back to Rennes to tell his friends and neighbours what he'd discovered. Within minutes the local seigneur was there. He descended on the boy in fury, brushed aside all explanations, and hanged him as a thief before he could disclose the exact whereabouts of the treasure. The buried treasure theory certainly has much to commend it.

Another aspect of the hidden treasure hypothesis is concerned with certain mysterious parchments that Saunière is believed to have found. There are two contradictory versions of their discovery. In the first account, a wealthy benefactress had called at Rennes shortly after Saunière was appointed as parish priest. She offered to pay for a little restoration work. The old church had been neglected for centuries: windows were missing, the roof leaked, the altar had slipped sideways. Bérenger asked her for a few francs to have the altar straightened. According to this version, a hollow Visigothic altar pillar held some mysterious coded parchments in Latin and Greek. The masons who discovered them took them straight to the priest. Within minutes he was in the church telling them to cease work, and that he would send for the masons again when he needed them. The first short manuscript was very easy to decode: certain letters were raised slightly. They spelled out the message "*A Dagobert II roi et a Sion est ce tresor et il est la mort.*" (Literally translated as "To Dagobert II King and to Sion is this treasure and he is there dead.")

What did it mean? Sion was once the Citadel of King David in Jerusalem, or perhaps the code referred to a supposed secret society known as The Priory of Sion. Dagobert II was allegedly an early French king of the ancient Merovingian line. Was something valuable buried with him — or in a secret hiding place in Jerusalem, below Solomon's Temple, where the original Knights Templar had had their headquarters in King Baldwin's time? Perhaps the mysterious Priory of Sion had hidden it in the Rennes area?

THE CURSED TREASURE OF RENNES

Did the phrase *il est la mort* mean "It is death" instead? Did the parchment indicate not so much that the treasure was in the royal tomb of Dagobert II, but that like the legendary treasure of Tutankhamen, it would bring death and destruction to any who tried to take it? Was it the curse on the treasure that had killed Ignace Paris?

The most intriguing theory of all, however, takes the Rennes mystery far back into the mists of time. Graham Hancock's brilliant research and his convincing arguments in *Fingerprints of the Gods* and his other excellent books and articles about such mysteries as the location of the lost Ark of the Covenant provide substantial evidence for the existence of a highly cultured and technologically competent civilization that may have flourished some fiteen thousand years ago on what is now the ice-shrouded continent of Antarctica. Traces of them may well lie waiting to be rediscovered below that formidable ice.

As the ice encroached remorselessly, we can imagine a party of well-equipped colonists moving north toward the warmth and safety of the East African coast, Egypt, and the Gulf. If Hancock is right, the technology they brought with them could well have been responsible for creating the Sphinx — millennia before the rise of the Pharaohs to whom traditional Egyptologists give the credit. Time passes. The "Mysterious-People-from-the-Far-South" gradually inter-marry and blend in with the peoples of Egypt and Northeast Africa. Some of their great cultural and technological secrets are carefully preserved by the inner hierarchy of Egyptian priests and courtiers, whose ranks Moses is eventually destined to join. Under his leadership, the great Hebrew Exodus gets underway.

When Moses leaves, he takes some great and vitally important "thing" with him. Glad at first to be rid of the troublesome nation-within-a-nation, Pharaoh suddenly becomes aware that this vital *thing* has gone with Moses. Does this traumatic discovery explain why he launched the flower of his charioteers to recover the mysterious and infinitely precious "thing" at all costs, risking military disaster to cross the perilous seabed in pursuit of it?

The unknown "thing" accompanies the Hebrews on their wanderings. It is, perhaps, even housed in their Sacred Ark alongside the Tablets of the Sinai Law. It is protected in their Tabernacle, then in Solomon's Temple. Centuries pass. Invaders come and go. Do the Romans carry it away, and do Alaric's conquering Visigoths take it from them to the remote safety of their citadel at Rennes-le-Château? Or is it in two or more parts, at least one of which stays concealed in a secret repository below the ruins of Solomon's Temple? Was that what the Knights Templar found when they dug there? Did they bring it to one of the Templar Commanderies near Rennes? And did Saunière succeed in finding and reuniting those pieces again after so many centuries of separation? Was that the secret that he learnt from the manuscripts?

So what did the longer and far more complicated coded manuscript reveal? It's currently surrounded by fierce controversy, but we'll start with the *assumption* that it's old and genuine for the sake of clarifying the basic story. The decoding process alone is an unsolved mystery in its own right. The cryptographer must begin by finding 128 letters that don't belong to the rest of the text. These have to be spread out symmetrically on two chess boards. The next step is to use the letters in *mort epée* (translated as "death sword" or "sword of death") as a key to another decoding process called the Tableau Vigenère. Here, alphabets, each beginning at a different letter, are arranged in a square, and one or another is selected by using the letters of the key words *mort epée*. To solve the labyrinthine codes on the longer parchment, further alphabetical shifts are needed, and finally a message emerges, lacking all accents and punctuation because of the decoding process:

Bergere pas de tentation que poussin teniers gardent la clef pax dclxxxi par la croix et ce cheval de dieux j'acheve ce daemon de gardien a midi pommes bleues.

One literal translation reads:

"Shepherdess without temptation to which Poussin and Teniers guard the key peace 681 by the cross and this horseman of God I have conquered the demon guardian at midday blue apples."

Dozens of possibilities now confront the researcher. There is a shepherdess in the centre of a famous painting by Nicholas Poussin, the seventeenth-century artist. She stands with three shepherds beside a tomb in a strange landscape, a landscape which just *might* be close to Rennes-le-Château. A curious bas-relief replica of that same tomb and the characters surrounding it stands in the grounds of Shugborough Hall in Staffordshire in England, where it is referred to in the guidebooks as the Shepherd Monument. A curious inscription is cut into the stone below the carving. The letters are D . O . U . O . S . V . A . V . V . M. The first and last letters are below the rest, and there is a centrally placed dot — like a decimal point — between each letter. Various suggestions as to their meaning have been put forward over the years, but so far there has been no definitive solution to the Shugborough riddle.

The great Staffordshire mansion was once owned by the Ansons, one of the earliest of whom was a contemporary of the mysterious Francis Bacon — sometimes credited with being the real author of the works attributed to Shakespeare. Francis Bacon had a brother, Anthony, who was engaged on the Elizabethan equivalent of CIA work in France. The Bacon brothers were very close. They were also, apparently, on the fringe of one or two seventeenth-century continental secret societies. Was the mysterious Priory of Sion around in those days? Did it know something vital about the Rennes treasure, and did the Bacon brothers latch onto it?

The mysterious and adventurous Admiral George Anson (1697–1762) was also frequently at the Bacon family home at Shugborough. He sailed around the world and came back with enough gold to have paid off the national debt had he been so inclined. Did that gold really come from pillaging the Spaniards, or did George have another older and more sinister source for his enormous wealth? There are links between the Rennes mystery and the equally intriguing riddle of Oak Island in Nova Scotia. Did coded information from Rennes via his Anson ancestors and their friends the Bacons enable George to exploit *something* of enormous value that was hidden on Oak Island?

The continental intrigues that involved the Bacon brothers are reminiscent of two other famous brothers, the Fouquets, who were similarly occupied. Nicholas, the elder, was minister of finance to the exceptionally powerful and successful Louis XIV, "The Sun King" of France. At the height of his immense power, there seemed to be almost nothing that Louis could not accomplish, yet it was said by many that Nicholas Fouquet was the *real* power in France at that time.

A letter written to Fouquet senior by his younger brother tells how he has met Nicholas Poussin, the painter, in Rome, and that Poussin has a truly remarkable secret, which he is willing to share with the Fouquets. Shortly afterward, Fouquet senior falls from power, and is replaced by the odious Colbert. Louis XIV acquires Poussin's strange, coded painting *The Shepherds of Arcadia*, which he keeps securely in the royal apartments at Versailles. Is it possible that it was Fouquet senior who became the hapless "Man in the Iron Mask"? It is hard to understand why Louis kept the notorious masked prisoner alive at all — unless whoever it was had some vital secret that Louis desperately wanted.

Suppose that the Man in the Iron Mask *was* Fouquet. Louis dared not risk letting him go, nor dare he take the chance of his communicating with his many powerful friends. If Louis believed that the secret Fouquet had learned from Poussin would have provided enough power to threaten Louis and his throne, it would naturally be safest to kill him, of course. Yet if he did, Louis knew he would never gain access to the secret he coveted so much. Hence the otherwise inexplicable, long-running standoff, with the king and his trusted prison governor, Monsieur St. Mars, on one side, and the mysterious masked prisoner (Fouquet?) on the other. The politically astute prisoner knows that once he has given the king the information he wants, death is his only reward. Louis knows that the masked prisoner is his only route to some great secret that he desperately desires to control. Kill the masked man, and you sacrifice all chance of ever gaining the secret.

The stranger and wilder the Rennes theories are, the more intriguing they seem to become. One tower of the ruined Château Hautpoul — which gives Rennes its name — is called The Tower of Alchemy. The Fatins who live there now kindly showed us around their crumbling, historic home. Monsieur Fatin, a talented sculptor, has a theory that the whole of Rennes-le-Château is one vast memorial to a long-dead king or some great ancient war leader. His skillfully drawn diagrams of the village certainly show the outlines of what could well be a classical Ship of the Dead.

Elizabeth van Buren, a descendant of President van Buren of the United States, has lived in the area and studied the Rennes mystery for many years. Psychically sensitive and very perceptive herself, she regards the mysterious village and its environs as a "gateway to the invisible" — and she could well be right.

Her theories include the idea that there is a vast ground zodiac below Rennes and the area surrounding it. It seems possible, according to her researches, that King Arthur of the Britons himself may lie beneath this enigmatic old French village.

Other theories involve the idea that a "magical" pentagon — formed naturally by several Rennes landmarks — may have rendered the area especially potent for "spells" to be worked.

Bremna Howells, who writes excellent and erudite books as Rosie Malone, is an acknowledged expert on magic, paganism, and ancient religions. She has carefully researched the hypothesis that Saunière and Marie Dénarnaud were secretly practising the sex-magic divination ritual known as The Convocation of Venus, which its protagonists claim is capable of remarkably accurate forecasts of the future.

Assuming for a moment that Bremna's theory is along the right lines, then Saunière's wealth may have come from selling accurate prophecies — rather like those uttered by Mother Shipton, the Wise Woman of Yorkshire, or Nostradamus.

Our own Rennes research goes back thirty-five years, and new information still continues to surface. Like any other research team, we could, of course, be wrong, but with the evidence currently available — and with due attention to all the rival theories — the best and most exciting of the probabilities seems to lean in the direction of Graham Hancock's bold Antarctic hypothesis. Is it possible that the Rennes treasure — whatever it finally turns out to be — is a mysterious, almost magically powerful artifact which originated in that pre-Ice Age culture? From Antarctica to Africa.... From ancient Egypt to Israel.... From Israel to Rome.... From Rome to Rennes-le-Château.... From Rennes to Oak Island, off the coast of Nova Scotia.... And have its equally mysterious guardians — sometimes calling themselves the Priory of Sion — been hovering around it for centuries?

The so-called Treasure of Rennes-le-Château is probably very much older and stranger than most of us can imagine.

12 MYSTERIOUS TREASURES

Centuries ago an unknown engineering genius hid something priceless in the labyrinth below Oak Island, Nova Scotia.

The modern end of the Oak Island story began innocuously enough one summer day in 1795. Three teenagers — Daniel McGinnis, John Smith, and Anthony Vaughan — had been given a day's holiday from the heavy manual work of Nova Scotian pioneers: fishing, farming, and lumbering. Life was tough for those eighteenth-century Canadians, but they had the will, the strength, and the tenacity to cope with it. When a brief opportunity to get away from their arduous labour came along, they enjoyed it all the more.

The three young men spent that fateful day exploring Oak Island — one of hundreds of islands scattered around in Mahone Bay on the Atlantic seaboard. This particular peanut-shaped island was about a mile long and a quarter of a mile wide at its narrowest.

The two broad ends of the island stood twelve metres above sea level, but the narrower central portion was low and covered by swamp. Clearly, as the centuries roll, Oak Island is destined to become two smaller islands.

The first thing that attracted their attention was a clearing toward the Atlantic end. In the middle of this clearing a saucer-shaped depression suggested strongly that someone had once dug there, and the earth had subsequently settled. Beside the sunken earth stood a large, sturdy oak tree, and one thick branch — its end deliberately lopped — extended across the low circle of ground. From that branch hung an old ship's block and tackle. Swiftly the boys drew an exciting conclusion: pirates or privateers must have buried their treasure there.

The Nova Scotian coast was rich with stories of pirates and smugglers. The very name Mahone Bay came from the "mahone," a type of ship

SINISTER THINGS ON OAK ISLAND

Oak Island was only a few hundred yards from the mainland, yet its prolific red-oak forest would have concealed anything suspicious from those who lived in the little fishing village of Chester. Besides, the island had a sinister, inhospitable reputation. The older members of the local community remembered a grim episode many years before. A party of fishermen had rowed across to investigate some mysterious lights on the island one night: those fishermen had never returned.

which privateers had traditionally favoured. The undeservedly notorious William Kidd was alleged to have buried his treasure there — but detailed research would seem to indicate that he had had little or nothing of any real value to bury.

In 1795, however, stories of the fabulous wealth supposedly accumulated by pirate captains like Kidd, Blackbeard, and Morgan, or bold adventurers such as Anson and Drake, were very much in the minds of young Nova Scotians like Smith, Vaughan, and McGinnis. The hope of discovering buried treasure was one of the counter-balances to an arduous life of hard work for subsistence returns. Digging up pirate gold meant a swift, almost miraculous escape from drudgery, into a life of luxury, comfort, and ease.

Eagerly, the boys began to excavate the circle of fallen earth below the oak tree. The first thing that encouraged them was the ease with which the soil came out: it was clearly soft backfill. As they cleared it away, the lads could see the original sides of the shaft: impervious, brick-hard clay that still bore the pickmarks of the original diggers. Whatever else they had found, it was not just some natural shaft or blowhole — someone in the past had excavated it deliberately.

Less than a metre down they hit a layer of flat stones, similar to paving stones, but the stone was not of a type found on Oak Island. It looked as if it had been brought there from Gold River, a couple of kilometres away. Was this a clue to suggest that gold from Gold River had been buried on Oak Island?

Encouraged by finding the stones, the boys dug on. Two and a half metres below the flat-stone layer, they hit a serious obstacle: a layer of horizontal oak logs had been let into the sides of the shaft. It was a struggle to get them out, but the young Nova Scotians were strong and keenly motivated, and eventually the oak platform came away — but the expected treasure was nowhere to be seen. The soil had settled and fallen half a metre or so below the oak obstacle, but that was all. Disappointed, they continued to shovel out the loose backfill, consoling themselves with the thought that whoever had gone to the trouble of going this deep — and putting an oak platform across the shaft, as well — must have buried something *very valuable indeed*. Mentally, they re-evaluated the hoped-for treasure: hundreds of thousands? *Millions even?*

Thus encouraged, they dug to the six-metre level, where they hit a second oak platform and removed it. Still no treasure chests — only more backfill. We can imagine them looking at one another grimly and accepting that this was more than the three of them could handle by themselves. They reluctantly accepted that it would require several men with special equipment and — above all — enough financial resources to pay for the digging time spent away from their essential regular work.

They marked the spot carefully and left the island. The demands of daily life meant that years rather than months passed before the first full assault was made on the Oak Island Money Pit.

BURIED TREASURE: TEN FILMS TO DIG UP

The Treasure of the Sierra Madre (1948)
Treasure Island (1950)
The Deep (1977)
Time Bandits (1981)
Raiders of the Lost Ark (1981)
Yellowbeard (1983)
Romancing the Stone (1984)
The Goonies (1985)
Pirates of the Caribbean (2003)
Pirates of the Caribbean: Dead Man's Chest (2006)

Simeon Lynds from Truro organized things. While visiting the Mahone Bay area, Simeon heard about the mysterious shaft from the three young men and visited the island with them. An article on Oak Island from *The Colonist*, dated January 2, 1864, more than half a century later, refers to him as "the late Simeon Lynds," and describes him as a relative of Anthony Vaughan's who was let into the secret because of those family connections.

Lynds organized an effective consortium of business and professional men into The Onslow Company. They included Sheriff Tom Harris and Colonel Archibald, the town clerk and a justice of the peace. The Onslow men worked hard and effectively. As the shaft grew ever deeper, they encountered not only platform after platform of oak logs at regular three-metre intervals, but inexplicable layers of ships' putty, coconut fibre, and charcoal.

Hiram Walker, a ship's carpenter who lived in Chester at the time and worked with the Onslow Company, told his granddaughter, Mrs. Cottnam Smith, that he had seen bushel after bushel of coconut fibre being brought up. Another eyewitness account referred to enough ship's putty being recovered from the shaft to glaze the windows of twenty local houses.

Close to the twenty-seven-metre level, the Onslow men unearthed a strange inscribed stone made of an unusual hard olive-grey rock — a form of porphyry unlike anything local. No one at the time was able to decipher the strange alphabet in which the inscription was written. Many years later, however, Professor Barry Fell suggested that it was a form of ancient Coptic script, and that the message was of a religious nature. This led to the theory that the Oak Island shaft and its ancillary workings had been created by a party of religious refugees from the eastern Mediterranean area. Another cryptographer deciphered the marks to mean "forty feet below two million pounds are buried." The suspicion was, however, that those markings had been superimposed over the original inscription after the stone had been in the hands of a later treasure-hunting company. Unfortunately, the stone has now disappeared.

Eventually it was decided that work would cease for the night and they would start again at first light. Just before finishing, however, one of the workmen probed the muddy floor with a long crowbar and reported striking something hard. Was it just another oak platform, or could it possibly be the lid of a treasure chest? It gave them all something to think about optimistically until sunrise.

First light brought a very unwelcome surprise: the pit was flooded to a depth of eighteen metres. The water was rising and falling gently with the tide. One unconfirmed account says that a workman leaned over too far and fell in. When his companions hauled him out again, his first words were, "Hey, it's salt water down there!"

That was the first clue to the amazing flood tunnels, which were discovered many years later. The lower levels of the Oak Island Money Pit were cunningly connected to at least two potentially lethal flood tunnels. Whoever had built the system had also created an artificial beach at Smith's Cove, at the far end of the island. Below that beach lay a fan-shaped pattern of drains that fed the first flood tunnel. Ingeniously packed with large stones and boulders to prevent collapse or blockage, while still allowing water to pass easily, the two flood tunnels led the mighty hydraulic power of the Atlantic itself down into the Money Pit.

The Onslow men tried bailing and pumping, but as one of them reputedly said at the time, "it was like trying to eat soup with a fork." Money ran out. Work had to be done back home. They were forced to give up for the time being — but they were more convinced than ever that there was some great treasure down there, if only some way of beating the flood water could be discovered.

The following year they tried again. Their plan this time was to dig a parallel shaft and then cut across horizontally and try to extract the treasure from below the flooded part. It was a desperate plan, but it seemed to work — up to a point. When they got down to the thirty-five-metre level and began tunnelling across, a sudden flood of water burst into their new workings, nearly drowning the diggers. That was the end as far as the Onslow Company was concerned, and the Oak Island treasure and its watery guardian were abandoned for the time being.

Daniel McGinnis was dead and Smith and Vaughan were both over seventy before another Oak Island expedition was organized. This was spearheaded by the Truro Company, which began work on the Money Pit in 1849. Both Smith and Vaughan were involved in the work, as was Dr. David Barnes Lynds, the son, or perhaps the grandson, of the Simeon Lynds who had led the Onslow men nearly half a century earlier.

This continuity factor is an important one. The new Oak Island treasure-hunting companies that were formed over the years almost invariably included veterans from earlier attempts. This was vital for such basic essentials as confirming the precise location of the site — not the easiest task in the world when so much digging, pumping, and bailing had been done all around it.

Under the leadership of Jotham McCully, a drill with a pod-auger was used to explore the flooded depths of the site. Some amazing discoveries were made. At the thirty-metre level — just where the Onslow men had thought it was years before — the drill went through layers of oak, and then loose pieces of unknown material that stubbornly refused to come up through the pod-auger. The Truro men were convinced that they had drilled through two treasure boxes piled one on top of the other.

Not long afterward, thinking he was unobserved, James Pitblado, a drilling foreman, took *something* from the drill tip, examined it carefully, and put it in his pocket. But John Gammell, a major shareholder in the Truro adventure, *had* seen him — and immediately challenged him about it. Pitblado stubbornly refused to show it to him, saying that it was so important he would show it only to a meeting of all the shareholders together.

He never did. He left the island that night and failed to return. He and his partner, Charles Archibald of the Acadia Ironworks, tried very hard to obtain an appropriate government treasure-hunting licence and even attempted to buy the whole island — but with no success. Shortly after this fiasco, Archibald left Nova Scotia to settle in England, and Pitblado was killed in an industrial accident, taking the secret of the drill-tip fragment with him. Whatever it was had been enough to convince him and Archibald that there was something very valuable down there.

When the Truro men ran out of cash, further exploration passed into the hands of a new company called The Oak Island Association, set up in April of 1861. Jotham McCully and other members of the 1849–50 group provided continuity yet again. John Smith, last survivor of the three original discoverers, had passed his Oak Island land to his sons before he died. They had sold it to Henry Stevens, and he in turn had sold it to Anthony Graves, who was now the principal landowner on Oak Island. Graves made a good deal with the Oak Island Association, one which entitled him to a third of anything they discovered on his land.

George Mitchell was now foreman on the island, and the association's plan was to cut off the flood water before attempting anything else. With nearly one hundred horses and men to do the job, Mitchell and his team tried to intercept and block the flood tunnel. They failed. Unbelievably, Mitchell then went for an option which had proved repeatedly disastrous with past expeditions: he attempted to sink a parallel shaft alongside the Money Pit and then cut across for the treasure horizontally. Abbott and Costello, the Three Stooges, or Laurel and Hardy would have known better than to try that approach again.

Two of Mitchell's intrepid tunnellers were digging horizontally toward the flooded Money Pit from the foot of their new parallel shaft when all hell broke loose in the deeply flooded shaft they were approaching. Eyewitnesses described the noise from the Money Pit as being "like an earthquake or a bomb exploding." A great surge of fast-moving mud hurled the two men back and almost cost them their lives. The area of the excavation where the possible treasure chamber had been detected by the pod-auger collapsed and crashed into the unknown depths of the Money Pit. It was followed by hundreds of metres of cribbing timber that had once lined the shaft. The water foamed and boiled madly: the lower levels were now a chaotic ruin.

Among fragments retrieved later from this cataclysmic mess were a few pieces of oak, blackened with age, and definitely far older than the recent cribbing timbers that had collapsed so dramatically. Had this ancient wood been part of the original treasure chamber? Other very old, pre-nineteenth-century pieces were found. These contained clear drill and tool marks, which also helped to confirm the conclusions drawn from the pod-auger samples.

For nearly a quarter of a century very little treasure-hunting work was done on the island, but there was a curious and significant accident. Sophia Sellers, daughter of Anthony Graves, was ploughing with a team of oxen barely one hundred yards from the Money Pit when the poor beasts and the plough crashed through a large hole, and nearly dragged Sophia down with them. The animals and equipment were later recovered — miraculously safe and uninjured — but the mysterious hole (referred to ever after as The Cave-in Pit) posed another intriguing problem for Oak Island researchers. Sophia's husband, Henry, filled it with boulders as a safety precaution, and nothing much was done about it until tireless and determined Fred Blair came on the scene in 1893.

Fred was one of the most dedicated and effective explorers to tackle the Oak Island mystery, and he worked there from 1893 until his death in 1951. At one point he dynamited the flood tunnels in an attempt to stop the water — but even that was only a partial and temporary success, and it probably achieved nothing except to scatter the remains of the contents of the supposed treasure chamber that had collapsed in 1861.

Blair drilled for samples as the McCully team had done fifty years before. His drill hit what seems to have been a cement treasure vault with impenetrable iron reinforcement at the fifty-two-metre level. Somewhere inside this mysterious space the drill's behaviour suggested that there were more boxes of the tantalizing loose metal that had failed to come up on the McCully drill.

Another strange discovery was a fragment of ancient parchment that came up in the core samples: it bore only two letters, "VI," but had evidently been torn from some larger document. The existence of this parchment opened up a whole new field of speculation.

As the years went on, Franklin D. Roosevelt, the future American president, became interested in the work, and was one of the shareholders in Captain Bowdoin's company, which made a brief and conspicuously unsuccessful assault on the Money Pit in 1909. A disappointed and disgruntled Bowdoin later wrote that there was no treasure down there and never had been.

A far more diligent and persistent later researcher was Mel Chappell, whose father had been a member of the expedition during which the parchment had been discovered. Mel and Blair worked together in 1931. A big new shaft was dug, but nothing significant discovered. Had the constant dynamiting, flooding, and pumping dispersed the treasure beyond any reasonable hope of recovery?

Gilbert Hedden also deserves honourable mention among the heroes in the Oak Island Hall of Fame. He had excellent management and engineering experience, and he was a thoughtful planner. He hired Sprague and Henwood of Pennsylvania to do the drilling and clearing work and they made an excellent job of it. At the forty-six-metre level and below, the drill encountered pieces of oak of various sizes, strongly suggesting that the remains of the old treasure chamber and its supports were down there somewhere. Hedden's team also discovered the remains of an ancient sea-ramp, jetty, or coffer dam, in Smith's Cove — where the artificial drainage beach and flood tunnels were located. The old timbers which Hedden discovered were massive. They were also notched, and labelled with Roman numerals. They have never been satisfactorily explained.

Unhappily, like so many others before him, Hedden ran into financial difficulties, curtailing his Oak Island work.

The next major player was Professor Hamilton, an Engineering teacher from New York University. He made meticulous explorations of many of the old shafts and tunnels, and drilled down to limestone bedrock sixty metres below the island, where oak chips continued to come up on the drill. There was, however, no other sign of the elusive treasure.

George Greene, a tough, cigar-chewing Texas oilman, made an attempt in 1955, but the skill and determination that had led him to succeed in the oil business didn't translate into success on Oak Island.

Then came Robert and Mildred Restall, daring and exciting show-business personalities. Robert was a motorcycle stunt rider and Mildred a beautiful seventeen-year-old ballerina when they married in 1931. With a little capital put up by loyal show-business friends, the Restalls came to work on Oak Island in 1959. Robert and his son, Rob Junior, died in a tragic accident in 1965, when some mysterious gas-poisoning caused Robert to fall into a flooded shaft where they were working. His son died trying to rescue him. Two of their loyal friends also died trying to get them out.

Including earlier accidents, that brought the total death toll to six — but the sinister legend of Oak Island prophesied that seven men would die and that the last oak tree would fall before the mysterious treasure was recovered. The last oak has already fallen …

Bob Dunfield was next to attack the Money Pit, and he went at it like Hannibal's elephants charging the Roman army at the Battle of Zama — with as little success as Hannibal had against Rome!

With massive financial resources and ruthless directness, Dunfield built a causeway to carry his huge clam digger across to rip the heart out of Oak Island. On October 17, 1965, Oak Island became part of the mainland of Nova Scotia. Dunfield's machine tore a hole thirty metres wide and forty-five metres deep where the Money Pit had once been. He created something that looked like a miniature Somme battlefield — or the site of tank warfare during a monsoon. He destroyed priceless clues and archaeological evidence that later researchers would have found invaluable. All his investment and all his energy achieved absolutely nothing. In the spring of 1966, he gave up and left the island. He died in Encino in 1980.

Fred Nolan, a skillful and talented surveyor, has worked on the island for many years, and has discovered numerous strange marker stones — some of which form a distinct Templar Cross of very large proportions. He believes that the treasure is more likely to be hidden under the swamp than in the depths of the Money Pit. Fred's hypothesis is that those who sank the shaft tunnelled upward again, at various angles, and concealed the treasure in several separate locations that could easily be reached from the surface if the diggers had the right directions. He thinks that his mysterious marker stones, together with an ancient stone triangle that was destroyed as a result of Dunfield's work with the clam digger, may hold the clues to these sites.

Next on the scene came a formidable combination of experts working as Triton Alliance — and the toughest and most formidable of them all was our good friend Dan Blankenship, former 1939–45 war hero. If any combination of courage, imagination, initiative, and engineering skills will ever solve the Oak Island Money Pit mystery, Dan has that profile.

But he almost became the seventh victim of the Oak Island curse instead when the steel shaft inside which he was working collapsed under the colossal weight and pressure of the mud surrounding it. His son's strength and determination — as he worked the cable winch that hauled Dan to safety with only seconds to spare — were the vital factors in the rescue. Even that hair's breadth escape failed to deter Dan and his team.

Their work continues, and when the Oak Island secret is eventually revealed, it may well turn out to be the eighth wonder of the world. What might it be? And who could have put it down there in the first place?

One of the best theories comes from another of our close Nova Scotian friends, George Young, a retired surveyor and Royal Canadian Navy officer, now sadly deceased. With his unique combination of professional knowledge of both sea and land, coupled with his linguistic skills in ancient Ogham, and an interest in unexplained phenomena in general, George's theories are always well worth considering. He wonders whether the Money Pit and its formidable defences were intended, not as a treasure cache, but as a securely protected burial place. If Professor Barry Fell was right and the ancient stone found at the twenty-seven-metre level contained a religious inscription, is it possible that a community of religious refugees from the eastern Mediterranean found their way through the straights of Gibraltar and across to the Nova Scotian coast long ago?

George's studies of prevailing winds, tides, and currents make this a feasible conclusion. Theoretically, at least, such a journey was possible.

The sturdy oak platforms at three-metre intervals are then explained as shields to prevent the weight of the earth from crushing the body of the *arif*, the revered leader of the community who his followers buried there. The artificial beach with its drains and flood tunnels can also be seen as precautions against grave robbers and desecrators. What the drill went through was not a treasure chamber containing chests of coins and jewels — but a burial vault containing coffins.

In the fascinating museum at Yarmouth, Nova Scotia, lies the famous Yarmouth Stone, discovered on the shore by a local doctor in 1812. It has what appear to be runic inscriptions engraved on it that suggest that an early Viking expedition made its way successfully to Nova Scotia centuries before Columbus reached America. So is it Viking treasure in the depths of the Money Pit? Did some ancient Norse sea-king once rest there, complete with his armour, his weapons, and his treasure?

The problem in trying to decide who originally excavated the pit and its associated flood tunnels and artificial beach drainage system is that it must have taken a large group of strong, intelligent, and disciplined people a long time to complete the work. Whatever else it is, the pit is not the quick, casual, haphazard work of swashbuckling pirates: a 1.8-metre hole under a tree and a few crude measurements on a rough sketch map are much more in keeping with traditional pirate style.

Another fascinating theory concerns the refugee Knights Templar. They left France after the treacherous Philip IV attempted to destroy their great and valiant Order in 1307. There is evidence that the noble and hospitable Henry Sinclair, ruler of Orkney, took them in and subsequently provided transport for them across the North Atlantic. He enlisted the help of the Venetian Zeno brothers, who were among the greatest navigators of their day.

The Templars were as famous for their building skills — some of their medieval fortifications are among the greatest military architecture of all time — as for their courage and prowess in war. They would have had the engineering knowledge, the time, dedication, and discipline to construct the Money Pit. They would also have had priceless treasure and holy relics from Palestine and the Saracen lands to conceal there. In the fourteenth century, a voyage across the Atlantic was as rare and daunting an enterprise as a trip to the moon today. Did the indomitable Templars conclude that the safest place for their treasure — the farthest possible hiding place from the avaricious Philip le Bel and his successors — would be on the far side of the Atlantic?

Or was it the work of Francis Bacon? Did that enigmatic Elizabethan statesman and scholar conceal secret manuscripts there, with the intention that posterity would ultimately rediscover them and give him what he considered to be his rightful place in history? Bacon, a pioneering scientist as well as a man of many other talents, had a theory about preserving documents in mercury. Among the strange things found on Oak Island in recent years were many old earthenware flasks that still held traces of the mercury they had once contained. Was that tiny scrap of parchment bearing the letters *VI* (recovered from the Money Pit in 1893) a fragment of one of Bacon's manuscripts?

Another tenable theory concerns King George III. Before his sanity left him, he was an intelligent and ambitious man. He wanted to reign supreme, as a true and decisive monarch, not a democratized and constitutionally restrained figurehead. He had learnt the lessons of Charles I. George knew well enough that to take power you had to take money first. Enough cash would buy enough mercenaries to subdue a kingdom. There is some evidence that with the help of a powerful secret cabal of statesmen — including the mysterious and incalculably wealthy Admiral Anson of Shugborough — George III had arranged for his "war chest" to be kept safely on Oak Island, to be drawn on as necessary when the power struggle against Parliament began, and mercenaries were needed. The insanity struck first, various vitally important plotters died or withdrew their support, and everything ended in ignominious failure. But does George's treasure still lie concealed below the Money Pit?

A closely associated theory suggests that either French or British military engineers constructed the great subterranean "safe" with its flood-tunnel "locks" to keep an army payroll out of reach of their enemies during the American wars of the mid-eighteenth century. Military engineers certainly fit the profile as far as skill and discipline are concerned.

Exciting theories abound. The most breathtaking of all is the possibility that some part of the ancient secret Arcadian treasure that was once concealed at Rennes-le-Château was smuggled across to Canada and buried below Oak Island.

This would link in with the curious geographical fact that there are *two* Oak Islands attached to the Nova Scotian peninsula: one on the Fundy side, the other on the Atlantic side. It has been suggested that those who knew about the secret over the centuries had deliberately planted oaks to mark the island for later travellers in their arcane organization. Near each of the two Oak Islands is a river that flows down from the centre of the peninsula. There is some archaeological evidence — albeit controversial — that a settlement or fortress once existed there in that central region. Some curious remnants remain today at New Cross, Nova Scotia.

The theory then goes on to suggest that something of immense value and importance — something that perhaps originated in the ancient pre–ice-age culture that supposedly flourished below the ice of what is now Antarctica, and of which Graham Hancock has argued for so logically in *Fingerprints of the Gods* — made its way first to Egypt, then to Palestine with Moses, later to Rome, and from there to the Visigothic stronghold at Rennes-le-Château. Templars, or the successors of other more ancient guardians, were later responsible for secreting part of it below Oak Island.

There are hints and suggestions that it was something so powerful that it was considered safer to have it in two separate locations, rather like keeping a gun in one steel cabinet and the ammunition for it in another. Were the oaks planted deliberately on those two Nova Scotian islands, both of which are now firmly attached to the mainland? Were those trees intended to show travellers from the Old World that they were in the right spot, and that they had only to sail up the adjacent river to find the settlement where other members of the group would welcome and protect them?

The final solution to the Oak Island mystery has yet to be revealed. When and if it finally is, there can be little doubt that it will be something truly momentous.

Co-author Lionel examining the New Cross ruins.

Top of the Oak Island Money Pit as it looks today.

The association of Arginy Castle with Templar treasure goes back to the attempted destruction of the order in 1307, when a loyal and fearless Templar, a member of the Beaujeu family, was said to have raced from Paris ahead of Philip IV's hoodlums and reached the temporary safety of Arginy Castle, where the Templar treasure he carried was skillfully concealed — most likely within the labyrinth under the castle.

Anne de Beaujeu was otherwise known as Anne of France (1461–1522). Her father was King Louis XI (1423–83), who earned the name "The Spider King" because of the webs of intrigue that were the main characteristic of his reign. Perhaps Anne also acquired some of those characteristics. In any event, having studied the traditions concerning the de Beaujeu who had fled from Paris with Templar treasure in 1307, Anne had all the underground passages below Arginy castle searched thoroughly. When nothing of any significance came to light — unless the prudent Anne was keeping it all secret — she ordered a wall be built, sealing off the access to the labyrinth below the castle.

Nothing further seems to have been done until 1914. In that year, Duke Pierre de Rosemont, who had acquired the property, demolished the barrier wall that Anne had erected, and sent men to explore the labyrinth. It was booby-trapped, however, like some of the tombs that Lara Croft and Indiana Jones raided in their adventure films, and this had tragic consequences for one of Rosemont's workmen, whose legs were badly injured when two massive stone spheres rolled out of an opening concealed in one of the labyrinth walls. It says a great deal for Rosemont's courage and unselfishness that he himself took on the next stage of the investigations so that no more of his men would be killed or injured.

Rosemont discovered an aperture that led him downward and provided access to a sinister tomb that he had been told was a vital clue to the whereabouts of the Templar treasure that de Beaujeu was believed to have hidden there in 1307. According to some chilling accounts of what happened next, Rosemont saw globes of coloured light and felt as though he was being attacked by an invisible force. He is also said to have heard strange cries emanating from below. To add to these unnerving phenomena, water began rising toward him, and Rosemont — never a man to lack courage — decided that this was one of those moments when discretion was decidedly the better part of valour. When he reached the surface, he decided that whatever was down there presented too great a threat to risk a second encounter — either for him, or for anyone else. He had the aperture closed, once again sealing off the access to the strange, sinister labyrinth below Arginy Castle.

THE TOWER OF ARGINY CASTLE

One of the oldest and most mysterious parts of the Arginy fortifications is a tower, variously known as the Tower of the Eight Beauties, The Tower of the Eight Beatitudes, and the Tower of Alchemy. This is quite intriguing, as one of the towers on Château Hautpoul at Rennes-le-Château is also referred to as the Tower of Alchemy. The old tower at Arginy looks circular from the outside, but proves to be octagonal inside. Although now faint and difficult to read, there are strange — possibly alchemical — symbols still visible on its ancient walls. Or could they be ciphers relating to Templar treasure rather than to alchemical formulae?

One of the most famous curses attached to a gem is the legendary curse of the Hope Diamond. It is not easy to unwind the strands of history and legend that accompany this exquisite stone. According to popular legend, the diamond, originally taken from the Kollur mine in Golconda, in south-central India, was serving as one of the eyes of an Indian idol. Stolen in the 1640s by a gem dealer named Tavernier, it was sold to King Louis XIV of France in 1668.

In legend, Tavernier later died of fever on a trip abroad, and his body was eaten by wolves. In fact, the records show that he lived to be eighty-four.

The ill-fated Louis XVI and his wife Marie Antoinette were guillotined; some said it was because of the Hope Diamond curse, but a great many other people who had never been within a mile of the Hope

The allegedly cursed Hope Diamond.

Diamond were also guillotined during the terror that accompanied the French Revolution. Having vanished during that revolution, the Hope Diamond resurfaced in London in 1823 in the possession of a jeweller named Daniel Eliason. It later seems to have become the property of King George IV (1762–1830), although there is some controversy about this. If it was one of his possessions, it seems to have been sold in 1830 to pay off a number of his debts.

The diamond later passed into the possession of Henry William Hope, from whom it got its name. Various other disasters and tragedies were associated with the diamond before it passed into the safekeeping of the Smithsonian Institute in Washington, where the authors inspected it. The Hope Diamond now seems to have settled down as nothing more than an interesting exhibit.

THE HOPE DIAMOND

The Hope Diamond is a 45.52-carat blue diamond. It is 25.6 millimetres in length, 21.78 millimetres wide, and 12 millimetres deep. It appears blue to the naked eye because of trace amounts of the chemical element boron found within its structure. Under ultraviolet light the diamond exhibits brilliant red phosphorescence. This "glow-in-the-dark" effect continues for several seconds after the light source has been removed.

Columbia City, in northwestern Oregon, stands on the banks of the beautiful Columbia River, about fifty kilometres north of Portland. One hundred kilometres east of the Pacific coast, Columbia City is close to coniferous forest slopes, and the Cascade Mountains are just across the river. The snow-capped peaks of Mount St. Helens, Mount Jefferson, Mount Rainier, Mount Adams, and Mount Hood are all visible from the city.

The curse of a Spanish treasure ship seems out of place amidst such outstanding natural beauty, but in 1841 the ship anchored by the riverbank where Columbia City stands today. It carried a dangerous and motley crew, and they had apparently discovered that there was treasure aboard. As soon as the anchors were down, they promptly murdered the captain and carried their looted treasure ashore. Quarrels broke out amongst the men, and several of them were killed during these savage internecine struggles.

At this point, a group of Native American warriors came into view, and the surviving thieves decided to bury their loot quickly in an area that was then known as Hez Copier's farm. When many more warriors appeared, the Spanish mutineers beat a hasty retreat to their ship. The thieves remained on board, hoping that the group would move on, but days passed and their tepees remained on the riverbank.

The Spaniards finally gave up and sailed away, bitterly disappointed — their greed had brought nothing but the death of the captain and many of their companions. They survived for two or three years as best they could, and then those who remained returned to the river in search of the buried treasure. Though the Native people no longer occupied the site, the murderous mutineers could not find the exact location of the treasure. The man who had been in charge of the actual burial of the stolen treasure moved away unobserved, and the mutineers did not realize that he was missing until they gave up the search and returned to their ship.

More than forty years later, during the 1880s, a group of gifted and perceptive spiritualists were at a meeting in Columbia City during the height of the nineteenth-century interest in séances and in the possibility of communicating with the spirits of the dead. One of the mediums felt certain that she had been given a psychic revelation of the exact site of the missing treasure. Treasure hunters followed her directions carefully and began to dig where she had directed. To everyone's consternation, one of the excavators suddenly fell dead. The medium felt certain that this was the work of the vengeful spirit of the murdered Spanish captain. All work ceased until 1890, when another party began excavating the site on Hez Copier's farm. A layer of shattered stones was removed, and below these were skeletons that were presumed to be those of some of the dead mutineers.

No one died on this occasion, but as the bones were being removed from the sinister excavation, one of the treasure hunters became wildly and dangerously insane. The search was again abandoned, as it was felt that some terrifying curse protected the dead captain's stolen treasure. The treasure would still seem to be there, waiting for a courageous treasure hunter with no fears of the paranormal — but it still might be a wise precaution to take a priest along to bless the ground and neutralize the curse. (Co-author Lionel would be very happy to help with this if invited!)

13 SPECTRES, PHANTOMS, GHOSTS, AND APPARITIONS

What is a ghost?

There are a number of theories that set out to explain what the phenomenon popularly described as a ghost might really be.

Some dismiss the phenomenon as a purely subjective mental experience: it's just one's imagination; you only *thought* that you saw or heard it; a ghost is merely the product of a malfunctioning mind. Materialistic prejudice assures us that ghosts do not and cannot exist. Therefore, those who *think* they see or hear them are suffering from some sort of mental abnormality. Against this explanation, of course, it may be argued that so many sane, rational, normal, and sensible people have reported experiencing the phenomenon that, if it is only a mental malfunction, the majority of people suffer from the condition. Dare it be suggested that it is more likely the inability to experience psychic phenomena which is "abnormal"?

Another explanation is the province of fundamentalist religious groups. They are either repelled by psychic phenomena, frightened of it, or both. They suggest that all supposed ghosts are demons, fallen angels, or evil spirits masquerading as departed human beings in order to mock and deceive the bereaved. This is a point of view that such groups are, of course, fully entitled to embrace, but it is not one which has any appeal to us as investigators of paranormal and anomalous phenomena.

If God is the loving, caring "Supra-Parent" that we believe him to be, then, like any other benign and caring parent, God's will for us is that we should all develop into happy, loving, independent, and autonomous beings. With that basic concept in mind, it should be possible to entertain the idea that the whole universe — physical and spiritual, material and mental — is one vast "adventure playground" in which we are free

PHYSICAL VISION AND PSYCHIC VISION

Using the analogy of full-colour vision, it is the colour-blind segment of the population who are in a minority. What if they were in the majority and didn't believe that full-colour vision existed except in the imaginations of those who proclaimed that roses were red and violets were blue? If the phenomenon of colour is experienced only by those who have the necessary optical and neurological equipment to receive it, how could they prove the existence of colour to those who do not have the appropriate biological equipment to share the experience with them?

to roam in order to learn. There's no part of it that we can't explore: there's nothing we can't do. There *are*, of course, eternal laws and divine principles by which we must faithfully abide if we are to get the best out of ourselves and out of God's universe.

Half a century of research into most aspects of the paranormal has led us to the conclusion that anomalous phenomena can be positive, negative, or neutral — rather like the human race itself. If ghosts are demons in disguise, many of them must be singular good-natured demons. In fact, the majority of the rest are so bland and ineffectual as to be practically innocuous.

So if ghosts are neither mental malfunctions nor evil spirits, what are they? A third theory suggests that they could be patterns or impressions left in the fabric of haunted sites. If audio and videotape can pick up the impressions that sound engineers and camera crews wish them to receive, why can't metal, stone, and wood pick up impressions naturally from events that are taking place in their vicinity? Then, when a sufficiently sensitive person comes within range of those recorded impressions, they are simply played back.

A fourth hypothesis uses the analogy of camera malfunction. It suggests that "seeing" and "hearing" are intellectual processes as well as physiological ones. On rare occasions some elaborate automatic cameras are capable of a sort of "internalization error" in which something inside the camera is "seen" by the film instead of the external object toward which the lens is pointing. The theory suggests that the human eye and brain can occasionally make that same internalization error. An internal impression is then registered as an external one: a memory, or creative thought, is seen as an external phenomenon or "ghost."

Theory number five involves telepathy and possibly an out-of-body experience. If a very sensitive and receptive subject picks up the powerfully transmitted thought forms of another person who is a strong telepathic sender, then the recipient might "see" either the sender or the image that the sender was transmitting.

After carefully examining and evaluating these five theories — interesting as some of them undoubtedly are — the authors' own conclusions (after half a century's research and evaluation) are that, although some reports of ostensibly psychic phenomena might be explained in other ways, there is enough strong evidence for genuine contact with departed human beings to make survival not only reasonable, but probable.

It would be possible to fill a vast library with first-hand eyewitness accounts of hauntings. One or two, even a dozen, might be dismissed as fanciful tales, but when the statistics rise into hundreds and then thousands of honest and reliable stories told by witnesses with integrity, then the evidence is not easy to dismiss.

Burke Hardison was driving home from Raleigh, North Carolina, one rainy night in the spring of 1924. He had spent the evening with some friends, and as he drove the fog came down thickly. Through that swirling mist he saw the Highway 70 underpass. The fog cleared just for a moment, and,

LIMITS OF FREEDOM

According to the theory of God's will, although freedom and autonomy are major virtues and highly desirable life targets, our individual, personal freedom ends at the point where it curtails someone else's. Our right to do what we like ends at the point where it prevents someone else from doing what he or she likes. Where resources are unlimited, we are free to take as much as we want. Where resources are limited, we are free to take our fair share — but not a pennyweight more.

to his amazement, in view of the time and the loneliness of the place, he saw a solitary girl standing by the side of the road. She was wearing a white evening gown and signalling frantically for him to stop. He slowed down and stopped the car beside her. When she spoke her voice was very soft, almost unnaturally quiet, and she had evidently been crying. "Please," she begged, "please, could you take me to High Point?"

Burke Hardison was a pleasant and good-hearted man, so he smiled reassuringly and helped her into the car: "I'm just on the way to High Point. I live there myself. It's no problem at all."

In spite of the fog and darkness, he could see the girl quite clearly. Her face was pale and her long, dark hair framed it attractively. Her full white evening dress billowed out on each side of her as she settled into the seat beside him. She gave him the address of a street that he knew in High Point and they drove on. The girl didn't say much, and over the noise of the engine it was difficult for him to hear her because she spoke so quietly. Burke said later that there was a strange *distance* about her voice; it was as though she was speaking to him down a poor telephone line from a long way away.

From the fragments that he could hear, he gathered that she was anxious because she knew her mother would be worried about her. Hardison also gleaned the information that she had just been to a dance

URBAN MYTHS AND LEGENDS

Variations of the story of ghostly hitchhikers have passed into urban legend, and some have been heavily embroidered. In some instances the girl who is hitchhiking borrows the driver's umbrella or coat because it's raining hard as he reaches her house and there is a long pathway or drive. When he returns a day or two later to collect the coat, he finds the house itself is no longer there. He asks in the village and is told that a young woman who once lived there was killed on that road. Out of curiosity he goes to look for her grave and finds that his coat, or umbrella, is resting against her headstone. Several interesting theories have been put forward to explain the spread and variations of these so-called "urban legends."

in Raleigh, but he could not make out from what she said how she had ended up standing there alone in the fog by the side of the road. He did not want to add to her distress by questioning her about something she did not appear to want to discuss. She did, however, say something very strange: "Nothing matters now except going home."

He reached the address that she had given him, stopped outside her house, and walked around to open the car door for her. As he did so, he found himself looking into the dark, empty interior of his car. The girl had gone; the car was empty. He couldn't understand how she could have got out so quickly and without his hearing the door. If she had slipped into the house, she must have moved unbelievably fast — how could she have done it without him seeing her?

For several minutes Burke could not make up his mind what to do, and then he took the bull by the horns and knocked on the door. It was a long time before it was answered. The woman who finally opened it bore a remarkable resemblance to the girl Burke had given the lift to, but she was much older. Hardison did not know what to say. At last, by way of explanation, he said, "I just gave your daughter a lift home, but when I opened the car door for her, she wasn't there." The woman in the lighted doorway was unable to speak for several moments, but then Hardison saw tears running down her cheeks. When she was able to bring her voice under control, she said, "I had an only daughter who was killed in a car crash near the underpass on Highway 70 in Jamestown — but that was over a year ago. She was on her way back from a dance in Raleigh."

She drew a deep breath and looked at Hardison. "You're not the first good Samaritan who has tried to give her a lift home. It's just that she never quite makes it."

The tendency of the human subconscious to dramatize, embroider, and exaggerate a narrative must be taken into account in this case. Nevertheless, a number of stories that have been dismissed as urban legends in the way that the tale of the female hitchhiker is often dismissed can occasionally be traced back to a time, an event, and a witness whose name can be placed firmly on the story.

Just as a verifiable version of the urban legend of the hitchhiking girl is one that demands to find its way into any collection of hauntings, so it would be equally difficult not to mention Borley Rectory in Suffolk, England, in the same context. Even today there are barely two hundred souls in the village and in the days of its paranormal fame in the 1930s and 40s there were a great deal fewer.

The name Borley comes from the Anglo-Saxon word *barlea*, meaning "the pasture or field of the boar." It found its way into the record books a thousand years ago when the owner of Borley Manor was recorded as a man named Lewin, who held it during the reign of Edward the Confessor. After William the Conqueror took over, he gave it to his half-sister, the Countess of Aumale, whose name was Adeliza. The village is even referenced in the Domesday Book in 1086.

In the robust Victorian days of the Anglican Church militant, the squire's eldest son inherited the estate, the second went into the army, and the third became a parson. Borley Rectory was built by the Reverend Henry Bull, known as Harry. He erected it in 1863, allegedly on the site of a much older structure. A mixture of legend and tradition maintained that a Benedictine Abbey had stood there much earlier, but the evidence for the existence of that abbey is scarce.

One day, around the year 1900, four of Harry Bull' daughters were walking on the grounds of the old rectory, when all reported seeing the ghost of the famous Borley Rectory nun. This strange figure was seen by many witnesses on numerous occasions, and the whole area became known as Nun's Walk.

The tragic story connected with a nun was told at a séance many years later. In this narrative the girl had been brought over from France,

THE DOMESDAY BOOK

The *Domesday Book* is the record of the great survey of England completed in 1086, executed for King William I of England (William the Conqueror). The king sent men all over England to find out what each landholder had in land and livestock, and what it was worth. This allowed him to figure out how much each landowner owed in taxes. Because no one could escape the survey and subsequent taxes, the book brought "doom and gloom" to the people of England — hence the name "Domesday Book." A complete online version of the *Domesday Book* is available at the U.K.'s National Archives.

The Wild Hunt is an ancient folk myth from Northern, Western, and Central Europe. In it a spectral group of huntsmen on horseback, carrying the weapons of the hunt and accompanied by hounds, race as if possessed across the skies or along the ground (or hovering just above it). The hunters were thought to be the dead, or fairies (often in folklore connected with the dead). The hunter may be an unidentified lost soul, a deity or spirit, or may be a historical or legendary figure. It was thought that seeing the Wild Hunt was a harbinger of some catastrophe such as a great plague or war, or simply the death of the one who witnessed it. Any who get in the path of the Hunt could be kidnapped and brought to the land of the dead, and some believed that people's spirits could be pulled away during their sleep to join the macabre parade.

---

ostensibly to leave her religious order and marry a member of the Waldegrave family, who were wealthy local landowners in the Borley area at the time. She had, however, been murdered, and her remains placed in the cellars. It is possible that the Waldegrave who sent for her had ideas other than marriage, and she was murdered when she refused to become his mistress.

Whether the famous Borley investigator Harry Price (whose reputation was not unblemished) actually *imported* some human remains from somewhere else and hid them in the cellars at Borley so that he could "discover" them later cannot now be decided. Certainly some human remains were produced from under one of the Borley cellars and Price arranged for a clergyman to give them decent burial.

Another of the Borley spectres was alleged to have been the ghost of a young servant girl seen at an upper window. A non-too-creditable tale attached to her sad little apparition suggests that she either fell from that attic window while cleaning it or that she was attempting to escape the amorous clutches of the virile Reverend Bull and went backward out of the window. Victorian "respectability" being what it was, and the Bulls' social position being pretty well unassailable in the district, the affair of the dead servant girl — especially if she was alone in the world, and had been hired from a parish orphanage or union workhouse — could have been quietly hushed up.

Another of the Borley hauntings concerned a coach driven by a headless horseman with headless horses and headless passengers. If such an apparition was actually seen by reputable and reliable witnesses in the Borley area, then it seems likely to have been allied with the far older story of the Wild Hunt (see sidebar).

A supposed explanation of the ghostly coach narrative is the romantic tale of a dashing young coachman endeavouring to elope with the nun who now supposedly haunts the Nun's Walk. He was captured and beheaded; she was bricked up alive in the wall of her convent.

Strange phenomena continued to be reported from Borley Rectory for many years after those sightings. When Harry Bull's son, Harry junior, died in 1927, his ghost was reported walking through the rectory corridors.

The headless lover of the imprisoned nun at Borley.

It was extremely difficult for the parish to find a successor to the Reverend Bull junior, and there is the inevitable debate about whether it was the ghostly atmosphere of Borley Rectory or the simple inconvenience of trying to keep such a vast old ruin of a house lit and heated that discouraged all those who saw it from accepting the living. From 1928–29, the Reverend Eric Smith and his wife reported various psychic phenomena: strange knocking noises, showers of coins, and footsteps made by no human feet. The phantom coach is also alleged to have turned up on the drive again during those few months.

The Borley coach did not seem to presage any particular doom or disaster for those who saw it, but the Norfolk phantom coach is considered to bring very bad luck, if not necessarily fatally bad luck, to those who witness it. Allegedly the coach hurtles from Great Yarmouth to King's Lynn with its headless horses, passengers, and coachman. According to the old Norfolk traditions, during the eighteenth century, a notorious poacher and petty criminal named George Mace was the leader of a gang of thieves and troublemakers based in the small Norfolk town of Watton. The local constables and magistrates all forecast that George Mace would end his days on the gallows. He didn't.

Local tradition says that George Mace was picked up by the phantom coach, driven away by its headless occupants, and dumped — stone dead — at Breccles Hall shortly before daybreak. It might be cynically suggested that the coach that picked up George Mace and disposed of him was a perfectly normal, material one, and that it was occupied not by headless ghosts but by hard-fisted gamekeepers who had had enough of George's troublemaking and had decided to take the law into their own hands — remaining blissfully anonymous in the shadow of the legend of the phantom coach. There were not very many mourners at George Mace's funeral. The general opinion in the Watton area was that it could not have happened to a nicer man and that it was certainly not before its time!

After Reverend Smith and his wife left Borley in 1929, the Reverend Lionel Foyster and his wife, Marianne (who was much younger than he was), moved into the rectory. Young and excitable, Mrs. Foyster appeared to be the centre of some quite formidable poltergeist activity, and strange messages addressed to her appeared on the walls.

A respectable justice of the peace named Guy L'Estrange paid a visit to Borley in the early 1930s and wrote an interesting account of poltergeist phenomena, including smashed crockery and bottles flying through the air like angry hornets. L'Estrange did not think that any human agencies were at the back of these phenomena, but Harry Price was rather suspicious of Marianne Foyster.

Price, himself, it must be remembered, was strongly suspected of fraud. He loved to be in the limelight, and certainly the alleged poltergeist activities at Borley did not hinder the sales of his two books about the old house.

Three men from the Society for Psychical Research, Hall, Goldney, and Dingwell, undertook an evaluative investigation of Price's work. Their report, published in 1956, accused him of being responsible for

GHOSTLY "LIVING SPACE"

The ability of some members of an investigating party to see psychic phenomena when others members cannot is reminiscent of the occasion at Bowden House in Totnes, Devon, where co-author Lionel, who was walking ahead of a small group of other psychic investigators, paused and sat down in a large armchair as he waited for the rest of the party to catch up.

Shirley Wallace, a very perceptive medium, was among those in the group. She looked toward the armchair in question and informed Lionel that he was sitting on the ghost of a Victorian lady wearing a voluminous brown crinoline dress. Shirley added that the ghost concerned appeared to be distressed because Lionel was in what Shirley described as the ghost's "living space"! It is therefore perfectly feasible that an experienced investigator like Andrew Green would have been unable to see the woman in the long white gown, whereas he was able to hear the inexplicable rustling of the leaves.

much of the Borley story. While it is true that he and a few like-minded characters may have amplified *some* of the Borley phenomena, there is more than enough evidence to indicate that a great many *genuine* hauntings took place there, as well. Although the rectory burned down in rather questionable circumstances in 1939, strange phenomena have continued in the district.

Andrew Green, an experienced investigator, went to Borley in the early 1950s accompanied by members of the Ealing Psychical Research Society. At one point in the investigation a friend grabbed Green's arm and pointed to what he described as a woman wearing a long white gown who had appeared at the far end of the Nun's Walk. Green himself could not see the figure, but he heard sounds from the bushes and shrubs as though someone or something was walking through them.

Stephen Jenkins, who has made a special study of ley lines (see sidebar), has put forward the view that Borley church is at a point where four lines intersect. A photograph of Jenkins taken in the late 1970s beside the wall of Borley cemetery seemed to show strange faces visible in the trees.

Another strange experience that the Jenkins family were involved in took place not far from Belchamp Walter Hall, less than five kilometres from Borley village. As they were driving, a group of men inexplicably appeared in front of them. They wore black cloaks and carried a coffin of a pattern not used in the twentieth century. This sinister group disappeared through the hedge and, although they did not get a long look at them, the Jenkins were convinced that at least one of the figures had a skull instead of a face.

Phantom funeral near Borley.

Ley Lines are a network of lines or ancient tracks connecting prehistoric sites, such as monuments or natural landmarks. The lines are thought to be ancient surveying or property markings, or could simply be commonly travelled pathways.

In South America, such lines often lead toward mountain peaks, with the Nazca lines of Peru being the most famous example. The site, located on a large plateau, is comprised of hundred of individual lines and figures, ranging in complexity from simple lines and geometric shapes to intricate outlines of spiders, monkeys, lizards, and sharks (the largest figure measuring more than two hundred metres in diameter). The shallow lines were made in the ground by removing the reddish pebbles common to the area, and uncovering the white ground below. They were thought to have been created between 200 B.C. and A.D. 700 by people of the Nazca culture. They have survived for centuries due to the dry and windless climate of the surrounding Nazca Desert.

Borley Church is as interesting as Harry Bull's rectory, and far older. There is evidence of a wooden building having been erected on the site in the middle of the eleventh century. Flint and rubble dating from a hundred years later was located in the south wall.

Ethel Bull told Harry Price the story of a nineteenth-century incident when Waldegrave coffins in their vault below the church had apparently moved of their own volition. This ties in with the unexplained mystery of the coffins in the Chase-Elliot vault in the Barbados that we investigated for our BBC documentary. This case is discussed in detail in Chapter 16. Similar moving coffin incidents have also been reported in connection with the Buxhoewden family vault in Osel, in the Baltic region, and from Gretford (near Stamford) and Suffolk, in England.

Various groups of psychic investigators have studied Borley Church, including film director Denny Densham. Tapes made there for a very effective BBC documentary recorded inexplicable rappings, knockings, and a heavy crash against the door, as well as a very strange human sigh.

Despite the disappearance of its famous haunted rectory, Borley is undoubtedly still well worth the serious psychic investigator's time.

Just as churches and rectories are frequently the sites of reported hauntings, so too are many ancient inns and taverns.

If ever an old inn enjoyed the most beautiful setting it must surely be the Anchor Inn at Tintern. The building stands on the banks of the beautiful River Wye, barely a stone's throw from the famous ruin of Tintern Abbey. Both are surrounded by scenic, forested hills, but although it is a perfect picture of what a country inn should be by day, in the depth of night it is a very different place.

The main bar of the Anchor Inn is at least as old as the abbey, and its restaurant was at one time the boathouse used by the monks. Tintern Abbey was built by Walter de Clare: it was raised as his penance for the murder of his wife, and many psychic investigators have wondered whether it was the unhappy Lady de Clare who became the frequently sighted spectral Grey Lady of Tintern.

Like many atmospheric old buildings of its kind, the Anchor Inn has intriguing tunnels and passageways beneath it. History asserts that the monks of Tintern hid in these tunnels when Henry VIII's men were after their blood. The abbey was eventually sacked and most of the occupants slaughtered, a number certainly killed in the tunnels where they had sought their escape from the king's men. The former boathouse, now the Anchor's restaurant, witnessed a number of desperate launches as the monks tried urgently to escape. Two arches, today discretely curtained off from the main part of the restaurant, mark the exact places where the monks boarded their boats.

It could well be argued that there are perfectly natural explanations for the feeling of intense cold which surrounds these curtained archways. Drafts of moist, cool air from the surface of the river on a winter's night could very well provide the logical, common-sense explanation for the coldness. Nevertheless, psychic investigators who have considered the area carefully wonder whether there is a paranormal reason for the anomalous temperature changes.

It is said in the village that some are not too keen to go into the cellars or backrooms of the Anchor after night has fallen. Alan Butt, landlord of the inn — a tough, rugby-playing sailor with common sense to match his physical strength — is not in the least nervous or imaginative, but he will tell in his typically quiet, sensible way about a dull winter afternoon when he saw the wraith of a woman in long grey garments looking through the doorway of the inn. As Alan looked back at the strange spectral form, a picture fell from the wall with a loud crash. It seemed inevitable that the frame would be broken and the glass shattered, but when he picked it up it was, to his great surprise, undamaged. He checked the cord and the strong, secure hook from which the picture had been hanging. The cord

Aerial view of Tintern Abbey.

THE DEVIL'S PULPIT

On the other side of the River Wye from the Anchor Inn is a curious outcrop of rock. It is known as the "Devil's Pulpit" and stands high on the cliff, offering an amazing aerial view of the abbey far below. According to legend, Satan himself stood there doing his eloquent best to persuade the monksof the abbey to change sides and work for him. There are some who sided with Henry VIII at the time of the Dissolution who would have argued that a number of the monks must have accepted the devil's offer when he harangued them from his strange "pulpit."

Several of the Tintern inhabitants, who know the area and its atmosphere well, wonder whether it is the troubled souls of these renegade monks that glide behind the inn when darkness falls.

was unbroken and the hook — as good as the day it had been put in — was still firmly embedded in the wall. Apparently, there was no logical reason why the picture should have come down so suddenly.

When Alan searched for the Grey Lady in the gardens next to the inn, there was no sign of her. She had vanished as suddenly and as inexplicably as Lydia the ghostly hitchhiker from Jamestown in North Carolina. In the same area where the landlord saw the Grey Lady, she was also spotted by an Anchor employee named Chris James, whose attention was drawn to her by a young child that he noticed running across the room while he was working in the tea shop. The child ran toward a lady in grey robes who was of above-average height. Chris had to attend to something else for a moment or two, and when he looked again in the direction in which the young child had gone there was no sign of either the infant or the Lady in Grey. The only exit was directly past the spot where Chris was working, and although his attention was on his work, he was positive that not a soul had passed him.

The wife Walter de Clare had murdered had been the mother of one small child. Was it the tragic Grey Lady of Tintern and her child who Chris saw in the tea room that afternoon?

Another strange occurrence at the Anchor Inn concerned the landlord's daughter, his wife, and his daughter's fiancé. They were the only three people in the inn at the time and the young man was asleep upstairs as the two ladies were talking together in the kitchen. It was just after midnight when he came down, sounding rather puzzled and asking why someone had come into his room and woken him!

In one ancient tradition, the grandfather of the legendary King Arthur was a good old king named Tewdric. In his day, Tintern was known by the Welsh name of Din Terwyn. After a lifetime of turbulence and battle, good King Tewdric went into semi-retirement and moved to Tintern, where he hoped to live out his declining years in tranquility. Tewdric's son, Meurig (in this version of the Arthurian legend), got himself involved in a huge battle being fought at Pontysaison, not far from Din Terwyn. (Pontysaison meant the "Bridge of the Saxons.") Like the good and protective father he was, old Tewdric came out of his semi-retirement and galloped to his son's aid, bringing with him his own loyal armed escort and his formidable royal bodyguard. A savage hand-to-hand fight ensued, as a result of which father and son together defeated the Saxon invaders. Tewdric, however, was fatally wounded during the sharp engagement, and was buried with royal honours at Mathern Church, less than sixteen kilometres from Tintern. There are some psychic investigators who wonder whether a few of the hauntings at the Anchor can be traced back to Tewdric's triumphant spirit coming home to celebrate that last great victory in which he did his father's duty so well.

If it is the monks of Tintern whose psychic presence troubles the old Anchor Inn to this day, does it seem strange that men supposedly devoted to the cause of holiness during their earthly lives would be such negative and distressing spirits after death? The original Cistercians were generally regarded as being a severe and pious order, who lived lives of the most rigorous religious discipline, giving away all their wealth and keeping strictly to vows of poverty, chastity, and obedience. In consequence, their lives were simple in the extreme: lives that the authors would personally regard as an infallible formula for chronic and abject misery — but there's no accounting for taste!

The Cistercians even wore robes that were woven from sheep's wool that had not been dyed, and this, too, was in accordance with their principle of simplicity.

Some investigators have put forward the theory that perhaps the strange figure in grey robes is not, after all, the unfortunate Lady de Clare, but a monk whose white robes have been glazed over with dirt until they look as though they are grey.

Although these original, sincere Cistercians seem to have followed the Order's rules of poverty, chastity, and obedience, poverty became an unwelcome stranger to Tintern Abbey as the years passed. Generous gifts and bequests of land made the monks wealthier, and with that wealth came power. Their original strictness and rigorous religious observations began to soften. They became "liberalized, progressive, and permissive" to use a kindly phrase. As their discipline faded and fell away, it was not only the king's propagandists and the monks' jealous enemies who talked about their gluttony and debauchery. It seemed that nothing and no one could keep these rapacious ex-holy men under control, and there are historians who suggest that this was one of the reasons why Henry VIII felt that the safest plan would be to execute them all.

If it is the souls of the Tintern monks who haunt the old Anchor Inn by the Rive Wye, it is very unlikely to be the spirits of the first generation of benign and pious men who are responsible for the uncanny events and strange phantom appearances there. There would, however, seem to be nothing to prevent the return of the restless souls of those *later* monks, seeking, perhaps, to find peace and tranquility in the same location. Was this the spot where their vows of poverty, chastity, and obedience went up the same chimney as the smoke from the geese and swans that were roasting merrily for them and their raunchy young tavern wenches?

During the 1700s, builders working in the grounds at Tintern discovered a ponderous stone slab beneath which a number of skeletons lay as though huddled together in death. There was no trace of any coffins under that great slab. Was it that some of the monks in conflict with Henry VIII had been killed and buried there in a great hurry? Or had they been trying to hide from their pursuers under that stone — and ultimately perished there?

While having a well-earned meal in the inn that night, the workmen who found the skeletons were discussing who they might have been and how they might have met their deaths. It could, of course, merely have been coincidence, but as they discussed the skeletons the sky darkened and a terrifying storm burst over the dining room of the inn. Great bolts of lightning flashed all around them, and the thunder sounded like a legion of skeletons dancing on a corrugated iron roof immediately above their heads. The men began to wonder whether the vengeful spirits of those whose bones they had inadvertently disturbed were seeking vengeance on them.

Another prime candidate for the cause of the ghostly disturbances reported at the inn might be John Callice. A Tintern man, Callice made even the most debauched of the monks appear pious and mild-mannered by contrast. Callice was a notorious Barbary Coast pirate and not averse to a little lucrative white-slaving on the side. Suitable girls aboard the ships he had captured would be auctioned off as sex slaves in North Africa. Like many similar boastful villains, Callice enjoyed shocking his listeners with stories — possibly wildly exaggerated — of the mayhem, rape, and murder he had committed at sea and along the notorious Barbary Coast.

Is it possible that the savage, restless spirit of John Callice returns to trouble the bar where he once told his picaresque tales?

Yet another candidate for the hauntings would be the fearless Sir Henry Wintour. During the English Civil War, Wintour, a bold, if reckless, Royalist, was galloping flat out to get away from a posse of parliamentary soldiers who were hot on his track. At the spot still known today at Wintour's Leap he urged his horse clean over the clifftop and down into the deep water of the Wye below.

Macaulay wrote a magnificent poem about Horatius holding the bridge in ancient Rome to keep the Etruscans at bay and defend the city he loved so much. At the end of the battle, when the bridge had fallen behind him and his task was successfully accomplished, Horatius deliberately dove into the River Tiber rather than surrender to Lars Porsena and his Tuscan horde. For a long moment there was no sign of the gallant Roman hero, and in Macaulay's words:

> No sound of joy or sorrow
> Was heard from either bank,
> But friends and foes in dumb surprise,
> With parted lips and straining eyes,
> Stood gazing where he sank.

Horatius, despite his wounds and the weight of his armour, made it safely back to Rome, where he was appropriately rewarded for saving his city.

Much the same thing happened with Sir Henry Wintour. Like Horatius centuries before him, Wintour and his horse disappeared beneath the deep, brown waters of the river. Unlike Horatius, however, from that day to this no one knows for certain what became of him. Was he somehow trapped by his horse falling on him on the riverbed and drowned at the point where he had leaped in? No substantive evidence either of his body being found, or of his survival and reappearance after Charles II came to power, has ever been put forward.

Did Wintour's wild leap generate such an explosion of emotion that it etched itself into the soil and stone of the riverbanks and bed? Is it Sir Henry's restless ghost that reportedly makes things leap about occasionally in the bar of the Anchor Inn as he once leaped to his death not far away? A good inn would be an irresistible attraction to a good, hard-riding, hard-drinking, cavalier hero.

Yet another candidate was a wonderful old character named Billy Budd, who lived in a cave in the woods less than a mile from the inn. The cave came to be known as "Billy Budd's Hole." He earned a few coppers by playing his penny whistle in the yard outside the inn, and good-natured staff, as well as kind-hearted visitors, would throw a few coins into his cap from time to time. Billy became such a landmark in the fifties that regular visitors who knew and loved Tintern and frequently returned to it would ask about him if he was not there. Old age and illness finally forced him into a nursing home. Could it be the restless ghost of Billy Budd that causes some of the paranormal disturbances in and around the inn?

There is one other strange event connected to the old inn at Tintern. A few years ago, in 1996, an outstandingly good guide book was produced by Grantley James. The date of its launch was Thursday, June 6. That evening, all hell broke loose in the sky at around seven o'clock in the form of a singularly violent and destructive storm. When the thunder, lightning, and rain were at their worst, the East Wing of the Abbey was struck, and nearly three tonnes of stone were dislodged: they hit the ground like a bomb. More lightning struck the inn, knocking out the electronic tills, the telephones, and all the lights. If the spirits in and around the inn at Tintern are as evil and vindictive as some psychical researchers suggest, then that storm — remarkably similar to the one that frightened the workmen when they uncovered the skeletons centuries before — may be regarded as a warning that the ghosts were angry because of the depth and accuracy of Grantley James's work.

A number of the famous stately homes in Britain have their fair share of reports of strange, supernatural happenings. One well-known and well-authenticated example is Bisham Abbey, not far from Marlow in Buckinghamshire. It is actually a fine Tudor house built on the site of an old abbey. The building that is there today was originally a gift from Henry VIII to one of his queens, Anne of Cleaves. When she died, the house became the property of Sir Thomas Hoby. During the reign of Queen Mary Tudor, Thomas Hoby was the official guardian to young Princess Elizabeth (later Queen Elizabeth I). Whether it was through enlightened self-interest or natural kindness, Sir Thomas was a caring, kindly, and thoughtful guardian. When turbulent Tudor politics performed one of their many dramatic somersaults and Elizabeth became queen, she made Sir Thomas her ambassador to France.

His old home at Bisham Abbey appears to be haunted by his wife, Lady Elizabeth Hoby. Like Shakespeare's Lady Macbeth, the spirit of Lady Hoby is reported to wander through the house and grounds washing blood from her hands in a bowl that floats mysteriously just ahead of her. Other witnesses have seen her in a boat on the Thames, which laps against the lawns of Bisham Abbey. Visitors staying at Bisham have been woken in the early hours of the morning by the sound of footsteps in corridors that are not there any more. At other times, witnesses have reported hearing desperately sad weeping. Those who have seen the spectre of Bisham Abbey have had no difficulty at all in recognizing her as Lady Elizabeth Hoby, as there is an old family portrait of her still hanging on the wall of the Great Hall. In the portrait, her face and hands are significantly white and she wears the wimple, weeds, and coif traditionally associated with a knight's widow in Tudor times.

It is particularly odd that when Elizabeth Hoby's ghostly form appears it is almost as though she had become a photographic negative. (Could there be a clue here to the strange negative appearance of the Turin Shroud?) The face and hands of the Hoby apparition are dark, and her black dress comes out as a startling, almost luminous, white.

Admiral Vansittart owned Bisham Abbey as the nineteenth century drew to its close. The gritty old sea dog had never believed in anything supernatural until the night that he saw Lady Hoby. He had stayed up until the early hours of the morning in an intensely absorbing game of chess with his brother. When they finished their game, the admiral's brother went off to his bedroom. Vansittart was alone beside Elizabeth Hoby's gaunt portrait in the Great Hall when he felt that someone was standing immediately behind him. Being a stalwart serviceman, and prepared to tackle anything, he spun around defensively, thinking an attacker had crept into Bisham Abbey — but it was no burglar that he saw.

The ghostly phantom of Elizabeth Hoby was standing behind him. With great presence of mind Vansittart looked up at her portrait as if to confirm that the female form was in fact Lady Hoby. Even his calm resilience and great presence of mind almost deserted him then — the frame where her portrait should have been was empty!

A moment later everything was back to normal, but Vansittart was convinced beyond a shadow of doubt that he had seen someone, or something, that his pragmatic common sense was at a loss to explain.

Reports of hauntings come from every age and every country. The great Roman author Pliny, whose work bridged the first and second century A.D., recorded the story of a spacious Athenian home that remained unoccupied because it was allegedly haunted by the ghost of a repellent old man who moaned and rattled his chains as characteristically as Marley's ghost in Dickens's *A Christmas Carol*. A number of courageous, if skeptical, young Greeks volunteered to spend the night in the house, but fled when the moaning old spectre turned up.

HAUNTING FILMS

Hollywood has long had a fascination with ghosts and hauntings. Here are ten creepy films about hauntings:

The Haunting (1963)
Burnt Offerings (1976)
The Amityville Horror (1979)
The Shining (1980)
The Changeling (1980)
Poltergeist (1982)
What Lies Beneath (2000)
The Others (2001)
Saint Ange (2004)
A Haunting in Connecticut (2009)

Even in the beautiful Greek climate the house began to crumble from neglect. Athenodorus, who was a Stoic, saw the place and decided that it had the great virtue of solitude. The unbelievably low rent made it even more attractive to him. The honest landlord explained to Athenodorus that the rent was ridiculously low because he was unable to obtain a tenant due to the alleged haunting. According to Pliny's account, on the first night that Athenodorus spent in the house working on his book he was interrupted by the rattling of chains. A few moments later the ghost of the repellent old man appeared before him and beckoned with a bony finger.

A Stoic philosopher is not easily disturbed, and Athenodorus simply waved one hand dismissively and carried on with his work. The spectre persisted in rattling its chains and making hideous noises until, rather wearily, Athenodorus followed him into the garden, where the spectre vanished amongst the undergrowth. The philosopher marked the place with a small cairn of stones and went back to his room. The next morning, Athenodorus went to consult the magistrates, and a number of leading Athenians returned with him to the spot he had marked in the garden. On their instructions, slaves began to dig. A metre or so below the surface their spades encountered something curious. What they unearthed was a skeleton encumbered with rusting chains. On the orders of the Athenian magistrates these pathetic remains were interred with honour and dignity and the proper ceremonies — and the spectre never again disturbed the house.

Athenodorus was one of the greatest of the Stoic philosophers. The way in which he ignored the persistent ghost that was interrupting his writing was typical of the man.

Ancient Greek skeleton in chains.

14 POLTERGEISTS, GHOULS, AND ZOMBIES

The word *poltergeist* is derived from the German *poltern*, meaning "to knock," and *geist*, meaning "a ghost, or spirit." Poltergeists are frequently associated with noise and mischief of a kind which is not rationally explicable. One such entity that co-author Lionel was called in to deal with in Cardiff moved food from the refrigerator to a wardrobe and wrote curious messages on the wooden floor underneath a carpet. It also moved clothes and shoes from the wardrobe into the refrigerator.

Strange, disturbing, poltergeist-type activities were part of the recorded paranormal events from the old Anchor Inn at Tintern. Most frequently these take place in the carvery. Janet Hill, who has been a member of staff at the Anchor for a number of years, witnessed a very strange episode, when a basket full of bread rose into the air for no apparent reason and emptied its contents all over the counter where Janet was working. Additionally, furniture has been seen to move, menu boards have vanished and reappeared, and episodes almost as dramatic as the Esther Cox poltergeist phenomena at Amherst, Nova Scotia, have been reported from time to time.

A London inn, the Grenadier, known as the Guardsman during the reign of George IV, has also had its share of reported hauntings. An old story suggests that the Grenadier, in Wilton Row, was once part of the old Knightsbridge Barracks. Some of Wellington's officers were said to have been billeted there, and the duke himself, it was alleged, often attended for a game of cards. In the small, panelled card room, preserved more or less in its original state, the legend of a tragic death is centred.

Reportedly, at the beginning of the nineteenth century, one of the guards officers billeted in the Guardsman was caught cheating at cards. The others decided that he deserved a sound thrashing for letting them down in this way. Unfortunatelhy, during the course of the punishment, he died.

No ghost has ever made its presence known visibly at the Grenadier, but there are so many records of minor poltergeist-type happenings that cannot be explained that it certainly seems as if *something* preternatural is lurking in the old inn. Lights switch themselves on and off for no apparent reason, small objects move — apparently of their own volition — from one room to another. Light bulbs have been observed turning in their sockets and then floating slowly to the ground, remaining intact.

Other Wilton Row residents whose homes are close to the Grenadier have also reported that lights and water taps have turned on and off without any visible cause. One of the strangest events in the history of the anomalous phenomena associated with the Grenadier was included in a report made by Tom Westward, one-time head barman there. It was during his lunch break, and Tom was sitting with another member of staff when suddenly he noticed what he described as a wisp of smoke. It was emerging from beneath a shelf near the door. Tom's first thought was that a customer had left a cigarette burning, but after close inspection of the area, he found no evidence of anything burning near it. It was as if the wisp of smoke had no origin: it was simply a wisp of smoke in the air with no apparent source.

Soon after Tom saw the strange phenomenon, an inspector from the brewery visited the Grenadier. He was standing near where Tom had seen the smoke previously. Suddenly the inspector winced and withdrew his arm as though it had been stung. There was a small round burn on his skin that looked as though it had been caused by a lit cigarette. It might, of course, simply have been an insect bite, but at the very least it was an extraordinary coincidence.

A very strange Canadian case was investigated and reported by the famous nineteenth-century artist Percy Woodcock, who lived at Waterniche in Brockville, Ontario. He became a full member of the Royal Canadian Academy in his early forties, in 1889. In addition to his considerable artistic talents, Percy was keenly interested in investigating psychic phenomena.

On the north side of the Ottawa River, not far from Shoreville, Quebec, lived George Dagg. He and his wife, Susan, had two young children — four-year-old Susan and two-year-old Johnny. They decided that it would be a good idea — useful as well as kindly — to adopt an older child from one of the orphanages to help Mrs. Dagg look after the two young ones and help out with the housework, as well.

Dinah Burden McLean was a Scottish girl who had recently arrived in Canada and had been placed in the orphanage at Belleville, Ontario. Dinah was a few months short of her twelfth birthday when she went to live with the Daggs, and it wasn't long before the paranormal occurrences began.

In November 1889, when Percy heard accounts of the strange events that were allegedly taking place in the Dagg household, he travelled to Shawville, then several kilometres farther to the Daggs' farmhouse. As Woodcock described it, the building was a single-storey log house with a storage shed at the rear and a small attic at the top. In his opinion the Daggs were ordinary, hard-working, intelligent farm people. He had no reason at all to doubt their honesty or integrity.

He was welcomed, as many sightseers had been over the past few weeks. They explained to him that they did not expect any phenomena to take place because Dinah — who seemed to be the centre of the activity — had gone to see Mr. Dagg Sr., who lived about five kilometres away. George and Susan had already noted that when Dinah was not in the house, nothing happened.

Percy was very disappointed. He had undertaken a long journey in the hope of seeing some unusual psychic events taking place. The Daggs felt sorry for him and sent a message to Mr. Dagg Sr., asking him to send Dinah back the following day. This gave Woodcock an opportunity to have a long talk with the Daggs and to record the experiences that they reported to him. As an artist, Percy Woodcock revelled in detail, and took particular care preparing his notes. He had been contracted to write an article about the events for the *Brockville Recorder and Times.* So he carefully recorded the tale told to him by the Daggs, as well as by other friends and neighbours in the vicinity who he was able to interview.

The story that George Dagg related to Woodcock had begun several weeks previously. He recalled distinctly that in mid-September he had given his wife a five-dollar bill and a two-dollar bill, and that she had put them carefully in the drawer of their desk. Several local farmers, who were as kind-hearted and generous as the Daggs, gave a few odd jobs to a young orphan lad named Dean. It was the Daggs' turn to provide him with accommodation and food in return for some light chores.

Dean was staying in the attic. He got up early and started to light the cooking stove for Mrs. Dagg. As he got down low on the floor to attend to the fire he claimed he spotted a five-dollar bill, which, being an honest lad, he took to Mr. Dagg, informing him where he had found it. Dagg checked the desk and found both the two-dollar and five-dollar bill were no longer there. He sent the boy out on an errand, then went and checked the attic. In Dean's bed he found the two-dollar bill.

It seemed obvious to the Daggs that Dean must be the culprit, although they were at a loss to explain why he would take the money and then claim to have found the five-dollar bill under the stove.

The next problem was rather more serious: excrement had been taken from the outside toilet and scattered about indoors. Criminologists and psychologists who specialize in the analysis of deviant behaviour are well aware that it is characteristic of a significant number of burglars to leave excrement at the scene of their crime — like an animal marking its territory. Experienced police officers tend to refer to this as the criminal's "trademark."

When accused of the crime, Dean denied it vehemently, but Dagg took him to a local magistrate and formerly charged him with stealing the two-dollar bill. While they were away, more excrement was scattered all over the house. It was perfectly obvious that Dean — who was at this time appearing in front of the magistrate — could have had nothing to do with the subsequent problem.

Matters became considerably worse: milk containers were tipped out, crockery was broken, and a quantity of water was thrown over Mrs. Dagg when there did not seem to be any possible local cause. While George was away, his father John and his wife came to stay with Susan and the children. While they were there a great many of the window panes were broken. Whatever was causing the disturbance then turned its attention to the children's hair. Dinah's long, braided pigtail was practically severed; young John had his hair cut crudely and painfully.

Upon his return, George went to consult Mrs. Barnes, who lived at Plum Hollow and was generally regarded as a source of folklore and wisdom about the paranormal. "Wise woman" Barnes told Dagg that in her opinion a woman, a girl, and a boy were involved in launching black magic against him.

Young Dinah was convinced that she could see a huge, dangerous, dark thing dragging the bedclothes away. Grandmother Dagg was nearby and, although she treated the girl helpfully and sympathetically, all she could see was that the bedclothes looked as if an invisible hand was lifting them up into the air.

The next piece of evidence was augmented by a young neighbour named Arthur Smart who was visiting the Dagg family at the time when Dinah thought she could see the large dark object. Grandmother Dagg, like Mrs. Barnes, was reasonably well versed in folklore. She went to fetch a whip, gave it to Dinah, and told her that if she struck at the evil thing she thought she could see, it would be driven away. Arthur was watching the performance and told Dinah not to be afraid but to strike hard at the tormentor that only she could see. All three of them heard a high-pitched shriek which they later described as similar to the squeaking and squealing of a pig. Dinah put the whip down.

"It's gone," she said. Sometime later a message was found on a piece of paper stuck on the wall. The words were: "You gave me fifteen cats." The reference was apparently to the cat-o'-nine-tails, which had been used for punishment for many years.

THE "SACRED" CAT-O'-NINE-TAILS

The legend behind the cat-o'-nine-tails was that nine — three times three — was a triple holy number, like the Holy Trinity, and a whipping with this "sacred" instrument was intended to drive out evil from the criminal or heretic being attended to.

Four-year-old Mary later said she could see the weird, dangerous haunter. She described it as roughly human in size but as having a head like a cow but with horns, and cloven hooves. She said she saw it standing by the front door. The second time she saw it, it said to her, "Little girl, would you like to go to hell with me?"

After this episode, a local minister named Horner was summoned. He was unable to attend, but sent his brother to help the family. The brother asked for a Bible and then began to say some prayers with the family. During these prayers the Bible mysteriously disappeared from the chair where he had placed it. It was found a few moments later in the oven. The minister's brother was unable to believe his eyes when, in addition to the movement of the Bible, an inkstand appeared to float, unsupported, from the table to the shed outside.

Once Mrs. Dagg Sr. was carrying a bottle of vinegar, and remarked, "I daren't put it down in case the goblin breaks it." As she spoke, a potato flew through the air — apparently without any normal physical cause — and struck her hand.

John Quinn, a neighbour, was carrying a halter when he called to see them. He put it down while he was talking and when he went to retrieve it as he left, it had disappeared. A few moments later, as he stood in puzzled conversation with four or five members of the Dagg family, there was a whistling sound in the air, and the halter that had vanished fell in the middle of the group.

But worse was to come.

Whatever strange presence was troubling the Daggs, it now began to speak. Like the evil force in *The Exorcist*, the words uttered by the strange voice were usually obscene and full of crudely expressed sexual innuendoes directed toward Dinah. At the end of Woodcock's investigation, a statement was obtained signed by seventeen local people, including the Dagg family, who had some experience of the strange entity and its voice to report.

There may perhaps be a curious parallel between the talking poltergeist which haunted the Dagg family and Gef, the strange "talking mongoose" that haunted Doarlish Cashen, not far from Cashen's Gap on the Isle of Man, in the following century. Doarlish Cashen was well over two hundred metres up the western heights, bleak and isolated. The nearest neighbours were out of sight and more than a mile away.

The family with the mysterious "talking mongoose" consisted of James Irving, a sixty-year-old retired commercial traveller, who made little money from his farm, his rather grim, prim wife, Margaret, and their teen-aged daughter, Voirrey, who was the one most closely associated with the weird creature called Gef. The talking mongoose may have existed in a real, objective sense: it might equally well have been a product of Voirrey's restless teenage mind. It could have been a poltergeist. It could have been a harmless deception created in the hope of bringing a little interest (and some much wanted fame and money?) into the boring, rural life of the Irvings.

Reports of strange creatures like Gef and ghostly hauntings of various types are not enough in themselves to provide irrefutable evidence of an alleged spirit world. Is there a case for a mysterious zone in which departed human souls share their psychic existence with curious elemental spirits and strange entities like Gef and the talking poltergeist that tormented the Dagg family?

Toward the end of the nineteenth century, the famous medium D.D. Home collaborated with William Crookes, who was widely recognized as outstanding by his fellow scientists. A Fellow of the Royal Society, he was the discoverer of the element thallium. Scientific accuracy was extremely important to him, and after nearly thirty scrupulously documented experiments, Crookes was convinced that Home really had the ability to alter the weight of various objects — including people — and to induce table rapping. So accurate and consistent were the measurements that Crookes recorded that he explained the phenomenon as an entirely new form of energy to set alongside light, heat, electricity, and the other energy forms already known to physics. Crookes called the new force "psychic force."

As a contemporary of Sigmund Freud and Carl Jung, Crookes was interested in studying the states of mind and psychological factors involved in the manifestation of this new psychic energy. He became particularly interested in the idea that the existence of such energy — which he felt that he had proved to his own satisfaction, at least — indicated the existence of other dimensions: psychic dimensions.

Of particular interest as far as the Crookes and Homes experiments were concerned is that a number of them — like valid laboratory experiments in the natural sciences — appear to have been repeatable. Sir Oliver Lodge, the physicist, was one of the contemporary scientists who seemed to have above average success with the experiments that Home and Crookes had pioneered.

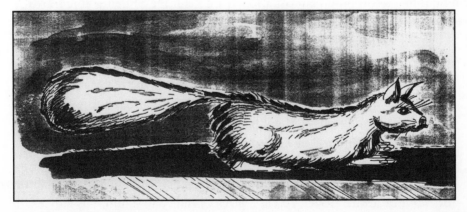

Gef, the talking mongoose.

Later work was done by Everard Feilding, who did a number of tests involving the medium Eusapia Palladino. Feilding later met and married Stanislawa Tomczyk — one of the most remarkable young mediums of the time.

In her normal, waking state, Stanislawa produced all kinds of séance and poltergeist-type phenomena in a rather haphazard, unexpected, and spontaneous way. What Feilding discovered was that under hypnosis she seemed to be able to produce the same phenomena practically at will and much more frequently. There is good evidence that Stanislawa was able to make small domestic objects such as buttons, spoons, and matchboxes move without being physically touched — and there are reports that she was also able to cause them to levitate simply by making a gesture close to them.

Poltergeist activity may be associated with an aspect of human personality that is non-material and which, therefore, has a strong chance of surviving bodily death. Poltergeist phenomena are among the most persistent and spectacular of all paranormal cases.

If ever one individual seemed to encapsulate the entire spectrum of poltergeist activities, it was Carmine Mirabelli. So many incredible reports were made about him and so many amazing stories told of his astounding abilities that his connection with poltergeist activity was almost a backwater to the great, surging, tidal river of his dynamic life.

Two of the most reliable and impressive witnesses to Mirabelli's vast range of paranormal abilities were Eurico de Goes and Miguel Karl. De Goes was a particularly well-read intellectual and an academic librarian who became interested in psychical research after the tragic death of his beautiful young wife. His attraction to investigations of paranormal phenomena was based almost entirely on his hope of being able to reach her in the spirit world.

Some of the materializations that Mirabelli is alleged to have been able to perform were said to be so realistic and durable that doctors were able to examine them. Mirabelli seems to have attracted as many rumours, myths, and legends as King Arthur and Robin Hood put together — but even when the most dubious of these have been discarded, there still remains a granite core of Mirabelli fact, particularly concerning poltergeist-type phenomena that obdurately refuses to dissolve away.

Mirabelli was born toward the end of the nineteenth century in the little town of Botucatu, about 240 kilometres outside São Paulo. His father was a Lutheran Pastor who was remembered mainly for his kindness, sincerity, and generosity. This generosity and kindness were also characteristic of Mirabelli. His first job after leaving school was in a shoe shop in São Paulo, where boxes of shoes literally flew off the shelves poltergeist-fashion while he was attempting to serve customers.

This report about him is remarkably similar to our own experience in the haunted bookshop that we investigated in San Antonio, Texas, close to the site of the Alamo. Books would move around in that shop apparently of their own volition, and those who knew the background of the strange episodes were of the opinion that their shop had been built over the site where the Mexican soldiers, having stormed the Alamo, had cremated the bodies of the defenders.

It is equally possible, of course, that a member of the staff unwittingly produced the phenomena much as Mirabelli apparently did in the shoe shop. So much wild talk followed Mirabelli when he was forced to leave his job at the shoe shop that it was generally suspected that he must be clinically insane — and the unlucky young man was incarcerated in Juquery Asylum. Here, Doctor Franco da Rocha wrote a report about him, as did his colleague, Doctor Felipe Aché.

Aché came very close to the theory of libido — or nerve energy — examined earlier. He believed that the strange phenomena that seemed to accompany Mirabelli was "the result of nervous forces radiating. We all have them," he wrote, "but Mirabelli has them in excess." Dr. da Rocha gave a detailed description of the kind of telekinetic, poltergeist-type displays that he witnessed while with Mirabelli:

A skull was placed on top of a glass, and when the doctor asked Mirabelli to make it rotate, *it did*. Both the glass and the skull balanced on it, then toppled over on the table. Dr. da Rocha picked them up again and the display continued. In his opinion, some sort of "psychic radiation" seemed to have come from Mirabelli and entered the skull.

In addition to these careful observations of Mirabelli, which de Goes carried out over an extended period, the medium and his work was also examined and analyzed by a professional conjurer, Carlos Gardonne Ramos, who was widely regarded as an expert in the field of stage magic and illusions. In Ramos's opinion, it was not possible that the feats Mirabelli performed were done by a professional conjuror by trickery or by sleight of hand. In other words, as far as one expert stage illusionist was concerned, whatever Mirabelli did was due to some strange psychic power and *not* to prestidigitation. Poltergeistic apports were part of Mirabelli's stock-in-trade.

One gentleman, Sir Douglas Ainslie, was attending a mediumistic session with Mirabelli in 1928. As he entered the house, there on the hall table was the small travelling clock that Sir Douglas had left safely inside his suitcase, in his bedroom ... *at his hotel!*

Some expert psychic investigators tend to the view that the *character* of the medium is to some extent reflected in the phenomena that he or she attracts. Occasional minor pranks and simplistic practical jokes are often associated with poltergeist phenomena. These minor events are by no means dangerous or malevolent. It is almost as if a schoolchild's sense of humour still clung vestigially to the adult. The most sombre and solemn among us may occasionally have minute humorous quirks that seem totally out of character.

PARLOUR TRICKS?

Did a powerful, serious, benign and highly intelligent medium like Mirabelli have a tendency to perform one or two of these minor practical jokes integrated into his personality? At some of his sessions things moved about the room from one shelf to another. A pair of glasses was mislaid and turned up again. Flowers drifted into a room through a window that was not only locked but *sealed*, and a religious carving weighing a good nine kilograms came in by the same route without damaging the window at all. According to the report, it floated, much as the flowers had done, toured the room like a sergeant-major inspecting his troops, and then drifted out again as quietly as it had entered.

Whatever Mirabelli attracted in the way of psychic forces, he was himself quite benign. If there is anything to the theory that mediums who have a sinister side to their nature are capable of attracting and using evil forces, a man with Mirabelli's massive psychic energy could have caused as much damage as a stick of dynamite going off in a confined space.

One of the most gruesome reports recorded by de Goes concerned parts of a decomposing corpse that filled the séance room with an indescribable stench and grotesque visual effects that would have gladdened the heart of any Hollywood horror filmmaker today. De Goes described it as reminding him of some of the worst excesses of Edgar Allan Poe.

GHOULS

A ghoul is a particular type of evil monster linked with tombs and burial places. They are believed to eat the flesh of the newly dead. Ghouls in their Arabian folklore origins are said to be shape-shifters that lure travellers out into waste places and then kill and eat them. The old Arabian word *ghúl* meant "demon." Ghouls are traditionally the servants of the evil god Ahriman.

Haitian voodoo and zombiism is best understood within its historical context because it played a significant role in the successful slave revolution that ended French rule on the island. In 1791 France was in revolutionary turmoil and the Haitian slaves were being inspired to rebel by a mysterious sorcerer-priest, Dutty Boukman. He led them into a secret rendezvous in the depths of the forest, where a terrifying storm acted as a dramatic background to their proceedings. Here Boukman sacrificed a pig, and his revolutionaries drank its blood. They then stormed many of the plantations, and the slave-owners — known as the plantocracy — were slaughtered.

Boukman was captured by the French soon after the start of the rebellion that he had inspired. They decapitated him and placed his head out for all to see in the hope of quelling the legend of his invincibility — but the gruesome display had the opposite effect, and the rebellious slaves fought harder than ever for their freedom. It took a further twelve years for the revolutionaries to establish their new Republic of Haiti under the leadership of President Toussaint L'Ouverture.

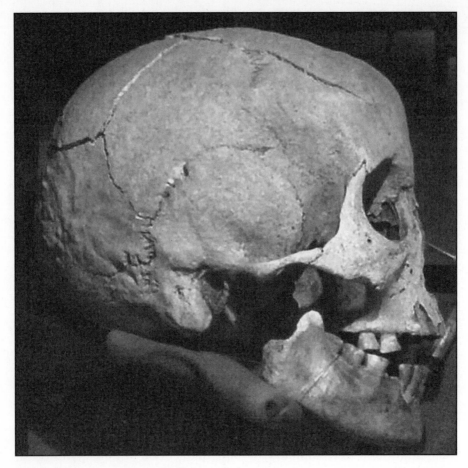

Dutty Boukman was decapitated.

In contemporary voodoo it is believed that the snake deity, or python god, is invoked to animate the zombie. The sorcerer, or enchanter, using the process is thought to have become the owner and master of the moving corpse. Ancient African religious and magical practices combine with equally old western occultism and certain aspects of traditional Catholicism to create the ceremony at which the zombie is reanimated and made subservient to the sorcerer.

The sorcerer or magician in charge of a zombie is known as a "bokor." Traditionally, the bokor removes a newly dead corpse from its grave and uses spells to rekindle a spark of life within it. For those who believe in the existence of zombies, the resurrected corpse can eat, drink, excrete, hear, and speak. According to voodoo folklore, the zombie does not know who it was prior to being zombified, and has no memory at all of its earlier, normal, human life. It lurches from side to side as it walks, and the rest of its actions are clumsy, awkward, and robotic in character. The voice, when it speaks, is decidedly nasal, and this is thought to be due to the funeral custom of padding out the nostrils of the corpse with cotton wool.

Rational explanations of zombiism involve the use of drugs similar to the one that Father Laurence gave Juliet in Shakespeare's play so she would appear to be dead. According to this theory, the bokor administers such a drug to the victim who is destined to become a zombie, and digs up the apparent corpse a few days later. Some partial antidote is administered, and the revived victim faces a life of mindless slavery to the bokor, or to some new owner to whom the bokor has sold that victim.

In Haiti, in 1937, a folklore researcher, Zora Hurston, came upon the case of a girl named Felicia Felix-Mentor. Felicia had "officially" died in 1907 when she was twenty-nine. Witnesses reported to Zora that they had seen Felicia wandering about in a zombie-like state thirty years after her body had supposedly been laid to rest. Some of Zora's informants suggested that powerful drugs might have been responsible for zombifying a victim like Felicia.

Another account tells the story of a hungan who was strongly sexually attracted to a girl who wanted nothing to do with him. He promptly cursed her, and a few days later she became ill and died. Her grieving family bought

HYPNOTISM

One theory of zombiism involves the use of hypnotism at a very profound level — so deep, in fact, that the bokor's victims never regain their original self-consciousness. This could be combined with the use of drugs to produce the traditional zombie-state in the victim. Fraud also needs to be considered as a possibility. There are accounts of a bokor — also referred to as a "hungan" — being caught out after opening a grave and apparently reviving the corpse lifted from it. The "corpse" turned out to be the bokor's accomplice, and a sharp-eyed examining magistrate found that an air tube had been connected to a hole in the coffin.

a coffin, but upon discovering that it was too short to fit the body properly, they had to pull her head down hard to one side so that her body would fit. During the family funeral party, a candle set fire to the lower end of the coffin lining and burnt her left foot quite severely.

Several weeks after being buried, the deceased was reported to have been seen with the bokor whom she had firmly rejected before her death. The family ignored these rumours and said that the hungan clearly liked girls of similar appearance, and must have found a new one. Several years later, however, the dead girl's brother saw a woman who looked very much like her. When questioned, she had no idea who she was, and no memory of any past life as his sister. She did, however, have a badly twisted neck and there were severe burn scars on her left foot. Taken home to what her brother believed was her family and his, she was loyally cared for until she died. During all this time, however, she failed to recall anything of her past life, and was able to exercise only the most limited mental functions.

The famous British anthropologist Francis Huxley reported a well-authenticated case of Haitian zombiism from the late 1950s. Huxley, a remarkable adventurer, had travelled thousands of kilometres in the Amazon Basin studying the indigenous population and their religion. He was also a friend and colleague of the brilliant and dauntless Canadian medical research scientist Humphrey Osmond, who had immigrated to Saskatchewan in 1951 and done so much to help patients at the Weyburn Hospital.

A Catholic priest reported to Huxley in 1959 that what appeared to be a zombie had been found wandering in a Haitian village street and had been taken to the local police station. It seems that the police did not wish to take any action, but eventually the apparent zombie managed to mumble the name of a woman living in the village. When enquiries were made, she recognized him as her deceased nephew — who had been buried *four years earlier*. The priest, however, took a keen and sympathetic interest in the zombie, who, unusually, was able to name the bokor who had enslaved him. The priest duly informed the police, but they were still apparently very unwilling to confront and antagonize a powerful hungan. Instead, they sent him a message offering to return the stray zombie to him! Two days later the zombie was found dead — really and finally dead. The hungan was arrested, but later released.

An equally impressive zombie report dating from the 1980s comes from the village of L'Estère in the Artibonite Valley in Haiti. A lurching robotic figure with a blank facial expression and staring eyes crossed the market square and spoke to one of the local women, Angelina Narcisse. She recognized him and let out a terrified scream. She identified him as her brother, Clairvius Narcisse, whom they had buried nearly twenty years before.

The head of the psychiatric centre in Port-au-Prince at the time was Dr. Lamarque Douyon, a gifted and rigorously professional Haitian psychiatrist who had trained in Canada. With proper professional scientific detachment, he had studied the phenomena associated with zombiism for over a quarter of a century. During the later stages, assistance came from his equally gifted colleague, E. Wade Davis, a botanist from Harvard.

Is this the face of a hungan?

When the case of Clairvius Narcisse was investigated in depth, it was found that he had been officially recorded as having died in the Schweitzer Hospital in Deschapelles in Haiti on May 3, 1962. Clairvius had arrived at the hospital three days earlier with a high fever and a body that ached all over. He was also spitting up a lot of blood. After the doctors officially pronounced him dead, he was placed in cold storage in the mortuary for a day before being handed over to his family for burial.

When giving an account of his grim experiences, Clairvius said that he remembered hearing the doctors announce that he had died. He also remembered his sister Angelina in tears beside his hospital bed when his death was pronounced. He was able to recall being buried because he said that despite being conscious he was totally unable to move or cry out. As he listened to shovelfuls of earth landing on his casket lid, he had the strange feeling that he was hovering above the grave.

There was a scar on his right cheek, and he said that this had been caused by a nail driven through his coffin lid when he was being sealed in. He then vividly recalled how a bokor, or hungan, had taken him from his coffin, revived him, and transported him to a sugar plantation in the north of the island. Here, with a several other zombies, he had worked in slave conditions until their overseer had died. This provided the zombies with a chance of escape, and Clairvius had finally found his way back to L'Estère.

As Douyon's research continued, he found that there was a socio-cultural factor in zombiism: in some areas it was regarded as a form of punishment for people who had contravened the social norms and mores of their community. From this perspective, it was apparent that Clairvius had appropriated land that was not legally his — at least its title was disputed. Had those who thought they had a better claim to it arranged for him to become a zombie?

Another apparent case of zombiism "punishment" concerned a woman named Francina Illeus, who was nicknamed "Ti-Femme." She had allegedly been zombified for refusing to marry the man who had been selected for her, and for giving birth to the child of another man. Hospitalized with symptoms similar to Clairvius's, but sent home on February 23, 1976, she died there a few days later.

It was almost twenty years later that her mother recognized the female zombie walking uncertainly through the village as Francina because of her distinctive birthmark. Her coffin was exhumed ... *but there were only stones inside it.*

15 VAMPIRES AND OTHER HORRORS

Vampires in legend go back a long way. Some versions of the myth of Lilith, or Lilis, supposedly Adam's first wife, suggest that she was a special type of vampire who was particularly dangerous to children. The Latin word *strix* was sometimes applied to a vampire, although it is more appropriately used for a screech owl, which also links it with the Lilith myth. Graeco-Roman literature contains a sprinkling of vampire stories, but there are earlier traces of them in the East. The word *vampir* is found in the Magyar language, and the Lithuanian word *wempti*, meaning "to drink," is also associated with it. A Russian document dating back to 1027 uses the phrase *upir lichy*, meaning "wicked vampire."

It is possible that the vampire legend originated in the Far East and travelled to Europe along the silk and spice routes. From the Mediterranean, the vampire tradition reached the Carpathians and became popular among the Slavs.

Another route may well have been the one thought to have been followed by the original Romany Gypsy tribes who migrated from northern India, and were thought to have arrived in Bohemia and Transylvania

VAMPIRES' PARENTS?

Some old traditions maintain that vampires are the offspring of a witch and a werwolf; others suggest that witches, wizards, and black magicians become vampires after death, or that suicides run the risk of changing into vampires.

during the thirteenth and fourteenth centuries — and Transylvania has been synonymous with the vampire legend ever since Bram Stoker introduced Dracula to the world.

The original form of the name was Vlad Dracul, known as Vlad the Impaler. Vlad was born in Sighisoara, or Schassburg, around 1413. His father, "Vlad the Devil" or "Vlad the Dragon," was a member of the Dragon Order, who pledged to make ceaseless war against the Turks. This is reminiscent of the Carthaginian Hannibal's sworn hatred of the Romans — as an impressionable boy he was made to take a solemn oath against them by his father, Hamilcar Barca.

Young Dracula was allegedly captured by his Turkish opponents when he was only thirteen, and seems to have acquired his notorious taste for torturing and impaling his enemies during that captivity. For several decades, from 1456 onward, he was the stern terror of Wallachia, where, even allowing for exaggeration and the propaganda put around by his enemies, he launched thousands of victims into eternity via the spikes below his castle walls. This accounts for his alternative title of *Tsepesh* or *Tepes*, meaning "impaler."

When the tomb of Dracula was opened in 1931, it contained a crumbling skeleton, a serpent necklace, a cloak of red silk with a ring sewn into it, and a golden crown. These unique souvenirs were eventually stolen from the Bucharest Museum, and have never been recovered.

Turning from the historical Vlad to the folklore of vampires in general, they were feared not only because they were deadly and secretive killers, able

DEATH OF DRACULA

Vlad the Impaler was said to have been killed by one of his own men by mistake. He had apparently disguised himself as a Turk to watch the outcome of a battle from behind enemy lines. He lacked all vestiges of mercy and morality but, like Macbeth, he wasn't short on crude physical courage. Seeing that the field was all but won, he raced to the top of a hill to watch the last few Turkish soldiers being slaughtered — fatally forgetting his own disguise. He was mistaken for a Turk and killed.

VAMPIRES ARE EVERYWHERE!

Vampire folklore exists almost universally. In Ashanti legends, for example, they are called *Asasabonsam* and live in trees deep in the forest. This African vampire tradition gives them iron teeth and feet like hooks, from which they dangle from trees to trap the unwary. And the southern United States — namely Louisiana — is home to the legend of a vampire-like monster called *Fifollet* or *Feu-follet*, thought to be the soul of a dead person sent back to Earth to do penance, or that of an unbaptized child. Most attacks reported have had them performing mere mischief, but on occasion, the *fifollet* became a vampire who sucked the blood of people, especially children.

to assume the form of a bat and fly up to the intended victim's bedroom, but because they carried with them the deadly infection of vampirism: once drained by a vampire, the victim was doomed to join the vampire's ranks. Traditionally, vampires show no reflections, cast no shadows, and are unable to cope with bright light.

It was believed that vampires were unable to enter a house unless they had been invited — but once the householder had made that fatal error, they were able to come and go at will.

The traditional vampire's longevity was so great that it almost amounted to immortality, and this was combined with massive physical strength and relative invulnerability. The rules of the game, however, were not loaded entirely in the vampire's favour. It disintegrated almost instantly in the presence of strong sunlight. A good sharp stake through the heart was also terminal: iron and wood being equally satisfactory. Beheading, severing the limbs, and burning the pieces of the dismembered torso were also considered effective.

Some vampires are said to be unable to cross water, refinements of this tradition say that the water has to be *flowing* in order to stop them. They are helpless between sunrise and sunset and must then rest in their coffins on some of the soil in which they were originally buried. Holy water sears them like concentrated acid. Being touched with a cross, preferably a silver one wielded by an ordained priest who sincerely holds the faith, burns vampires as devastatingly as a red hot branding iron. Like werebeasts, they can be shot with silver bullets or cut with a silver knife. They are deterred by garlic, but not totally halted by it.

A particularly interesting Bulgarian vampire was known as an *ustrel*, and was believed to be the spirit of an unbaptized child. Slowly working its way out of the grave, an *ustrel* would emerge on the ninth day after death to attack sheep and cattle in order to drain their blood.

This links in with the sinister *chupacabras*, or "goatsucker," reported recently from Mexico, Puerto Rico, and parts of Central and South America. Numerous reliable and reputable witnesses have described the *chupacabras* they saw as resembling an enormous porcupine, but with disproportionately powerful hind legs like a wallaby or kangaroo, and strange-looking appendages — almost like thin horns — all the way down its spine. It attacks by day as well as by night, and seems to live on a diet of goats, chickens, and household pets.

Despite every effort by the authorities, no specimen of *el chupacabras* has yet been killed or captured. Some researchers have suggested that it may be a genetic engineering experiment that has gone horribly wrong and broken out of a laboratory. Was someone attempting to create a monster that would be ideal to launch against enemy troops? If such a

---

VAMPIRES DOWN UNDER

In Australia there are stories of *Yara-ma-wha-who*, a small red humanoid, not much more than a metre tall. The mouth is exceptionally large and the hands are covered in suckers. When it captured someone by dropping down from its perch in a fig tree, it would drain the victim's blood until the unfortunate man or woman was helpless. *Yara-ma-wha-who* would return later, swallow the victim whole, take a long drink of water (an interesting practical detail from a terrain where water was particularly scarce), and then sleep. When it awoke, the undigested portion of the victim would be regurgitated — *still alive!* This swallowing and regurgitating process was repeated until the victim had shrunk to the size of a *Yara-ma-wha-who* and slowly turned into one. Although many factors here differ from the European vampire legends, the *Yara-ma-wha-who* shares the traditional power to infect and transform the victim.

creature could be bred, and programmed to attack selectively, it could be much less dangerous to the user, and much more useful militarily than indiscriminate germ or chemical warfare. It would also be tactically preferable to unleashing any type of nuclear radiation to blow around indiscriminately for years after the conflict — contaminating friends and foes alike with grim impartiality.

Other theories suggest that it has alien origins: some reports describe it as resembling a hybrid between one of the "grey" ufonauts and an unspecified terrestrial animal.

So far, no human beings have been attacked by *el chupacabras*, but a young girl in Cumbria, England, was not so lucky when something thought to be a vampire appeared at Croglin.

Some popular accounts of the Croglin Grange or Croglin Low Hall vampire that attacked her date from the 1870s. Augustus Hare presents most of the facts in *The Story of My Life*, and he says he obtained his account from a Captain Fisher, who once lived at Croglin Grange.

The whole Croglin story is shrouded in mystery and misunderstanding. To begin with, there's a bloodcurdling mid-nineteenth-century "penny-dreadful" called *Varney the Vampire, or the Feast of Blood*. Written by James Malcolm Rymer (1804–82), it certainly contains a few minor parallels to the Croglin story, and some researchers have regarded *Varney* as evidence to invalidate the entire Croglin account.

Rymer was a successful and prolific writer: his 220 chapters, first published in 1847, were republished as "penny parts" in 1853. They then amounted to nearly nine hundred pages.

To seek to discredit a factual, historical episode on the grounds that someone has written a piece of fiction that is vaguely similar, and that the real-life history, therefore, is not history at all but just additional fiction

A **penny dreadful** (also referred to as penny horrible, penny awful, penny number, and penny blood) was a type of British fiction publication in the nineteenth century that usually featured lurid serial stories appearing in parts over a number of weeks, with each part costing a penny. The term soon came to encompass a variety of publications that featured any cheap sensational fiction. The penny dreadfuls were printed on cheap pulp paper and were aimed primarily at working-class adolescents.

based on the first piece, is not a substantive argument. Fictional stories of espionage, detection, warfare, or romance cannot invalidate the historical truth of Rahab and the Israeli spies who visited her establishment on the walls of Jericho, of P.C. Edward Robertson's courageous arrest of multiple murderer Charles Peace, of the memorably gallant charge of the Light Brigade at Balaclava, or of Edward VIII's choice of the lady he loved rather than the British Crown.

It would be as just as rational to argue that the *Titanic* never existed simply because Morgan Robertson had written a novel in 1898 in which a giant liner called the *SS Titan* hit an iceberg and sank in the Atlantic on her maiden voyage with terrible loss of life.

More confusion arises because there are *two* Croglins. When we made our first research visit to the village in the early 1970s, it was clear that the Parish Church of St. John the Baptist was not the church toward which the vampire had fled. The church we studied then had been built in 1878 on the site of an old Norman church, which had itself replaced a Saxon one.

CROGLIN IN THE PAST

There were people living in and around Croglin in the Bronze Age — one of the moulds from which they cast their spearheads was found in the 1880s. Opposite the church stands a house called "The Old Pele" that dates from 1400 and was once the rectory.

On subsequent research visits we discovered that a mile or two downstream was the *second* Croglin, the tiny village of Croglin Parva. All that remains of it today are two large farmhouses, known respectively as Croglin High Hall and Croglin Low Hall. It is to Croglin Low Hall in Croglin Parva, and to the old church with its ancient vaults that once stood near it, that the historical episode of the vampire rightly belongs — and there is every indication that the attack occurred long before the 1870s. Croglin Low Hall is at least as old as nearby Carlisle Castle (*circa* 1100), and — originally a fortified farm — must now be one of the oldest working farmhouses in Cumbria.

Another problem associated with the Croglin vampire episode is the difficulty of pinpointing *which* Captain Fisher of Croglin gave the facts to Augustus Hare, and exactly who the three Cranswells were — if indeed their name *was* Cranswell — who took Croglin Low Hall from the Fishers on the seven-year lease that plays an integral part in the story. It is also of major importance to try to ascertain *when* they lived there.

Croglin was originally part of the Barony of Gilsland. The Lordship passed to the de Vallibus family and from them to the de Hastings family. In 1214 it changed hands yet again and passed to the Whartons of Westmoreland. In later times it became the property of the Fishers, and the house that went by the name of Croglin Low Hall seems to have belonged to the Fisher family since at least 1730.

The Captain Edward Fisher of the vampire story — whose full title was Edward Rowe Fisher-Rowe, late captain of the 4th Dragoon Guards — seems to have been the grandson of Edward and Deborah Fisher, whose graves are in Ainstable churchyard. He made the acquaintance of Augustus Hare in 1874 when he married Hare's cousin, Lady Victoria Liddel. The newly married Fishers then moved to Thorncombe, near Guildford, where Edward eventually died on his seventy-seventh birthday, November 8, 1909. Victoria survived him until 1935, and they now lie side by side in Holy Trinity Churchyard at Bramley.

The dating difficulty in Augustus Hare's account may well have arisen because he had assumed that Captain Fisher's narrative coincided with his own move from Croglin to Thorncombe. There is a substantial body of evidence, however, that seems to suggest that Fisher knew the story well as an old established tradition in Croglin — and the account of the vampire's attack on Amelia was considerably more than a century old when Fisher first heard it as a child.

The Fisher ancestors from the relevant period were wise in their choice of tenants for Croglin Low Hall. We shall continue to use the name Cranswell for convenience, as that name was associated with the vampire episode by local residents to whom we spoke in Croglin village. The family consisted of two brothers: Michael, stocky and muscular, and Edward, rather slimmer and more athletic. The Cranswell brothers lived with their attractive younger sister, Amelia, an intelligent and practical girl with conspicuous courage and resourcefulness.

The Cranswells were popular in the district. They had a reputation for being unfailingly generous and helpful to their less fortunate neighbours, and they were popular members of the local social circuit — always welcome as dinner guests, at house parties, concerts, or card evenings. They were regarded as sociable, sensible, and totally acceptable. One summer evening, after a particularly sultry day — not the usual Cumberland weather — they had dined early and gone to bed. Amelia was propped up on her pillows, looking out across the lawn toward the derelict church beyond. Her casement window was secured, but she had not fastened the shutters. It was not the kind of area where that sort of security was necessary.

She became aware of what she described later as two points of light moving toward the house from the direction of the old, abandoned churchyard. They seemed to be glowing in the way that an animal's eyes sometimes glow when caught in the beam of a lantern. As the lights drew nearer, Amelia could see that they were quite unmistakably eyes, and they were set in one of the most frightening faces she had ever seen.

There was nothing in the world she wanted more at that moment than the reassuring presence of her two loyal and protective brothers, but her bedroom door was locked on the inside, and before she could get it open, the *thing* with the gleaming eyes was unpicking the lead of her ground-floor bedroom window.

What she later described as a claw-like, skeletal hand came through the aperture left by the removal of the small diamond pane that the creature had unpicked, and undid the catch. Something like an animated scarecrow entered her room, gripped her hair, and forced her head back. By the time Mike and Ed had been awakened by her screams, she had been savagely bitten about the face and throat and was unconscious and bleeding profusely. Even as the brothers broke the door down and rushed to help Amelia, the *thing* was escaping across the lawn. Edward raced after it, surprised by the speed with which it covered the ground. As far as he could tell, it was heading for the churchyard, and he thought he saw it disappear over the wall with a surprisingly powerful bound. He did not pursue it farther, but ran back to see how badly Amelia had been injured.

Although in considerable pain and shock, and bleeding profusely from the bites to her face and throat, Amelia's strength and courage pulled her through the crisis. In an era long before the discovery of antibiotics, infection from bites could sometimes prove life-threatening, but Amelia's strong mind and robust constitution saw her well on the road to recovery within a matter of weeks. There was, of course, the question of permanent scarring at a time when cosmetic surgery was either very basic or non-existent. A girl's appearance — and its effect on her marriage prospects — were highly significant.

In the days that followed, news of the attack on Amelia became the central talking point in the Croglin area. Two or three neighbours called to see the Cranswells with information about similar attacks that had occurred over the past two or three years.

The doctor advised a good, long holiday for the family, so that Amelia could convalesce and recuperate fully. The Cranswells were comfortably off and decided on a few weeks in Switzerland. While they were there, it was Amelia who insisted that they return to Croglin Low Hall instead of wasting the rest of their seven-year lease on it. It was also said that the quick-minded and resourceful Amelia devised a very successful contingency plan to be put into action if her attacker returned.

Another of the research problems connected with the Croglin adventure is that traditionally — and it is an important factor in the investigation — the house was said to be only a single-storey building. Croglin Low Hall is *not* a single storey building today, as the photographs we took on a recent research visit clearly show. However, when writer and researcher F. Clive-Ross examined the building carefully in 1962, he observed a large corbel in the room with the bricked-up window that is traditionally associated with the vampire. The most common architectural purpose of such a corbel is to support a roof. It is, therefore, highly likely that at some period well before the nineteenth century Croglin Low Hall had been a one-storey building, just as the legend maintains it was at the time when the vampire attacked Amelia.

Amelia's plan was that all three of them should arrange to sleep in adjacent downstairs rooms so that both brothers would instantly hear her shout for help. The bedroom doors were also to be kept open so that they could reach her quickly if they were needed. While in Switzerland, the family had purchased a matching pair of boxed pistols, complete with ammunition and cleaning equipment. The lead from which this ammunition was made had a distinctive greenish tinge — quite unlike standard British lead — and this made it readily identifiable. The guns were kept primed and loaded on the brothers' bedside tables.

Should Amelia's attacker return, the plan was that Mike would rush immediately to her side to protect her with one of the pistols, while Edward would race outside to cut off the monster's retreat with the other.

The Cranswells returned to Croglin, and in due time, Amelia again saw the weird, gleaming eyes approaching her window from across the lawn. Her contingency plan worked to perfection. The bulldog-like Mike was at her side in a matter of seconds, with his gun grimly raised. Ed was away through the front door and racing after the intruder before the thing realized its danger. Aiming for its legs, Ed fired from close range. There was a scream of pain and the creature limped away across the lawn in the direction of the church.

Ed pursued it doggedly, but his single-shot pistol was now empty. He was no coward, but he was nowhere near as powerful as Mike, and he knew from what Amelia had said after the first attack that the *thing* — whatever it was — was both dangerous and abnormally strong. He watched it clear the wall of the churchyard and vanish into a tomb. His understandable reaction at this point gives the whole account a clear ring of truth.

Uncertain of what to do next, Ed stood in the darkness outside the door of that sinister old vault, listening and watching. His dilemma was whether to go for help and so risk letting their quarry escape, to take his chance against it in a hand-to-hand fight and go straight in after it, or to wait and watch in the slender hope that someone would come that way so that he could send a message to Mike.

He eventually decided that the best course of action would be to go and get help. Perhaps the pistol ball had done the thing more damage than it first appeared. Was their opponent already dead or dying from loss of blood? Ed finally left the tomb unguarded and went in search of Mike and whatever other help he could find.

Not long after, a determined party consisting of the Cranswells and their more venturesome friends broke into the tomb that Ed had seen the wounded creature enter an hour or so before. The interior was filled with old, broken coffins and their decaying contents — with one exception. According to the Croglin tradition, what the men saw was a sort of raised dais in the centre of the tomb, on which lay just one sturdy old open coffin containing a dried and wizened — but otherwise remarkably well-preserved — corpse. The light from their lanterns revealed fresh red blood on the lips and skeletal fingertips. Again, according to the Croglin tradition, the men carried this corpse to the crossroads, where they grimly dismembered and burned it. During this macabre destruction rite, a pistol ball of greenish Swiss lead was discovered in one of the creature's withered legs.

Too many factors make it difficult if not impossible for this to have been a late-nineteenth-century adventure. Single-shot muzzle-loading pistols were far more common in the seventeenth and eighteenth centuries than in the late nineteenth. The Cranswell brothers would have been far more likely to buy a six-chambered revolver each if they had made their purchases in the 1870s.

There is strong historical evidence via Mrs. Parkin, whose husband, Inglewood Parkin, owned the estate containing Croglin Low Hall in the 1930s, that the old church of Croglin Parva had been ruined by Ireton, Oliver Cromwell's brother-in-law, at the time of the civil war. She recalled that in her early days on the Parkin Estate, there were many stones from this church lying about in an area adjacent to Croglin Low Hall and known then as the Church Field. Local tradition asserted that there had been tombs and graves there — including a Fisher family vault.

After the dismembered corpse had been burned, no further vampire attacks were reported in or near the village.

If the Croglin vampire is taken back to the seventeenth century, where he more than likely belongs historically, the whole story becomes far more comprehensible and believable. But what *was* the horrifying scarecrow-like creature that almost killed young Amelia Cranswell on that hot summer night?

Croglin Grange, close up.

When we were lecturing on the Croglin vampire phenomenon in the 1970s, an ingenious young medical practitioner in the audience put forward a fascinating — and totally rational — theory. He suggested that there was nothing paranormal about the case: Amelia was attacked by someone mentally ill who had, as part of that mental illness, made a den or hiding place among the tombs surrounding the derelict church adjacent to Croglin Low Hall. After Ed shot him in the leg, the psychopath retreated to the vault where he had been living for some time. His mental illness did not mean that he was stupid — far from it. He had no more idea what Ed was doing outside the vault than Ed had of what was going on inside the vault. It was a guessing game for them both.

The "vampire" gets a sudden bright idea. Having used the vault as a hideout for weeks, he knows all about the one old but well-preserved body: inspiration strikes. They want a vampire — they'll get a vampire! The psychopath extracts the green lead pistol ball from the wound in his leg. He smears fresh red blood from that same leg wound onto the mouth and hands of the long-dead corpse. Then inspiration really strikes. He takes the Swiss lead pistol ball that he has prised from the deep flesh wound on his injured leg and thrusts it into the dried parchment-like flesh of the long-dead occupant of the coffin on the central dais. Then he peers very cautiously around the door of the vault … He's in luck! The dangerous young man with the gun has gone! The psychopath sneaks silently out and puts as much distance as he can between himself and Croglin.

"And," said the doctor, thoughtfully, "the gangrene which he had caught from handling an open wound with fingers that had just been touching a corpse killed him a few days later. A poor vagrant is found dead in a ditch. Apart from an acrimonious argument about which parish he belongs to — the one with the responsibility for his funeral fees — no real notice is taken of him. Not surprisingly, no more vampire attacks occur in the Croglin district. Those who helped to dismember and burn the innocuous old corpse at the crossroads are delighted that their work has been so successful. No one associates the nameless dead tramp found in a ditch forty miles away with the Croglin vampire."

As the old fairground-stall proprietors used to say, "Yer pays yer money and yer takes yer choice!" So it is with the Croglin Low Hall vampire. The weight of evidence suggests that *something* odd and disturbing happened there three centuries ago, something involving an attack on a girl and her brothers, and their final vengeance on the creature. Whether it was paranormal, an extraterrestrial, a pan-dimensional voyager, or just a traditional vampire along the lines of Dracula or Varney, cannot be fairly proven by the evidence. Open-mindedness combined with sharp critical appraisal of *all* the known facts will usually take the honest researcher to the truth in the end.

Highgate Cemetery in London is by no means an ancient or even a medieval cemetery. By the 1750s there was considerable public concern because burial places in city centres were reaching a crisis point. From the beginning of the nineteenth century the press was taking an active interest in the unhygienic state of many London churchyards, and parliamentary committees were also investigating them.

Under the pavements of many churches and their limited surrounding areas, the vaults were literally crammed with coffins. The air in many of the buildings was so badly polluted that it was a major cause of death and disease. In the churchyards, coffins had to be piled one above the other until they were within a few inches of the surface: the ground level frequently had to be raised to correspond with the sills of the churches' lower windows in order to fit still more coffins. Crafty sextons surreptitiously removed bones and decaying remains to make room for fresh interments, and in many instances bodies were simply tipped out into pits nearby. The gravediggers' perks on these sordid occasions were the coffin plates, nails, and handles, which they salvaged and sold for their scrap-metal value. Consequently, churchyards and their immediate environs became dangerously unhealthy and hideous eyesores.

HIGHGATE IN LITERATURE

In Bram Stoker's gothic novel *Dracula*, the count's young victim, Lucy Westenra, is buried in Highgate Cemetery, where she later preys on young children as a vampire. More recently, Audrey Niffenegger published her second novel, *Her Fearful Symmetry*, a ghost story set in and around Highgate Cemetery.

This was the situation in many major cities in the first few decades of the nineteenth century. Because of its vast population and high mortality rate, London suffered worst of all. The old churchyards were finally closed by Act of Parliament, and the cemeteries on the periphery of the city took over from them. Kensal Green Cemetery, for example, is roughly the same age as Highgate, and dates from 1832.

Highgate itself goes back only as far as 1836, when Steve Geary of the London Cemetery Company bought nearly twenty acres of land on a hillside. For almost a century things went very well indeed with the new burial site. Expert landscape gardeners worked hard to create a peaceful and beautiful setting to ease the grief of loved ones who came there to mourn and to remember. Well-placed and well-tended trees and shrubs added to the quiet, dignified ethos that then prevailed.

It was not until the First World War that things began to go wrong at Highgate Cemetery. It was no longer possible to obtain enough staff, very few plots were left for sale, and cremation was proving a popular alternative. Neglect and vandalism inevitably followed — reaching a level that forced the cemetery to close to the public in 1975.

In response to these problems, a group of public-spirited volunteers known as The Friends of Highgate Cemetery was created in an attempt to solve the problems that plagued the site. They coped exceptionally well with a long list of daunting tasks, and when we made a research visit to the cemetery in 1998, we found their representatives very helpful, informative, and co-operative.

BURIED AT HIGHGATE

Many of the good, the great, and the famous were buried in Highgate Cemetery, including Cherkassky, a concert pianist; Elizabeth Lilley, midwife to Queen Victoria; Karl Marx, philosopher, economist, and politician; Sir Ralph Richardson, actor; Christina Rossetti, poet; Topolski, the painter; Max Wall, comedian; Mary Ann Evans, a.k.a. George Eliot (novelist); and more recently Douglas Adams, author of *The Hitchhiker's Guide to the Galaxy*, and Malcolm McLaren, punk impresario and former manager of the Sex Pistols.

It was in the bleak and desperate period before The Friends began the daunting work of restoration that stories of the Highgate vampire began to circulate. But a general look at vampire myths and legends is an essential introduction to the specific Highgate Cemetery episodes, if the Highgate reports are to be understood and placed in their proper perspective.

Like werewolves, leopard-people, and other shape-shifters, the vampire is credited with the ability to change its bodily form: a bat being a favourite alternative. According to the "rules" of this traditional vampire folklore, the vampire must be safely back in its grave, or tomb, before dawn breaks. Sunlight is fatal. When travelling, it needs to be accompanied by its coffin, containing soil from its original burial place to provide it with this essential diurnal refuge.

Although widely known throughout Asia and Europe, vampire legends were particularly prolific in Slavic and Hungarian mythology, and a great many cases were reported.

In May of 1730, the Austrian Count de Cadreras turned up at the University of Fribourg in Switzerland, where he allegedly dictated notes to the university's librarian, notes that became the notorious *Cadreras Manuscript*, which told an amazing story of apparent wholesale vampirism.

Some ten years earlier, the Habsburg Empire of Austria — having fought long battles against the Turks and the French — was enjoying a period of relative peace and tranquility. The army was quietly being brought up to strength and retrained. It was during this period of calm that a young Austrian soldier from Vienna was stationed at the village of Haidam near the Hungarian frontier. The soldier's name was Joachin Hubner, and he was billeted with a friendly local farming family.

Joachin was drinking wine with the farmer and his teenaged son while the ladies of the house were clearing away the evening meal in the adjacent kitchen. The farmer was facing the open doorway, and his son and the young soldier had their backs to it. The farmer suddenly broke off what he was saying in mid-sentence and froze with a look of horror on his face. The boy turned to follow his father's gaze and did the same. Joachin then craned his neck around and saw only a harmless-looking old man moving slowly into the room. He touched the farmer's shoulder and then walked silently away. Joachin saw him vanishing among the gathering shadows outside.

The farmer, normally robust and vigorous, staggered upstairs as though he had aged forty years in as many seconds. His teenaged son and the women ran up after him. The farmer died during the night.

Horrified, Joachin asked who the old visitor had been, and whether he had had anything to do with his host's death.

"He was my grandfather," replied the teenaged lad, "and he has been in his grave for ten years."

When Joachin Hubner's story went the rounds, the Count de Cadreras — a capable, sensible, and experienced commander of an Alandetti infantry corps — was sent to investigate. He took several other officers with him, plus a military doctor and a lawyer. Hubner and the farmer's family were closely interrogated. A solemn party gathered at the cemetery and the grandfather's corpse was exhumed. Despite being buried ten years previously, it looked as though it had been dead only a few hours. The amazed military doctor made a small incision in one arm. According to the *Cadreras Manuscript*, fresh red blood trickled from the cut. The body was duly staked through the heart, decapitated, and re-interred.

When Cadreras made his official report, its impact was so sensational that it reached the emperor, Charles VI, who reigned from 1711–40. Charles was a particularly pragmatic, shrewd, and able statesman. Not surprisingly, this practical and prosaic ruler was disinclined to believe the bizarre evidence that Cadreras had laid before him. A Royal Commission was established and charged with the task of reinvestigating the Haidam phenomenon — the implication being that should this commission fail to confirm Cadreras's findings, the count would be looking for another job. The commissioners were highly skeptical during the long journey to Haidam, but when they arrived they were confronted by a greater and more sinister mystery than that which young Hubner claimed to have witnessed in the farmhouse.

Many cottages had been abandoned, and others had had their doors barred and their windows shuttered. There was scarcely a soul to be seen, and only a handful of men had remained loyal to their officers in the small garrison. Despite the severe penalties for desertion, many of the troops had simply run away from the village. The commissioners were amazed. Skepticism turned to fear and incredulity. The few villagers whom they could find, along with the remaining members of the garrison, told incredible tales of long-dead relatives from the cemetery visiting family members, who themselves would die shortly afterward. It appeared that the village, according to the witnesses, was being attacked by a battalion of reanimated corpses.

VAMPIRES IN FILM

The most popular cinematic adaptation of vampire fiction, of course, has been from Bram Stoker's *Dracula*, with more than 170 versions released to date. Beginning with the first silent vampire film in 1909, *Vampire of the Coast*, and classics *The Vampire* (1913) and *Nosferatu* (1922) that followed, throughout the twentieth century the subject of these blood-sucking creatures of the night has gripped the imagination of both filmmakers and audiences. The genre has remained prevalent throughout the past century with releases such as *The Fearless Vampire Killers* (1967), *Salem's Lot* (1979), *The Hunger* (1983), *The Lost Boys* (1987), *Buffy the Vampire Slayer* (1992), *Interview with the Vampire* (1994), *Shadow of the Vampire* (2000), *Let the Right One In* (2008), and the currently popular Twilight saga (2008–10).

The commissioners made a careful list of the alleged "undead," opened their graves, and staked and decapitated each occupant in the prescribed manner. On every occasion it was reported that the bodies so dealt with had been found in an unusually good state of preservation. There were no further reports of vampire problems from Haidam after the grisly work in the cemetery had been done.

Understandably, the story grew in the telling and became distorted and wildly exaggerated. Cadreras, in an effort to clear his name, asked Charles VI to publish the Royal Commission's findings, but the politically astute old Habsburg remained obdurately silent. It was that stubborn silence which prompted the count to travel to the University of Fribourg to record the facts as he understood them and to preserve the report for academic posterity.

In 1746, Dom Calmet, a French monk, studied vampirism and became something of an authority on it. According to Calmet there was adequate evidence that what he called the walking dead were able to return and drain the blood of both men and beasts. He also subscribed to the popular theories of vampire disposal, involving staking, decapitating, and burning.

Much more remarkable is the evidence for vampires presented by Jean-Jacques Rousseau, who wrote, "If ever there was in the world a warranted and proven history, it is the history of vampires … the judicial evidence is all-embracing."

Montague Summers, a clergyman, and Reverend Neil Smith of Hampstead both studied vampirism in some depth — broadly concluding that in all probability the creatures really had existed in the past, and might still be around today.

Returning to the modern vampire of popular legend, much is owed to the depiction of Dracula in Bram Stoker's novel, published in 1897. The theatrical version of the story reached the stage in 1927 and was followed by Tod Browning's film, which starred Bela Lugosi, in 1931. It was characteristic of this stereotyped stage and screen vampire to have a pale face, protruding fangs, and glaring eyes.

In a number of pieces of relatively recent fiction, reference has been made to a creature known as a *drud* — a vampire's vampire — that is said to live on the refined blood of the vampire itself. It is possible that the drud, the vampires' predator, has some tenuous basis in myth and legend rather than being a creation of fantasy fiction. The drud apparently resembles a normal human being in most respects and is entirely benign to *Homo sapiens*, whom it protects. Its only distinguishing feature is a total absence of eyebrows. According to this tradition, vampires are terrified of the drud.

Researcher David Farrant reports that he was called in to help a number of residents in the Highgate Cemetery area in 1969. These witnesses told Farrant that they had seen a tall, dark, cloaked human shape — nearly seven feet tall — in the vicinity of the cemetery. Their reports included details of its ferocious, glaring red eyes — a feature which Amelia Cranswell also reported in connection with the Croglin Grange vampire attack many years earlier. The reports that reached David Farrant also said that the strange cloaked figure had faded mysteriously into the darkness after being observed.

On a bitterly cold December night in 1969, Farrant went to the Highgate Cemetery entrance, where several witnesses had reported seeing the bizarre figure. David's main motive at the time was to see whether there was some rational explanation for the strange reports. As he passed the cemetery's top gate on his way down Swains Lane, he reports that he saw a tall shape in the darkness. It seemed so real at the time that he was convinced it was someone dressed up to play an unwelcome practical joke to frighten passersby.

David reportedly saw two red eyes set in a dark object that looked only vaguely like a head. This globular, dark object was not easy for him to describe. He felt that it was strangely *vague* — neither opaque nor translucent — but that it was quite definitely *alive*, sinister, and very hostile. It seemed to him to be hovering above the ground and to be shaking or vibrating in a very menacing manner. To him the glaring red eyes seemed wolf-like, baleful, and malign.

David also recorded a sharp drop in temperature — noticeable on even such a cold night. He was convinced that he was in the presence of some very real and particularly foul evil entity. He reports feeling that he was very definitely exposed to some sort of dangerous psychic attack, and instinctively exerted his willpower against his supernatural antagonist. David reported that, as he focused his own spiritual and mental powers against the sinister Highgate entity, it slowly faded and vanished into the darkness.

In 1970 the London *Evening News* published a front-page account of a hundred-strong vampire hunt in Highgate Cemetery, which must have looked very similar to the finale of a classic Hammer horror film. Despite their enthusiasm — and a formidable array of sharpened stakes and heavy mallets — the Highgate vampire hunters did not meet with any notable success. The *Evening News* report made reference to the possibility that the supposed vampire sightings had been the result of a movie club using the cemetery to make a film called *Vampires at Night*.

However, no movie club was involved in another strange episode connected with Highgate Cemetery that preceded the 1970 "vampire hunt" by about a century.

The artist and poet Dante Gabriel Rossetti had buried his beloved Lizzie Siddal there and had placed a manuscript of his poems in the coffin with her. Unfortunately these were the only copies in existence, and as his literary career took off he discovered he needed them. With the help of a young friend named Howell, who obtained permission from the Home Secretary for the exhumation to take place, the vital Rossetti manuscripts were duly recovered. Rossetti had remained at Howell's house while the work took place. Howell assured him that Lizzie's hair still retained its original beautiful colour and that her body was not corrupted.

There have been other cases of inexplicably uncorrupted bodies over the centuries. The Princess Withburgha of East Dereham in Norfolk was one, and St. Edmund was another. Where artificial means such as embalming fluids have been ruled out by scientific tests, researchers are left to contemplate the possibilities of abnormal conditions in the tomb, such as natural currents of warm, dry air or abnormally high levels of background radiation. Where all other explanations fail, paranormal possibilities may be considered.

There are other rumours and legends about Highgate Cemetery that also predate the great 1970 vampire hunt. Some refer to a spectre with a top hat and cloak reported from two local pubs: The Flask and Ye Olde Gatehouse.

This latter hostelry is also alleged to be haunted by the ghost of Mother Marnes, which always appears dressed in black, gliding along a gallery. According to the legend, the old lady was murdered there along with her pet cat by a callous thief who killed her for her savings. Perhaps because of the old lady's love of animals, it is generally maintained that her wraith will not appear if children or animals are in the inn.

CERUNNOS, THE HORNED GOD

In Celtic mythology, Cerunnos represents the spirit of horned male animals, especially of stags. In Wicca and other pagan religions, the horned god is representative of the seasons of the year and is closely associated with the cycle of life and fertility. Because of his association with animals, Cerunnos is sometimes referred to as the "Lord of the Animals" or the "Lord of Wild Things."

Ye Olde Wrestlers pub, which dates from the seventeenth century, is a reminder that Highgate was once an important point on the drovers' road. There was a rather curious initiation ceremony conducted there at one time known as "Swearing on the Horns." Although this is generally thought of as a drovers' custom, it is possible that it is the vestigial trace of something far older and more sinister. Might the horns in question have been those of Herne the Hunter, or of the terrifying horned god of the witches, Cernunnos of the Celts (see sidebar)? Yet another possibility is that swearing on the horns is connected with Mithras, a god of light, in whose honour a bull was slain. A cattle cult such as Mithraism might have remained underground for centuries with the droving fraternity, and thus have survived the inroads made by the early Christian Church.

HERNE THE HUNTER

In English folklore, Herne the Hunter is a ghost-rider said to have antlers on his head. In life, Herne was the favourite huntsman of Richard II. Mortally wounded while saving his master from a charging stag, he was miraculously cured by a stranger, who tied the antlers of the dead stag to the dying man's head. As payment from the king, the stranger claimed all of Herne's hunting skills. Crazed by the loss of his talent for the hunt, Herne fled to Windsor Forest and hanged himself from an oak tree. But it is said that every night he returned at the head of a ghostly hunt. He is, in Celtic mythology, a god and protector of the forest, sometimes called the "lord of the trees."

Herne the Hunter.

Some researchers have suggested that Highgate Cemetery was once the site of an ancient manor house rather than empty hillside land. It was also put forward that this ancient manor was a focal point for many hidden evil deeds. There are rumours of a mysterious coffin having been transported from the East and buried somewhere in or near this sinister old manor house. According to other legends, when the real, historical Vlad Dracula died during the fifteenth century, he was buried on the island of Snagov. But there were sensational reports from the island in 1931 that when his supposed tomb was opened, it was found to contain the remains of a bull. So where was Dracula? Was it the mysterious "father of all the vampires" who had been transported to the weird old Highgate manor in that legendary coffin? And what became of him when that eldritch manor became part of Highgate Cemetery?

Bram Stoker, who wrote his bestseller *Dracula* in 1897, is said to have written it while living in Highgate. Other strange rumours and legends link the Highgate vampire with Jack the Ripper, the notorious Victorian serial killer.

Queen Victoria employed Robert James Lees as a medium and, according to the records left in his diary, Lees had visions of the Ripper. It was said that he eventually led the police to Dr. Gull's house at 74 Brook Street. It was subsequently "suggested" that a false funeral took place, and it was further hypothesized that the *real* Dr. Gull was buried under the name Mason some years later — *in Highgate Cemetery*. On the basis of this version, it has been suggested that the Highgate vampire-spectre is none other than the ghost of Jack the Ripper.

So what conclusions can be drawn concerning all the varied vampire stories circulating around Highgate Cemetery? The location is undoubtedly very atmospheric and mysterious. The human mind seeks to create explanations for stimuli that can, in fact, have sources that are perfectly normal and innocent. It is possible to sit in a train and to interpret the rhythmic rattling of the wheels over the tracks as speech patterns. It is equally possible to see everything from enchanted castles to flying monsters in cloud formations and glowing coals in an old-fashioned grate. The branches of trees, combined with glowing cigarette ends in the distance could possibly be interpreted as a strange creature with malevolent red eyes. *But is there more to it than that?*

An experienced investigator like David Farrant reports that he felt an evil presence and a dramatic drop in temperature. Many other sane and sensible witnesses have described inexplicable sightings in the vicinity of Highgate Cemetery. If there really *was* an ancient manor on the site centuries ago, does something weird and dangerous still linger in the area? The Highgate Cemetery vampire has not yet been laid to rest, and the data is well worth further investigation.

Highgate Cemetery.

16 UNSOLVED MYSTERIES

The strange brigantine seemed to be jinxed.

The *Mary Celeste* was built by Joshua Davis (spelled Dewis in some accounts) — the first of twenty-seven identical vessels — on Spencer's Island, Nova Scotia, in 1861, where it was originally christened *Amazon*. Constructed from strong Nova Scotian beech, birch, spruce, and maple, the cabins were finished with pine. The ship was said to have been a few inches short of a hundred feet long, and just over quarter of that in width. The depth was fractionally less than twelve feet, and it was close to two hundred tons displacement.

The *Mary Celeste*.

The corvel-built (planks edge to edge, not overlapping like a clinker-built ship) *Amazon* was technically described as a two-masted brigantine, although the records of the Atlantic Mutual Insurance Company listed it as "a half-brig." The ship was officially registered at Parrsboro on June 10, 1861.

There are sailors with great knowledge and long experience who wonder whether certain ships carry a jinx, or curse. There were many of them who thought that about the *Amazon*: the first skipper, a Scotsman named Robert McLellan, died within forty-eight hours of taking command; on its maiden voyage, a great gash was ripped down one side when it collided with a fishing weir off the Maine coast; fire broke out and caused severe damage; and, while the hull repairs were still being done, the captain, John Nutting Parker, was dismissed.

It crossed the Atlantic uneventfully, but a collision in the channel not far from Dover sank the brig with which *Amazon* had collided, leading to yet another change of skipper. Under his command the ship ran aground just off Cow Bay, part of Cape Breton Island, Nova Scotia, in 1867, and was at first regarded as a total wreck. Incomplete records suggest that two men, Haines and McBean, attempted to salvage it, but the deal went disastrously wrong, and they went bankrupt.

The next owner was John Beatty of New York, who sold it on again to James H. Winchester and his associates, Sylvester Goodwin and Daniel Sampson. By this time various structural alterations had been made: the ship now had two decks; the length had increased to 103 feet, the depth to sixteen feet, and the breadth by a few inches. The displacement had increased dramatically to 282 tons. The ship was now American-owned and registered, and flew the Stars and Stripes, and the name had been changed to *Mary Celeste*. Lloyds of London had once listed her as *Marie Celeste*, and there is a minor mystery about the name. One theory is that the odd mixture of French and English was simply due to a painter's error, even more oddly it has been put forward that the real name was intended to be *Mary Sellers*.

When Winchester and his associates discovered dry rot in the hull, they promptly rebuilt the bottom with a strong copper lining. In their hands the *Mary Celeste* became as stout, as seaworthy, and as reliable as any vessel of its size at that time.

For some two years it was under the command of Rufus Fowler, who had also acquired a share in it on January 11, 1870. On October 29, 1872, he was replaced by Captain Benjamin Spooner Briggs, who also owned a few shares in the vessel.

Born at Wareham, Massachusetts, on April 24, 1835, the second of Captain Nathan Briggs's five sons by his wife, Sophia, Benjamin was thirty-seven years old, the product of a New England puritan, seafaring family. His brothers also went to sea, and by the time he took over the ill-fated *Mary Celeste*, Benjamin had already commanded the schooner *Forest King*, the barque *Arthur*, and the brig *Sea Foam*.

Just before sailing into history, the *Mary Celeste* was anchored at Pier 44 in New York's East River. On Saturday November 2, 1872, the ship was loaded with 1,701 red oak casks of commercial alcohol, and everything in the hold was made secure. The shippers were a firm of New York merchants, Meissner Arckerman and Co., and the alcohol was destined for H. Mascerenhas and Co. of Genoa, in Italy.

Although the *Sandy Hook* pilot ship took the *Mary Celeste* from Pier 44 to Staten Island's Lower Bay on November 5, the Atlantic was so rough that Briggs decided to wait for two days before taking his ship out into open waters on November 7.

Twenty-eight-year-old Albert G. Richardson, the first mate, had been a soldier in the American Civil War, had married the niece of James H. Winchester (owner of the *Mary Celeste*), and was generally regarded as a brave and reliable seaman. He had sailed with Briggs before.

The second mate was twenty-five-year-old Andrew Gilling, a New Yorker of Danish origins. He, like Richardson, was highly regarded, both for his character and seamanship. Edward William Head, aged twenty-three, served as cook and steward. He came from Brooklyn, and enjoyed

CAPTAIN BRIGGS AND HIS FAMILY

Besides Briggs himself, the *Mary Celeste* carried his thirty-year-old wife, Sarah Elizabeth (daughter of the Reverend Cobb, a Congregationalist minister in Marion, Massachusetts), and their infant daughter, Sophia Matilda. Their son, seven-year-old Arthur Stanley, had been left at home in the care of his paternal grandparents. Poignantly, in her last letter, posted on Staten Island, Sarah Briggs said how much she was looking forward to getting a letter from her little son.

Albert G. Richardson, first mate on the *Mary Celeste*.

Sarah Briggs.

the same good reputation as the three officers. The remaining crew members were German: Volkert Lorensen and his brother, Boy, were both in their twenties; Gottlieb Goodschall was twenty-three; and Arien Martens, around whom there was a slight air of mystery, was thirty-five. Although Martens was a qualified and experienced mate, he had signed on with Briggs as an ordinary seaman.

Before setting out on their last voyage, Briggs and his wife had dinner with Captain David Reed Morehouse — a Nova Scotian friend — and his wife. The two ladies were also friends. Morehouse was skipper of the *Dei Gratia*, carrying a cargo of petroleum to Gibraltar, and his ship was coincidentally moored not far from the *Mary Celeste*. Ironically, Morehouse was destined to be first on the scene after the tragedy. The four friends dined together for the last time at Astor House.

The *Mary Celeste* finally left port on November 7. The *Dei Gratia* sailed on November 15, and for nearly three weeks the voyage was completely routine and uneventful. Then, just after 1:00 p.m. on December 5, John Johnson, who was helmsman at that time, sighted a ship about eight kilometres off their port bow. They were approximately 960 kilometres off the coast of Portugal. Johnson's keen, experienced eyes detected immediately that there was something amiss with the other vessel. She was yawing slightly, and her sails did not look right. He called John Wright, the *Dei Gratia*'s second mate, and as soon as Wright had had a good look, they sent word to Captain Morehouse. He inspected the other ship for a few moments through his telescope and then decided that they needed assistance.

By 3:00 p.m. the *Dei Gratia* was only about four hundred yards from the stricken ship. Having hailed her several times and received no answer, Morehouse sent a boat to investigate.

Oliver Deveau, the first mate, went across with Johnson, the helmsman, and second mate John Wright. As they closed the distance, they saw that the other ship was the *Mary Celeste*, which had left New York eight days before them. Johnson stayed in the dinghy, while the first and second mate climbed aboard.

First mate Oliver Deveau of the *Dei Gratia*.

Oliver Deveau, a big, muscular man who was afraid of nothing, led the exploration. They searched the ship from end to end, but found nobody aboard — alive or dead. They sounded the pumps to see how much water lay in the hold. One pump had already been withdrawn to let a sounding rod down, so Deveau and Wright used the other. Recent storms had left a fair quantity of water between decks — but it was no great threat to the ship's buoyancy and stability.

They found the main staysail lying across the forward housing, but the upper foresail, and the foresail itself, had apparently been torn away by the recent storms and lost overboard during the time the *Mary Celeste* had been deserted. The jib was set, as were the fore-topmast staysails, and the lower topsail. All the other sails were furled. The running rigging was in a chaotic mess. Much of it was fouled, some was dangling forlornly over the sides, and the rest had been blown away and lost like the foresails. The vitally important main peak halyard, more than 325 feet long — used to hoist the gaff sail's outer end — had snapped off short, and the greater part of it was missing. The binnacle had been knocked or blown over, smashing the compass, and the helm was spinning freely as wind and tide moved the rudder randomly.

Although the main hatch was in good condition and securely fastened down as it should have been, some ancillary hatches were open and their covers were lying on the deck. When Wright and Deveau checked the galley they found less than thirty centimetres of water in it, and almost all of the provisions were intact and usable. There was also a plentiful supply of fresh, clean drinking water aboard.

When they searched Captain Briggs's family cabin, they discovered the temporary, or slate, log, which showed that on Monday November 25, the *Mary Celeste* had been close to St. Mary's Island in the Azores on a bearing of east-southeast. At 8:00 p.m. on the same day they had been within ten kilometres of Eastern Point on a bearing of south-southwest. A child's garment, partly finished, lay in the sewing-machine, which had not been put away.

The mate's cabin contained an unfinished calculation, which looked as though he had been called away very suddenly, and there was also a chart with a tracing of the *Mary Celeste*'s track up until November 24, when it had been 160 kilometres southwest of San Miguel Island in the Azores.

In the crew's quarters, razors had been left out as though their owners had been about to shave when the disturbance occurred. Laundered underclothes still hung on a line to dry. Sea chests and treasured personal possessions like oilskins, pipes, and tobacco pouches had also been left behind. An open bottle of medicine seemed to indicate that whoever had been taking it had deemed the emergency too acute to waste time putting the cork back in.

Two sections of rail had been removed to make space to launch the boat — a small yawl, which was normally kept above the main hatch cover. Wherever the passengers and crew had gone, some at least appeared to have left in that yawl. They also seemed to have taken essential documents and equipment with them. The bill of lading had gone, so had the navigation book, the sextant, and the chronometer. It was reasonable to assume from this that Briggs and his crew had abandoned ship for some reason that seemed vitally important to them at the time, and had taken with them the means of navigating their way into a main shipping lane to be rescued by another vessel, or to the nearest port the inadequate little yawl could reach.

Having discovered all they could, Deveau, Johnson, and Wright returned to the *Dei Gratia* to report their findings to Captain Morehouse. After some discussion, it was agreed that Deveau and two other men — Augustus Anderson and Charles Lund — would try to sail the *Mary Celeste* to Gibraltar to claim the salvage money. This was a risky undertaking for all concerned. Three men were a bare minimum skeleton crew for the *Mary Celeste*, while Morehouse would be left with barely enough men to handle the *Dei Gratia*. If the weather turned really bad, or if some other kind of emergency hit either vessel, they would be in desperate trouble. The safest thing seemed to be to sail in convoy.

This worked well until they reached the Straits of Gibraltar, when a fierce storm separated them. The *Dei Gratia* arrived in Gibraltar on the evening of December 12, and the *Mary Celeste* struggled in about twelve hours later.

The salvage claim should have been simple, straightforward, and relatively generous. By great strength, courage, stamina, and expert seamanship, the mighty Oliver Deveau had saved not only a valuable ship, but its cargo as well. He and Morehouse and their men merited heroes' welcomes and substantial gratitude. What they got instead was the odious Frederick Solly Flood, whose arrogance and pomposity were inversely proportional to his IQ. Within two hours of their arrival, the *Mary Celeste* was placed under arrest by Thomas J. Vecchio of the Vice-Admiralty Court.

Fred Flood had the grandiloquent title of Attorney General for Gibraltar and Advocate General for the Queen in Her Office of Admiralty. He simply could not see that the *Mary Celeste* would have been abandoned unless there had been foul play. He obstinately refused to accept any explanations that did not involve murder and piracy or, at the very least, criminal collusion between Morehouse and Briggs.

Fred's first broadside was fired at the *Mary Celeste*'s crew, who were, of course, unable to be in court to refute his wild accusations. He was convinced that they had broken into the cargo of crude industrial alcohol, got raging drunk, and murdered Briggs, his family, and first mate Richardson. When it was pointed out to him that raw industrial alcohol is not only very unpalatable, but so toxic as to produce severe internal pain long before it produced intoxication, he grudgingly abandoned that theory and looked around for another avenue of attack.

At Fred's request, marine surveyors examined the ship thoroughly. They reported her to be in excellent condition, with no sign of collision damage. However, they did comment on a curious groove which seemed to have been cut deliberately on either side of the bows. It did not damage or weaken the ship in any way: it was just inexplicable. Another marine carpentry expert, Captain Schufeldt, gave his opinion later that it was probably just the way that the curved timbers had naturally cracked and dried as a result of exposure to wind, sea, and sun.

Fred's next line of attack was to suggest that some brown stains on the deck were blood. He also pointed out stains on the blade of an ornate Italian sword found in Briggs's cabin under his bed. Once more he put the circumstantial evidence together and saw only foul play. To everyone else's annoyance, Fred refused to disclose the results of the analysis: an almost certain indication that it was wine, paint, or ship's stain and varnish — unless the cook-steward had spilt some brown soup while taking a tray to the captain's cabin in rough weather!

It was the great good fortune of Morehouse, Deveau, and their men that the actual members of the Admiralty Court were experienced and level-headed seamen, and totally unlike the obnoxious Fred Flood. The court eventually found in favour of the *Dei Gratia*'s captain and crew, and awarded them £1,700 salvage money: a considerable sum in those days, but only a fraction of the true value of their work.

What might have happened to the unfortunate people onboard the *Mary Celeste* when tragedy overtook them in mid-Atlantic? One theory

ERGOT POISONING

Human poisoning due to the consumption of bread made from ergot-infected rye and other grains was common in Europe in the Middle Ages. The epidemic was known as Saint Anthony's Fire, named for the monks of St. Anthony's hospital in France who were adept at treating the condition. Some historical events, such as the Great Fear in France near the start of the Revolution, have been linked to ergot poisoning. What are referred to as "convulsive" symptoms of ergotism may include painful seizures and spasms, diarrhea, itching, headaches, nausea, and vomiting, in addition to hallucinations resembling those produced by LSD (lysergic acid diethylamide), psychosis, and mania. Symptoms categorized as "gangrenous" can cause the loss of fingers, toes, or ears as the poison constricts the blood vessels leading to the extremeties. The decreased blood flow causes infection and burning pain, and gangrene sets in. If the affected limb is not removed, the infection will continue to spread.

concerns ergot poisoning. It was not uncommon in Victorian times for ergot to infect the food supply, especially bread. The resulting toxin has grim effects on the victims. It produces agonizing stomach pains, and hallucinations related to them. The victim may, for example, imagine that he is being attacked by a dangerous carnivore, an alien, a werebeast, a vampire, or a demon that is biting or clawing at his stomach.

Sometimes the hallucinating patient sees his family, friends, doctors, or nurses in these terrifying roles, and tries to defend himself against them accordingly. The ergot theory of the *Mary Celeste* explains the tragedy by saying that there was ergotine contamination aboard, and that the captain and crew saw one another as monsters or demons as the agonizing stomach pains and accompanying hallucinations took hold of them.

Perhaps one or two uninfected survivors of the initial outbreak tried to escape in the yawl, only to find that they, too, were carrying the disastrous toxin with them.

Ergot fungus poisoning provides a useful and sensible explanation, but the problem with it is that Oliver Deveau and his crew lived on the provisions on the *Mary Celeste* — and they suffered no ill effects whatsoever. If ergot fungus had been present, it would certainly have affected them, as well.

Sea monsters have always been mentioned alongside the *Mary Celeste*, and there can be little doubt that the oceans hold many secrets of which we know little or nothing. There may well be gigantic and terrifying marine life forms capable of destroying Briggs, his family, and crew. There are, however, problems with that explanation. For what reason would the monster also have taken the chronometer, the sextant, the navigation book, and the bill of lading?

A third theory concerns alien astronauts. Did someone or some*thing* from another world abduct Briggs and his people for reasons unknown? Curiously enough, this was the theme of one of the authors' early science-fiction novels, *Fiends*, published in the 1950s. In our novel we suggested that the curious marks that existed on either side of the bows were where the alien abductors in their UFO had extended a gigantic pincer-like appliance and gripped the *Mary Celeste* while the people were removed.

Along similar lines, theories have been put forward to explain the disappearances as the work of visitors from parallel worlds or other probability tracks, from other dimensions, or from the past or future: imaginative and remotely possible, of course, but not very probable.

One of the strangest theories ever advanced concerned the cargo of industrial alcohol and a horde of dangerously intoxicated rats. In outline, it suggested that carnivorous rats had broached the cargo, become dangerously aggressive and uninhibited as a result of drinking the crude alcohol, and swarmed out of the hold to attack the passengers, captain,

THE PONT-SAINT-ESPRIT OUTBREAK

As recently as 1951, a bakery in Pont-Saint-Esprit in southern France was infected with ergot poisoning. Many of the victims hallucinated so badly that they leaped into the river to escape their imagined pursuers: the outbreak affected more than 250 persons and led to seven deaths and fifty persons being interned in "asylums."

and crew. They had taken to the boat to escape, but the rats had swum after them and swamped the tiny yawl.

What about an armada of flesh-eating crabs? Even before brilliant horror writer Guy N. Smith had so much success with *Night of the Crabs*, a theory was put forward to explain the *Mary Celeste* tragedy in terms of an attack by an armada of flesh-eating crabs: unfortunately, like all the other theories, it doesn't comply with all the facts of the case.

The vanishing island theory has several classical precedents, including ancient legends of whales so large that they were mistaken for islands, but when they finally submerged, inadvertently drowned the sailors who had gone "ashore" to explore them. There is also the legend of the submergence of Atlantis to consider in these latitudes. Were the present-day Azores once the mountain peaks of that mysterious lost continent?

One of the most ingenious and elaborate theories was in the form of a superficially plausible story told by various lovable old rogues who pretended that they had been stowaways aboard the *Mary Celeste* and subsequently not only the sole survivor, but the only person who knew what had *really* happened. With minor variations from one telling to another, the story went like this:

There was friendly, sporting rivalry between Captain Briggs and first mate Richardson as to which of them was the better swimmer. The sub-plot of this imaginative drama was that baby Sophia Briggs loved to toddle up to the bowsprit and watch the water rushing past the bows. This naturally perturbed her parents, so Briggs ordered the ship's carpenter to build a little platform under the bowsprit with a good, strong safety rail around it. The infant Sophia could then enjoy watching the water in perfect safety. This platform was duly constructed and let an inch or so into the ship's timbers for added strength and security.

It was a relatively warm day for November in those southern Atlantic seas; there was only a slight breeze — ideal conditions for a swimming race. Briggs and Richardson decided on the spur of the moment to dive in off the bowsprit and race around the ship. The first man back at the bowsprit would be the winner. Word spread like wildfire. Sarah left the little dress half finished in her sewing machine, Richardson had already left his half completed navigational calculations, a crewman who was shaving put his razor down and walked up on deck to watch the race, another crew member hastily swallowed his medicine and placed the bottle down uncorked so as not to miss anything.

Briggs and Richardson were neck and neck all the way. It was a truly great race. In order to get a proper view of the finish, the eight spectators moved down onto the little platform. Just as the two powerful swimmers reached the finish line together, the platform collapsed on top of them.

Everyone except the unknown stowaway was floundering helplessly in the water. Risking punishment and imprisonment, he crept from his hiding place to see what all the desperate shouting and splashing was about. He was intending to throw a rope for them, or to try to launch the yawl to rescue them, but before he could do anything, a sudden squall hit the *Mary Celeste*. The wind drove her a hundred yards away from the strugglers in the water. The only two men who might have caught her again had been badly injured when the platform fell on them. The wind rose and the *Mary Celeste* glided unheedingly away from her drowning complement.

It was no easy matter for one man to get the yawl into the water, but the stowaway cut down some of the ship's rail and managed eventually. He rowed back to look for the others, but found nothing except the little platform, still floating pathetically.

He rowed and drifted for days, finally landing on a deserted part of the Azores. Looked after by kindly locals, he gave a false name and said nothing about the *Mary Celeste* for several years in fear of the legal consequences of his having stowed away.

It's a very *neat* story, and even its preposterous, but beautifully dove-tailed, details — such as the captain and his first mate having a swimming race in November, and the carpenter building a playpen under the bowsprit — are almost credible because they fitted together so well. But that's its problem: it fits *too* perfectly. Truth *is* probably stranger than fiction, but the strangeness of the stowaway's story is the strangeness of well-crafted fiction, rather than the rougher strangeness of natural truth.

Some authorities have suggested that the passengers and crew of the *Mary Celeste* were abducted by pirates or slave traders. Female slaves were still being traded illicitly along the North African coast in the 1870s. Was Sarah Briggs sold into what nineteenth-century New England puritans would have euphemistically called "a fate worse than death"? And did the others just walk the plank? But surely no pirate would have left the money or the other valuables behind on the *Mary Celeste*? They'd have been far more likely to have taken the ship and the cargo, changed the ship's name board and flag, and sold it in a port where no questions would be asked.

CAPTAINS IN COLLUSION?

One of the darker theories that floated across the suspicious little mind of Fred Flood was that Briggs and Morehouse were in collusion to collect the salvage money: but Briggs's own shares in the *Mary Celeste* were more valuable than his percentage of any salvage money could have been — plus, he and Morehouse were both men of excellent character and unblemished reputation. They had far more to gain from pursuing their marine careers than from grabbing a few risky dollars of salvage money. As even Fred had to admit eventually, the collusion and conspiracy theory was far less watertight than the copper-bottomed *Mary Celeste*.

This slave trader theory, however, is supported by another strange version that purports to be an eyewitness account given by a seaman called Demetrius, who was one of the crew of the slaver concerned. He first told his story in 1913 — more than forty years after the tragedy. In outline, he claimed that when the *Mary Celeste* was near the Azores, she encountered another brig, which flew a signal: "Short of provisions. Starving." The *Mary Celeste* signalled back: "Send a boat." A boat duly arrived with one man visible and a tarpaulin draped over what looked like empty cases to hold the requested provisions.

As it drew alongside the *Mary Celeste*, the tarpaulin went sideways and several armed men boarded Briggs's ship. He and his family and crew were ordered aboard the other brig. This was a slaver with fever aboard that had decimated the former captives and crew. The *Mary Celeste*'s people also succumbed to it, and were flung overboard one by one as they died. The slaver itself was run down and sunk by a large steamer that did not stop, and Demetrius was the sole survivor of the collision. Not wishing to broadcast his criminal role in the tragedy, he had kept the facts to himself for forty years.

Other theories concern whirlwinds and waterspouts somehow sucking the hapless human beings away while leaving the ship itself relatively untouched. It's difficult to imagine a waterspout or whirlwind being so selective, and it's also pertinent to ask why everyone stood meekly on deck

291

at the same time, passively waiting to be absorbed like inert biological dust into some huge, maritime vacuum cleaner. Loving and protective parents like Benjamin and Sarah would undoubtedly have got baby Sophia safely below decks — as far away from the thing as possible.

Another idea put forward by some researchers was that Briggs — admittedly a deeply religious man, although not a fanatical one — had succumbed to a bout of religious mania and thrown everyone else overboard as a sort of divine punishment for their real or imagined sins. In the first place, it would have been completely out of character: Briggs was a very steady, quiet, sensible, and reliable man. In the second place, it would have been difficult if not impossible to carry out. He was only of average size and strength — unlike the massively powerful Oliver Deveau of the *Dei Gratia* — and any two crewmen could easily have subdued and restrained him.

Mutiny has been put forward as another possibility. Was there some sort of plot being hatched by the four German sailors? Martens was a well-qualified and experienced mate who could have taken command and navigated the *Mary Celeste* without difficulty. But it wasn't the ship that vanished — it was the people. Mutineers characteristically make off with the ship, abandoning their rightful captain and those loyal to him — as was the case with Bligh (1754–1817) of the *Bounty*.

The most logical and rational explanation would seem to be the one connected with the nature of the cargo itself. As the ship moved toward warmer waters, the casks might well begin to sweat and leak a little. Potentially explosive fumes would accumulate in the hold. There would be disquieting noises, like old timbers settling into slightly different positions in a centrally heated house when the system is switched off or on.

Winchester himself testified that, although Briggs was an excellent and experienced master, he had never carried a cargo of industrial alcohol before. If there had been a lot of visible vapour, or small explosions from the hold, Briggs might well have decided that the whole 1,701 casks were in imminent danger of going up — taking the *Mary Celeste* with them. His decision would have been influenced by the presence of the wife and baby daughter that he loved more than his own life. He would have launched the yawl, packed everyone into it, and secured it to the *Mary Celeste* with the longest line that was available — the missing halyard. The cargo did not explode, but the halyard broke. Desperately, Briggs and his crew row in pursuit of the *Mary Celeste*, but wind and current are against them. Their yawl overturns in heavy seas. The *Mary Celeste* sails on alone into legend.

After the lengthy and totally unnecessary difficulties with the unpleasant Fred Flood in Gibraltar, the *Mary Celeste* was sent back to James Winchester, and her new skipper, Captain George W. Blatchford safely delivered her cargo to Genoa. Glad to be clear of the problem — and probably half-convinced that there really was a jinx on the *Mary Celeste* — Winchester then sold her at a loss, and concentrated on making a fair profit from his other vessels. During the following thirteen years the unhappy ship had seventeen different owners, and her maritime history was a miserable trail of disasters. She lost men, sails, and cargo. She ran aground and caught fire.

The end came in 1884 when she was purchased very cheaply by a Boston consortium, who was supposed to have loaded her with bread, beef, ale, codfish, and expensive furniture. All of these goods were very heavily insured. Her unscrupulous captain, Gilman C. Parker, ran her onto a coral reef off the coast of Haiti, but the underwriters were highly suspicious and sent an investigator. Unfortunately for Parker and the other conspirators, there was plenty of the *Mary Celeste* left to investigate. What was supposed to be very expensive cutlery turned out to be cheap dog collars. Casks labelled ale were full of water: nothing was what it seemed, and nothing was half as valuable as it had been declared to be.

Captain Parker and the first mate both died before they could be charged. The majority of the traders involved in the attempted fraud went bankrupt, and one of them committed suicide. It was almost as if the ill-fated *Mary Celeste* had brought her destroyers down with her.

Certainly, loneliness and tragedy seemed to extend to the families whose people had vanished from the *Mary Celeste*. Benjamin Briggs's mother had already lost her eldest son, Nathan, who had died of yellow fever in the Gulf of Mexico. Maria, her only daughter, had drowned in a shipwreck, and Benjamin's brother Oliver went down in the Bay of Biscay. Albert Richardson's heartbroken widow, Frances, never remarried and died at the age of ninety-one in Brooklyn in 1937. The grieving parents of the Lorensen brothers did not learn of the tragedy until 1873.

As a footnote or corollary to the story of the *Mary Celeste*, it is interesting to recall what happened — and what may yet be happening — to a much more recent mystery ship, the *Baychimo*. It left Vancouver on July 6, 1931, with a crew of thirty-six, under the command of Captain John Cornwall. It travelled through the Bering Strait and on into the notorious

Northwest Passage. Thousands of dollars worth of furs were purchased all along the Victoria Island coast, but on her return journey the *Baychimo* was caught in the pack ice.

According to the records of the Hudson's Bay Company's Digital Collection, history was made when Captain Cornwall and his men were rescued by air. The previously ice-locked *Baychimo*, however, had mysteriously slipped away from her icy shackles and vanished. The following spring, it was observed 480 kilometres to the east, near Herschel Island. Leslie Melvin, a trapper, found and boarded the *Baychimo* and reported that the ship had seemed to be in first-class order, and totally seaworthy. A party of Inuit found it in 1933, but it disappeared again in the ice. Elizabeth Hutchinson, a Scots botanist, reported seeing the ship again in 1934. Over many years, sightings continued from trappers, whalers, prospectors, and explorers. The last recorded sighting was in 1969, when it was found frozen in pack-ice in 1969, some thirty-eight years after she was abandoned. In 2006, the Alaskan government initiated a project to locate the *Baychimo*, whether still afloat or on the ocean floor. At the time of writing, no sign of the ship has been found, and the mystery of the "Ghost Ship of the Arctic" is still unsolved.

If Fred Flood doubted that the *Mary Celeste* could have gone on for ten or eleven days without a crew, he would have found it impossible to accept the amazing saga of the *Baychimo*.

The *Baychimo* certainly moves mysteriously, as though guided by some unknown power. Its strange ability to move is reminiscent of the movements of the notorious Barbados coffins within their sealed vault!

What unknown power could have moved these massive lead coffins? In a universe where common sense cause and effect seem to govern most phenomena, the moving coffins of Barbados would appear to be an unexplained effect with no known cause.

The outline of the event is that in the Christchurch parish burial ground at Oistin Bay in Barbados — a bay that looks for all the world like a Caribbean holiday poster — the coffins inside one strangely troubled vault shifted repeatedly but inexplicably between one interment and the next.

In Barbados at that time it was customary for the coffins of wealthy plantation owning families to be massively heavy, lead-lined constructions, requiring a group of six to eight men to move them.

The first person to be buried in the notorious vault was Mrs. Thomasina Goddard, in July 1807. A year later, the pathetic little coffin of two-year-old Mary Anna Chase was interred. On July 6, 1812, Dorcas, her elder sister, followed her. There were dark whisperings that Dorcas had succumbed to an early-nineteenth-century medical problem that might have been diagnosed as anorexia in our own time. Some said that her father's brutality had led her deliberately to starve herself to death in a final desperate effort to escape from him.

THE VAULT

The Christchurch Vault at the heart of the mystery was built of large coral stone blocks and closed with a ponderous slab of blue Devonshire marble. It was partly below ground level, and its approach was via a short flight of steps. The interior was four metres long and two metres wide, with a roof that arched slightly when seen from inside, while appearing flat outside.

Up until that time, all the burials in the notorious vault had been perfectly normal. In August of 1812, everything changed.

The Honourable Thomas Chase, reputedly the most thoroughly detested man in all Barbados, was being laid to rest in his infamous vault. When the chamber was opened, it was evident that the tiny coffin of Mary Anna Chase had been thrown clear across the room and was now propped upside down in a far corner. Mrs. Goddard's coffin had been rotated ninety degrees so that it lay on its side with its back against the wall.

The first reaction of the members of the burial party was to blame the "coloured" graveyard labourers, who denied it vigorously. Despite their understandable and fully justifiable resentment of their treatment at the hands of the plantation owners and managers, the labourers were anxious to put as much distance as possible between themselves and this unquiet tomb. It is highly improbable that somehow they would have made their way secretly into the vault prior to Thomas Chase's burial and moved the previously interred coffins.

All the coffins were returned to their proper places, and Thomas was laid reverently alongside the earlier occupants of the vault. Time passed.

On September 25, 1816, approximately four years later, eleven-month-old Samuel Brewster Ames was carried to the crypt for interment.

The April before little Samuel's death there had been a brief but bloody slave rebellion — quite common in early-nineteenth-century Barbados — which had been quelled by the plantation owners with their usual ruthlessness and brutality.

When the vault was opened, the coffins were once again in complete disarray. Once more the workers were unjustly blamed for the desecration. This time the plantation owners believed that the vault had been violated as an act of vengeance on behalf of those slaves who had been killed or maimed during the recent abortive uprising.

Upon reflection, however, this explanation failed to satisfy the investigators. It was recognized that the vault had only one entrance, and the ponderous marble slab was still securely in its place, showing no signs of having been disturbed.

Then there was the question of the sheer weight and awkwardness of the coffins themselves. Mrs. Goddard's casket was only a relatively light wooden affair — flimsy compared to the others — and easy enough to move, but the unpopular Thomas Chase had been a big man, weighing well over one hundred kilograms. His remains lay inside a solid wooden coffin encased in lead. It required nearly a dozen men to move it. When the vault was opened for little Samuel Brewster Ames on that fateful day in September, Thomas Chase's massive lead-covered coffin was several feet from its original resting place and lying on its side.

Six weeks later the vault was opened again. Samuel Brewster, father of little Samuel Brewster Ames, had been killed — clubbed to death by his slaves during the unsuccessful April rebellion — seven months previously. As a temporary measure during the emergency at that time, he had been buried elsewhere. Now he was being transferred to his final resting place in the family crypt.

The marble slab was examined carefully, but seemed firmly in place. A crowd of curious onlookers followed Samuel's coffin as the slab was slowly moved aside. Sunlight revealed the interior of the vault, and *again* the coffins had been radically disturbed, and were randomly strewn about. Mrs. Goddard's wooden casket had now disintegrated — the pieces subsequently had to be tied together and propped against one wall!

Thomas Orderson, rector of Christ Church, along with three other men searched the vault thoroughly. Flooding was one possibility that occurred to them, and they tested for signs of dampness or recent moisture. But everywhere was perfectly dry inside the vault. Walls and floor were checked for any tell-tale cracks — nothing was detected.

There were some peripheral voodoo traditions on Barbados at the time, but they were much less common than on Haiti. The plantation workers were convinced that some form of supernatural curse was affecting the Chase vault, and they kept as far away from it as possible. Meanwhile, plantation owners, managers, and visiting sailors all expressed a high level of interest and curiosity: the next interment was awaited with ill-concealed enthusiasm.

It happened on July 17, 1819. Mrs. Thomasina Clarke had recently died and the vault was to be reopened for her. Understandably, there were a great many excited and curious onlookers, and the burial party included Lord Combermere himself, the then governor of Barbados and a former cavalry commander in the Peninsula War, where he had been one of Wellington's bravest and most reliable officers.

As before, the coffins were in disarray — all except for the pathetic bundle of wood that had once contained Mrs. Goddard. That was standing where they had left it propped against the wall three years previously. If anything would have moved easily because of some natural tremor, disturbance, or flood, it would have been the precariously propped planks of the Goddard coffin. But that was the only one that still stood — unmoved as a Roman sentry at his post at Pompeii.

Once more, a thorough examination of the coffins and the vault was carried out. No clue to the disturbance was found. The coffins were once again laid back in their proper places, with the three large leaden ones forming the foundation layer. Above them were placed the children and the disintegrated pieces of Mrs. Goddard's casket, tied together as before.

On Combermere's orders, further precautions were taken. A thick layer of fine white sand was sprinkled over the floor to show footprints or drag marks. The heavy marble slab was cemented in place yet again, and Combermere and his party made distinctive marks in the wet cement using their seals.

Feelings of excitement and curiosity on the island were now running too high for Combermere to wait for the next interment. On April 18, 1820, after he and a party of the island's leading citizens had been discussing the moving coffin enigma, they decided not to wait for another family death, but to reopen the vault and inspect its interior straight away. Neighbouring citizens were notified of the governor's intentions, a party of very reluctant plantation labourers was assembled, and the grim work began.

The blue Devonshire marble door proved to be a major problem. All the distinctive seals in the rock-hard cement were undisturbed and clearly visible, but after the cement was chipped free the door was still very difficult to move. The reason soon became all too clear: Thomas Chase's huge lead coffin, weighing the better part of a ton, was wedged up against it at a steep angle. That in itself was totally inexplicable, but with the single exception of the fragments of Thomasina Goddard's wooden coffin, everything else was also in wild disarray. The sand, however, was undisturbed. There were no signs of dragging, of intruders' footprints, nor of flooding. Every part of the vault was as sound and solid as the day it had been built: there were no loose, movable stones, and no secret passages.

Combermere and his distinguished guests were completely baffled — and so were the onlookers. The tough old cavalry veteran, who feared nothing *physical*, decided that enough was enough. He gave orders for all the coffins to be reverently reinterred elsewhere and the Chase vault to be left empty — and so it has remained until the present day.

A number of theories have been put forward over the years — the best of them are not entirely adequate: the worst are at least 180 degrees off target.

Wherever and whenever there is a really challenging and inexplicable phenomenon, there seem to be those who claim that it never really happened at all. A classic example is the eager denial by some atheists and agnostics of the very existence of the historical Christ — let alone his miracles and his resurrection. The fragile argument that the Barbados coffins never moved around in their vault relies mainly upon the supposition that there was a sinister, but totally motiveless and unsubstantiated Masonic Plot: Lord Combermere, the Reverend Thomas Orderson (who officiated at the interments), Nathan Lucas, Major Finch, Bowcher Clarke, and other honest, respectable, and reliable contemporary participants and witnesses were all said to have been Freemasons and to have concocted the whole story as a sort of Masonic fable about death and resurrection. That theory disintegrates more speedily than the unfortunate Mrs. Goddard's wooden coffin.

What next? Of much more substance is the idea that giant tropical puff-ball fungi were responsible. An account of the Barbados coffins, written by Valentine Dyall, appeared in *Everybody's Weekly* on July 19, 1952. Shortly

THE FUNGUS THEORY TESTED!

While giving a series of lectures on unexplained phenomena in East Anglia in the 1970s, we mentioned the Barbados coffins and the Ames letter. A member of the group who was a farmer brought in a very large British puff-ball fungus that he had found in one of his barns. We duly sealed it inside a large plastic sack and the group kept watch over it week by week. At the end of the two-term course, it still showed not the slightest sign of disintegrating into an undetectable nothingness.

afterward, Dyall received a letter from a Mr. Gregory Ames, from Middlesex, England. He enclosed a copy of a letter written by his great-grandfather on Christmas Day 1820. The writer, a close relative of the interred infant Samuel Brewster Ames, and almost certainly an eyewitness to the events in the Barbados vault, believed that huge fungi of a type known to grow in caves in Honduras were responsible for moving the coffins. He said that a very old plantation labourer told him that, although the vault was originally built to hold the remains of the Honourable John Elliott, the mysterious sounds like muffled explosions that came from it led to John being interred elsewhere in 1724 — long before the Chase/Ames phenomena began. Were those unexplained "muffled explosions" really caused by the sudden collapse of enormous puff-ball fungi?

When Combermere and his team searched the vault and checked out the sand on the floor, they would have been certain to see and recognize the remains of any puff-ball fungi large enough to have moved coffins weighing up to a ton apiece. No one at the time reported seeing such debris. The fungus idea is, nevertheless, tenable, but far from conclusive.

Seekers after a supernatural explanation have laid great emphasis on the behaviour of Mrs. Goddard's wooden coffin. It alone did not move when the heavier metal ones did. It was widely surmised at the time that the unhappy Mrs. Goddard had taken her own life. If she had, there are precedents in the archives of supernatural case studies for strange disturbances and paranormal phenomena attending suicides. Yet, if Mrs.

Goddard's restless, earthbound spirit *was* somehow responsible for moving the Barbados coffins, that raises more questions than it lays to rest.

Where do such unhappy spirits obtain their psychic — and physical — energy? (In this case, very significant amounts of energy.) Why, when so many unfortunate people take their own lives, are cases like the Barbados coffins so rare? To what extent — and this links across to poltergeist phenomena — can purely mental or spiritual energy possibly affect such large masses of matter? To "explain" the Barbados coffin phenomena in terms of Mrs. Goddard's troubled spirit is like trying to explain the nature of water by saying that it has come out of a tap. To say that the power "came out of" Mrs. Goddard's suicide, is not a full or satisfactory explanation of the true nature of that power.

Was it, after all, despite the vault being tightly sealed, the vengeance of those plantation workers who had been abominably treated by Thomas Chase? They had the motive, but they were undeniably afraid of the "dark powers" that they believed the vault contained. It seems far more likely that they would have avoided the place rather than find a way to creep in and vandalize it without being detected. The vengeful labourers theory fails to explain the sealed door, the sound masonry (totally lacking in loose stones or secret passages), and the carefully sanded floor that showed no tell-tale marks.

Some researchers have suggested that the coffins were moved by natural forces, as yet not understood by orthodox mainstream science. Ill-defined things like "negative gravity bubbles" have been proposed. Admittedly, they seem far more probable than the Masonic fable theories, but they're significantly less likely than Honduran puff-balls.

FLOODS AND EARTHQUAKES?

Flooding and minor earthquakes have both been suggested as causes, but the great difficulty here is the localized nature of the disturbances. One vault does not flood, leaving dozens of others perfectly dry. One set of coffins is not shaken violently out of position by an earth tremor that leaves all the adjacent vaults unaffected.

Inevitably, intrepid travellers on the boundaries of von Däniken Land will suggest that extraterrestrial aliens were responsible. To give that hypothesis the modicum of respect that it deserves, it is just about possible to imagine the alien observers carrying out a few simple experiments. Did they try out some sort of highly advanced, long-range tractor beams? Perhaps they were able to move *metal* cases more easily than wooden ones — hence Mrs. Goddard's coffin remaining in its place while the leaden ones shifted significantly.

As a corollary, might it be suggested that there were also psychological and sociological dimensions to those entirely hypothetical extraterrestrial experiments? As well as trying out their tractor beams, were our postulated aliens studying the reactions of Combermere and the other investigators? Were they trying to find out how the human mind responded to a series of phenomena which it couldn't explain? Were they conducting some kind of cosmic IQ test on Combermere and his contemporaries? It's not high on the scale of probabilities, but it's not impossible given the great weight of pro-UFO evidence that has steadily accumulated over the centuries.

The overwhelming weight of evidence leads to the inescapable conclusion that the Barbados coffins were real, and on several occasions they moved significant distances inside a sealed vault. They do not seem to have been thrown around by vengeful intruders, by flood water, by giant fungi, by localized earthquakes, by extraterrestrial aliens, or by nil-gravity-bubbles. Today, the tomb is empty — except for the intangible mystery which still clings to it.

But the Barbados vault is not unique. There are reports of *other* vaults where coffins were alleged to have moved — and they are situated a long way from Barbados.

During July 1844 — nearly a quarter of a century after the strange events in the Chase family vault — odd things happened at Kuresaare, formerly called Ahrensburg, on what is now Saarema, but was then identified on maps as the island of Osel in Estonia. There were reports from visitors to the Ahrensburg cemetery that their horses were behaving strangely. They seemed nervous and unsettled when they were tethered after their riders had dismounted to attend the graves of family or friends. One report states that some horses went crazy with fear, and adds that at least one of the horses died in its frenzied efforts to get away from the hitching rail near the cemetery.

When a member of the Buxhoewden family was being interred there on July 24 the vault was duly opened. There were sudden cries of anger

301

and amazement: most of the previously interred coffins had been stacked up untidily in the centre of the vault like logs on a bonfire. The coffins were reverently re-placed, and the family made a formal complaint to Baron Guldenstubbé, president of the consistory. His colleagues included the mayor, a local doctor, two craft guild representatives, and an official secretary. Their formal verdict was that ghouls (either human or supernatural) had been responsible for the vandalism and desecration. Guldenstubbé acted swiftly — as determinedly and effectively as Lord Combermere had done on the other side of the world. New locks were added to the vault door and guards were positioned in the cemetery.

This had also been done — with great effect — in Bacton in Norfolk, England, in 1828, when body snatchers had attempted to steal corpses from the village churchyard during January of that year. The night guard had fired at the intruders, peppering them with heavy buckshot before they galloped away, never to trouble the Bacton dead again.

The carefully guarded Osel vault was inspected three days later. The soldiers reported no problems: all had been quiet while they had been on duty. All the locks were secure. But most of the coffins were again piled in a heap in the centre of the tomb; two or three others lay nearby on their sides.

Guldenstubbé and the local Lutheran bishop questioned everybody who might have had the slightest knowledge of the strange events. As in Barbados, a thorough search was made for a secret tunnel, but no trace of one was ever found. Guldenstubbé and the bishop ordered two or three coffins to be opened: only naturally decomposing bodies were found inside. As in Barbados, a thorough check was made for flooding — it revealed nothing. Even the base of the vault was dug up and replaced. The chapel above was also carefully examined. Guldenstubbé made a third and final attempt: new locks were provided, a ring of soldiers surrounded the vault, and dry wood ash was sprinkled liberally across the floor as sand had been spread in Barbados.

Three days passed and the vault was opened again: once more chaos reigned supreme. Coffins were scattered, some were upended, and some had sprung open. The ashes on the floor showed no trace of footprints or of any other type of disturbance. Just as in the Barbados case, the coffins were reinterred elsewhere and the Buxhoewden vault was left empty.

Another strange parallel with the Barbados case was that one of the young Buxhoewdens buried in the disturbed vault was rumoured to have shot himself.

Barbados and Osel were by no means the only sites where coffins were reported to have moved inexplicably. Notes and Queries for 1867 contained some correspondence from F.C. Paley, son of the rector of Gretford near Stamford, England. He reported that his father had told him of several heavy lead-lined coffins being disarranged in a vault in his parish. One was so heavy that six men could move it only with considerable difficulty. As in Barbados and Osel, some of these Gretford coffins were also found on their sides.

Yet another case was reported in *The European Magazine*, dated September 1815, and commented on by Algernon E. Aspinall in his book *West Indian Tales of Old*. This time the vault concerned was at Stanton in Suffolk, England. Once again, the coffins were lead-lined and standing on biers inside the vault. On several occasions when the vault was opened they were found to have been displaced. At least once, a coffin was found resting on the fourth step of the flight that led down from inside the door to the floor of the vault. Subterranean flooding seems to have been the most popular explanation at the time — although witnesses noted that there was no sign of any such flooding when the Suffolk vault was opened.

The "moved-by-water" hypothesis, however, does have some unexpected support from an unusual and bizarre quarter: *The London Evening Post* of May 16, 1751, carried a report that the *Johannes*, under Captain Wyrck Pietersen, retrieved a floating wood-encased lead coffin containing the body of Francis Humphrey Merrydith. A month or so earlier, he'd been buried in the Goodwin Sands in accordance with his last request. Commander Rupert T. Gould, an authority on unsolved mysteries, and a very knowledgeable professional seaman, also supports the idea that such coffins can float. He made some reliable buoyancy calculations and reached the conclusion that a typical lead-lined wood-encased coffin weighed around four hundred kilograms, but had a displacement of nearly five hundred kilograms. If the average corpse weighed less than ninety kilograms, that would make such a coffin reasonably buoyant.

There is an account of the Baltic mystery in S.R. Vale Owen's book *Footfalls on the Boundary of Another World*. He was an American diplomat who obtained the information from Guldenstubbé's son and daughter in 1859. Reliable and well-documented accounts of the Chase vault incident appear in the *Journal of the Barbados Museum and Historical Society, Volumes 12 and 13*, published in 1945.

On more than one occasion, and in more than one vault, heavy lead-lined coffins have reportedly moved. If they were moved by some as yet unknown *natural* force, it could prove to be well worth pursuing. A close study of light brought in the miracle of the laser. An examination of silicon semi-conductors introduced the computer revolution. Fleming's observation of the behaviour of micro-organisms in the presence of certain moulds heralded the life-saving arrival of powerful antibiotics. A boy watching a kettle lid moving as the water boiled grew up to develop the steam engine … What might a perceptive and imaginative engineer discover from trying to replicate the Barbados vault phenomena on a scientific basis? If only Tesla had heard of the enigma and visited Barbados to investigate!

As we were putting the finishing touches on this manuscript, and making the final revisions, we received a very interesting phone call from Simon Probert and Pamela Willson of Penarth. Our lecture to the Annual Fortean "UnConvention" in London had been widely advertised, and this year the subject was the Barbados coffin mystery. Simon and Pamela had seen a press report, and invited us to call and see some photographs of the disturbed vault, which they had taken in September of 1996. As a well-qualified and experienced funeral director, Simon is especially knowledgeable about coffins. Pamela, a talented artist and expert picture restorer, is also a sensitive psychic and psychometrist.

It was after lunch on that mid-September day that they visited the little church and graveyard at Oistin in Barbados. Having looked around the church first, they went to inspect the infamous Chase vault. Surprisingly, as an iron grid is normally kept locked across it to prevent vandalism and damage, they found it was unbarred and open that afternoon. Simon took a photograph, which came out quite normally, and then Pamela descended to inspect the interior. She felt that the atmosphere was strangely *wrong*, and decided not to go in. Simon, however, did go in, and Pamela took a photograph of him in the actual doorway where the blue Devonshire marble slab once rested, his hand raised in a cheery wave. When this picture was developed, Simon seemed to have faded away into the darkness of the tomb's interior, while a curious, amorphous, wraith-like figure — not unlike a dead woman in a shroud — was standing on his left, on the right side of the print. When this picture was subjected to computer enhancement, the shrouded woman could be seen quite clearly — with a skull for a head.

Another strange object behind her could have been a second skull. It appeared to Simon and Pamela, as the four of us studied the picture together, to have a look of menace as though it was threatening the spectral woman. If the unfortunate Mrs. Thomasina Goddard had taken her own life because of Thomas Chase's cruelty, then the photographic evidence seemed to be suggesting that death had not ended her suffering.

The very least that can be said about Simon and Pamela's photographs and the computer enhancement is that the pictures are inexplicably strange, just as the coincidence of their visiting the open vault that afternoon was strange, and my choice of lecture subject for the Fortean meeting was strange, and Simon and Pamela's seeing the note about that lecture in the *South Wales Echo* was strange — almost, perhaps, as if we were *destined* to meet and discuss the sinister Barbados coffin mystery.

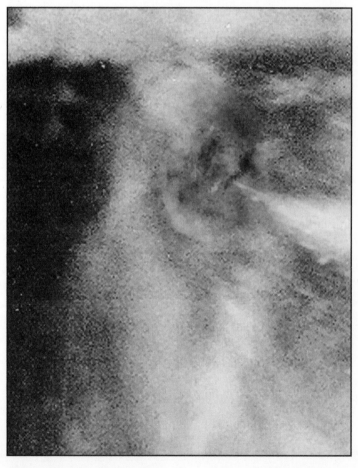

Simon and Pamela's strange photo taken at the Barbados vault.

17 MYSTERIOUS APPEARANCES

King Stephen of England (born 1094, crowned 1135, died 1154) did not enjoy a particularly prosperous or peaceful reign — and the most memorable event in it was an extremely unlikely one: two green children, a boy and a girl, reportedly arrived mysteriously in a Suffolk harvest field. Reliable twelfth-century records exist that explain the story of the bizarre appearance.

The chronic problem throughout the whole of Stephen's reign was Matilda, daughter of Henry I, who reigned from 1100–35. By any standards of justice and fair play, she should have been queen. Stephen had, in fact, promised her his allegiance and full support until his brother Henry had prompted him to go for the throne himself.

While Stephen and Matilda were fighting for the crown like the Lion and the Unicorn in the famous old nursery rhyme, there was no strong central power to keep the barons in check. With every local baron able to behave more or less like an absolute and autonomous monarch in his own little kingdom, life for the majority of ordinary people was hazardous and uncertain.

Social and psychological historians occasionally comment that at times of uncertainty and weak central government, there is a tendency for strange and inexplicable phenomena to be reported. It is almost as though cultural and political instability encouraged a crop of weird Fortean phenomena as welcome diversions and distractions from the general threats of war and exploitation that most citizens have no control over. Were the "Green Children of Woolpit" perhaps a response to social anxiety rather than tangible, objective phenomena?

In this case, the chronicler is Ralph, who was abbot of the Cistercian monastery at Coggeshall. He lived and worked close enough to Stephen's unpropitious reign to have known eyewitnesses to the Woolpit episode. During the reign of Stephen, the local supremo appears to have been Sir Richard de Calne from Wikes, or Wyken Hall — twelfth-century spellings are notoriously variable — and Ralph the Chronicler may have known one of his descendants, although traditionally he obtained the story from Sir Richard himself.

Another chronicler was William of Newburgh, or Newbridge, Priory. His account is preserved in Manuscript Number 3875 in the Harleian Collection in the British Museum. Freely translated from the Latin it says:

Concerning the Green Children.... It does not seem right or proper to leave out a miracle unknown for centuries which is said to have happened in Anglia during Stephen's reign. For a long time I hesitated about recording it although many people knew and spoke of it. There is no rational explanation for it, and it seemed foolish to me to present such an obtuse matter to people as though it deserved belief. At last, however, I was compelled to accept it because of the overwhelming weight of evidence. I was amazed by events which I cannot understand or fathom out, no matter how hard I concentrate my mind upon them. There is an East Anglian village a few kilometres from the Monastery of the Blessed Martyr King Edmund. Close to this village there are some ancient excavations, which in English are referred to as "Wlfpitts," which means wolf pits. From these the village takes its name. At harvest time, while the harvesters were busy in the fields collecting their crops, two children appeared — one boy and one girl — with completely green bodies. They were also wearing clothing of a strange colour made from unusual material. As these bewildered children wandered through the fields, the harvesters caught them and took them to the village. Many people gathered to see the strange sight. It was a long time before they would eat anything, although it was clear that they were almost fainting from hunger. Food was offered to them in plenty, but they would touch none of it. It was discovered by accident, while beans were being gathered in from the fields, that the children tried to eat the pith from inside the stalks. They cried with great sadness because they could not find any. However, one of the harvesters took pith from a pod and gave it to them. They ate this eagerly. For some months they ate nothing except this, but gradually they got used to bread, and their colour slowly changed until it was like ours. They also learned to speak our language, and were baptized. The boy, who appeared to be the younger of the two, died soon afterward, but the girl who now looked indistinguishable from our women married a man from King's Lynn. When they had mastered our speech, they were questioned about who they were and where they had come from. They said that they came from The Land of St. Martin, a place where that Saint was greatly venerated. They had no idea where their own land was, nor did they know how they had come to be in the field where they were found by the villagers. They recalled that they had been tending their father's animals in the fields of their own country, when they had heard a great noise like the bells ringing from our Monastery of St. Edmund. While they were puzzling over this sound, they found themselves in the Woolpit fields with harvesters all around them. When they were asked about the faith of the people of St. Martin's Land they said that they were Christians and that there were churches there. When questioned about the movements of the sun, they replied that it did not rise in their country as it does in ours. They said that the light is much weaker than ours: about the same as early morning or just after sunset. They also said that they could observe another country across a wide river. These things and many besides were spoken of by the children when people asked them about their country. Readers can say what they will as they think about these very strange things. I do not regret writing down these astounding events: the story is too strange and complicated for human intelligence to unravel.

Piecing together the records and traditions, the two children with green skin and perhaps green clothing of some unusual material, turned up in the harvest fields.

They seemed to have thought that they had come through a tunnel or passageway of some kind. Their description of their home in St. Martin's Land makes it seem a very normal and terrestrial place, but there are odd discrepancies. If there was little or no light there, how did the necessary photosynthesis in the grass take place to enable their father's animals to graze it? What was "the bright country," which they claimed to be able to see in the distance? If it was the simple Suffolk harvest fields of Woolpit, what "great river" lay between?

Again, if it was merely a terrestrial tunnel that separated their father's mysterious land from Woolpit, why could neither the children nor their new friends in the village find the entrance again?

Several ingenious theories have been advanced over the years. There was alleged to have been a similar episode in Spain, where two green children appeared in Banjos in Catalonia. In this account, some agricultural workers found two strange children crying at the entrance to a cave. They spoke a language that the villagers could not understand, and nor could experts from Barcelona. The children were wearing clothes of an unusual fabric, and their skin was green. Just like the Woolpit children, they went hungry for days, finally eating beans. The boy soon died, but the girl survived and learned enough Spanish to tell her friends in Banjos about her homeland. Her description of it was exactly like the St. Martin's Land of the Woolpit story: twilight, a wide river, and a

The pit in Woolpit.

bright country in the distance. There was also a reference to a loud noise that had immediately preceded their arrival in Banjos.

The villagers failed to find the entrance to the mysterious "tunnel" that had transported the children to Banjos. Just as in Woolpit, the girl lost her green colour, but died after five years instead of marrying a local man as the Woolpit girl had done. The Spanish children were said to have had almond eyes, but otherwise they resemble the Suffolk children very closely — rather too closely, perhaps. The mayor of Banjos, who took the lead in befriending them, was said to have been a certain Ricardo de Calno — which sounds uncannily like a Spanish version of Sir Richard de Calne in Suffolk. In fact, the whole Spanish tale seems to have been only an imported version of the Woolpit story, and to have no foundation in fact. The Catalonian village of Banjos does not even seem to exist — unless a very strong magnifying glass has to be applied to the map of Catalonia.

So who might the Green Children of Woolpit have been, and where did they come from?

The Green Children of Woolpit made their-surprising entrance to the Suffolk harvest fields about three centuries before Robert de Grey arranged for the murder of his orphaned nephew. However, the idea that the Babes and the Green Children might have been one and the same involves a poison theory rather than the more widely known death from exposure hypothesis. If Robert had attempted to use cyanide or something similar on the Babes, the argument goes, the toxicity might have accounted for their green colouring. It doesn't, of course, account for their description of the twilit St. Martin's Land and their story about looking after their father's farm animals. Neither does it contribute any solution to the problem of their diet.

So, if confusion with the Babes in the Wood can be discounted, where *did* the Green Children come from?

In what appears to be the historically valid version of the event, although the boy died shortly after being rescued by the Woolpit villagers, his sister grew up, lost her green colour entirely, became a happy, healthy young woman, and married a man from King's Lynn.

Sir Richard, who employed her for a few years before her marriage — and it is necessary to remember that in Shakespeare's Elizabethan world Romeo and Juliet were married in their early teens — said that she was inclined to be "somewhat loose and wanton in her ways." Sexual behaviour tends to vary from culture to culture, and Sir Richard's remark may be one of the most significant in the whole record. Were the Green Children from somewhere — call it St. Martin's Land, or whatever we choose — in which a different code of sexual ethics was the norm? In the records of the Kaspar Hauser case, the Mystery Boy of Nuremberg would perform his excretory functions in public without the slightest idea that it was not acceptable in the culture of early-nineteenth-century Nuremberg. Is it sensible to ask whether the Green Girl was sexually uninhibited because she had been reared in a more open and permissive culture than that of twelfth-century Suffolk?

It is extremely unlikely that the Green Children travelled through time, across whatever barrier exists between parallel worlds and probability tracks — if, indeed, such tracks do exist, from another dimension or from another planet. Yet how else can the so-called "tunnel" connecting Woolpit with a twilit land bounded by a great river be explained?

Folklorists and students of myth and tradition will suggest that there are several features in the account that point in legendary or supernatural directions. "Martins" were imps or little demons. So was the strange, dimly lit St. Martin's Land meant to symbolize the outer boundaries of hell? Perhaps it was purgatory? In C.S. Lewis's *The Great Divorce* he describes purgatory as a huge, sprawling, twilit city in the grey, drab, industrial midlands of the 1930s Depression.

Beans were also the traditional food of the dead, and green was the colour of fairies, gnomes, elves, leprechauns, and "little people" in general. Can the green children be explained in supernatural terms? Again, it seems highly improbable.

WORKING IN A COPPER MINE

It has been suggested by some that the green children were escapees from one of the notorious early copper mines that employed enforced child labour. Snow White's seven dwarfs were thought by some researchers to have been child miners whose growth had been stunted by long, arduous toil and exposure to huge amounts of copper. Could those conditions have induced a green pigmentation as well?

The mystery is as deep now as it was during Stephen's reign. Researchers remain as puzzled as the Woolpit harvesters of almost nine centuries ago.

We now move on to another curious, unexplained appearance: that of Kaspar Hauser, who arrived suddenly in Nuremberg — metaphorically from nowhere.

One of the most picturesque cities in Bavaria, Nuremberg has a long and fascinating history, complete with other mysteries reported in the vicinity long before Kaspar arrived. Nuremberg had been important and prosperous. That era was over by 1828, the year that Kaspar arrived, and the Bavarian industrial revolution — which would bring a different kind of fame and prosperity to Nuremberg — still lay a few decades in the future. In that sense, at least, the timing of whoever, or whatever, had brought Kaspar to Nuremberg was fortuitous.

On May 28, 1828, the city was almost deserted: it was Whit Monday — a public holiday, the *Ausflug*. Georg Weichmann, a shoemaker, was practically the only citizen in Unschlitt Square at the time of Kaspar's arrival.

Strolling into the square, Georg noticed a youth of about sixteen leaning weakly against a building and moaning softly, as if ill or greatly distressed. The kindly Weichmann walked over to the young man and offered assistance. Was he ill? Did he need a doctor? Was he hungry or thirsty, perhaps? The only answers the friendly shoemaker received were unintelligible mumbling sounds, but the boy had an envelope in his hands and Weichmann read the address on it. The letter was intended for The Captain of the Fourth Squadron of the Sixth Cavalry Regiment, Nuremberg.

Weichmann was sturdy as well as good-natured and, according to one account, he supported the staggering youth all the way to Captain Wessenig's house. He was out, but his servants said he was expected back shortly, and invited Georg and the stranger to wait. Hospitably, they produced the customary refreshments for their visitors.

Georg and Wessenig's servants watched with amazement as the newcomer wolfed down bread and water as if there was never likely to be any more on Earth, but he shied away from cold meat and beer — apparently revolted by the smell of them. When cooking odours drifted in from the kitchen, he almost fainted. He was also very nervous of the big grandfather clock, treating it like some monstrous beast that was capable of attacking him.

Curiosity prompted him to try to pick a candle flame as though it were a flower. He cried out in pain and surprise when the flame burnt his finger. Every time Weichmann or members of Wessenig's staff asked him a question he responded with "*Weiss nicht*," meaning "Don't know."

Captain Wessenig then arrived, listened attentively to what his servants and Weichmann had to tell him, looked quizzically at Kaspar, and opened the mysterious envelope. There were two letters inside. The first, in an illiterate, disguised hand, ran as follows, and purported to be from the boy's mother:

> This little one has been baptized. He is called Kaspar, but you must give him his second name. Please take care of him. His father was once a soldier in the cavalry. Take him to the 6th Cavalry Regiment at Nuremberg when he is 17. That was his father's old Regiment. Please, I beg you, look after him until he is 17. His birthday was April 30th, 1812. I cannot care for him myself because I a very poor girl, and his father is dead.

The second letter, ostensibly from the mysterious guardian to whom the impoverished young mother had sent the infant Kaspar, said:

> Honourable Captain,
>
> I am sending to you a young man who wishes to serve his king by joining the Army. A poor young woman brought him to me on October 7, 1812, and I myself am only a poor workman with a family of my own to raise. His mother begged me to take care of him, so I have tried to treat him as a son. I have never let him outside my house, so nobody knows where he was brought up. He does not know the name nor location of our home. No matter how you question him, Honourable Captain, he will not be able to show you where my home is. I brought him at night so that he will not be able to retrace his steps. Because I have nothing, I have not been able to give him any money at all. If you do not wish to keep him, you can hang him or strike him dead.

Both letters appeared to have been written by the same person, whose clumsy attempt to disguise the style and degree of literacy was an abject failure.

All that Kaspar was able to add were the words "Horse, horse," and "Want to be a soldier like father."

Wessenig concluded that the young stranger was either "a primitive savage or an imbecile" and sent him to the police station, where he was given a pencil and paper. He managed to write the words "Kaspar Hauser," but simply answered "Don't know" to all questions. Sergeant Wüst stripped and searched him, and wrote an official report:

> He is a sturdy, broad-shouldered boy of 16 or 17, with a healthy complexion, light brown hair and blue eyes. His hands and feet seem to be disproportionately small. Although at first he appeared to be crippled, closer inspection revealed that his feet were badly blistered as though he were unused to walking. His hat and shirt are too large for him. His boots are too small. His shapeless jacket and trousers are too large, and the jacket appears to have been cut down from an old frock coat.

The sergeant and other officers compared Kaspar's childish, irregular scrawl with the writing on the letters. There was no possibility at all that Kaspar himself could have written either of them. Not quite sure what to do with the lad, the Nuremberg police decided that the best course of action was to keep him in a cell for a few days to give higher authority a chance to come to a decision.

Herr Hiltel was the experienced old warder who kept Kaspar under observation during these early days. His report of the young man makes for very interesting reading:

> He can sit for hours without moving his limbs at all. He does not pace the floor nor does he attempt to sleep. He sits quite still and rigid without appearing to be uncomfortable. He prefers it to be dark rather than light, and he can move in the dark as well as a cat can.

Apart from repeating "Want to be a soldier like father," Kaspar's only replies to police questions were the monotonous reiteration of "Don't know."

Kaspar, however, suddenly caught the public imagination, and the citizens of Nuremberg began to take a keen interest in him. This was due in part to the theories of Jean-Jacques Rousseau (1712–78), the writer responsible for putting forward "the child of nature" myth. According to Rousseau, it was civilization and society that "corrupted" people. Then it may be likely that, if the Mystery Boy of Unschlitt Square had indeed grown up largely insulated from these "corrupting" influences, he might turn out to be one of Rousseau's almost perfect "children of nature."

Crowds of sightseers visited Kaspar daily. They gave him pieces of paper on which he wrote "Kaspar Hauser" but nothing much else. Many of his reactions were characteristically infantile, as though he were somehow compensating for having missed out on his normal childhood development.

KASPAR'S STRANGE HABITS

The boy was fascinated by a ticking watch. He built coins into little stacks. He was engrossed by the pictures of kings, queens, and jacks on ordinary playing cards. He did not at first seem to recognize any difference between the genders, but referred to both male and female visitors as *junge*, the word for "boy." He did not seem to have any awareness of the passage of time, and knew nothing of day and night, or of hours, minutes, and seconds.

At first he showed no preference for privacy with toilet functions, but would excrete and urinate in public as unaffectedly as he would eat or drink.

The greatest success, and for Kaspar the major stimulant of these early days in Nuremberg, was a wooden horse. He adored it. He festooned it with ribbons. He played with it constantly like a happy toddler. He "fed" it each time he ate.

His learning curve was a steep one. By July he was able to talk fluently enough to give Bürgermeister Binder and the town council an account of his past life. They issued an official version of what Kaspar told them and called it "Bulletin Number One":

> He knows neither who he is nor where he came from. It was only here in Nuremberg that he first entered the world. Before coming here he always lived in a hole and sat on straw on the ground. During that time he heard nothing, and saw no bright lights. He would wake and sleep and wake again. When he woke he would find a pitcher of water and a piece of bread beside him. Sometimes the water tasted unpleasant. Then he would sleep. When he woke again he would be wearing a clean shirt. The face of the man who came to him was always hidden. He had ribbons and two wooden horses to play with. He does not remember ever being ill or sad in his hole. The man brought a wooden table into the hole and put it over Kaspar's feet. There were pieces of white paper on this table and the man made marks on them with a black pencil. When he had gone Kaspar copied the marks the man had made. Finally the man taught Kaspar to stand and then to walk. At last he carried him out of his hole. Kaspar is unsure of what happened after that until he found himself here in Nuremberg carrying the letter.

The Nurembergers adopted Kaspar and placed him in the care of Professor George Friedrich Daumer, who enjoyed something of a reputation as a philosopher and educationalist. Daumer — like many of his contemporaries — was a committed passenger on the Rousseau bandwagon. He regarded Kaspar as a prime example of a feral child, and studied him accordingly, keeping meticulous records as he did so.

Daumer discovered that Kaspar's natural senses were unusually well developed. The young man had exceptionally acute hearing and could see in the dark. Conversely, he had difficulty at first in adjusting to normal light. His sense of smell was abnormally keen, almost as good as a hound's. He could track an animal by its scent, and he could recognize human beings in the dark in the same way. He was also able to distinguish different trees merely by the scent of their leaves.

Daumer and Kaspar decided to collaborate on his autobiography, which was duly completed in August of 1829. It proved to be something of a disappointment and anticlimactic. Perhaps the rumours and speculation surrounding Kaspar had led readers to expect something far more sensational, or at least some significant *new* disclosures as the boy's vocabulary and powers of expression and comprehension increased. The book was much longer than Kaspar's original statements had been, but it contained nothing fresh.

On October 7, Kaspar was found unconscious in Daumer's cellar with a head wound. On regaining consciousness, he was unable to give much information to the police other than that he had been attacked by a "man with a black face." This undoubtedly referred to a mask, and tied in with Kaspar's account of the masked man who had brought him his bread, water, and changes of clothes while he was confined in his straw-lined hole. The Nuremberg authorities took the attack seriously and moved Kaspar to a safer location with two policemen as bodyguards.

A curious incident that Hauser found hard to explain involved what he said was the "accidental" discharge of a pistol. Hearing a shot from Kaspar's room, the two guards rushed in to investigate. They found that

WHY DID KASPAR KNOW NOTHING OF THE NORMAL WORLD?

If Kaspar's natural animal senses were strong, his knowledge of basic physics and of simple cause and effect in the ordinary world were almost totally absent. He was unsure of the difference between living things and non-living matter. He would look behind mirrors to try to locate the person he had seen reflected in them. He thought that a rubber ball was alive and was bouncing because it wanted to jump. According to Daumer's reports, Kaspar was highly intelligent and learned fast. Certainly some of Kaspar's surviving drawings show that he was capable of finely detailed and accurate artwork.

he was unharmed but very shaken and upset. He told them that he had been looking out of the window, had leaned over too far, and consequently clutched wildly at the wall as he feared he was going to fall out. In his frantic attempts to get a grip on something to prevent the fall he had inadvertently snatched down the pistol from its support and it had gone off.

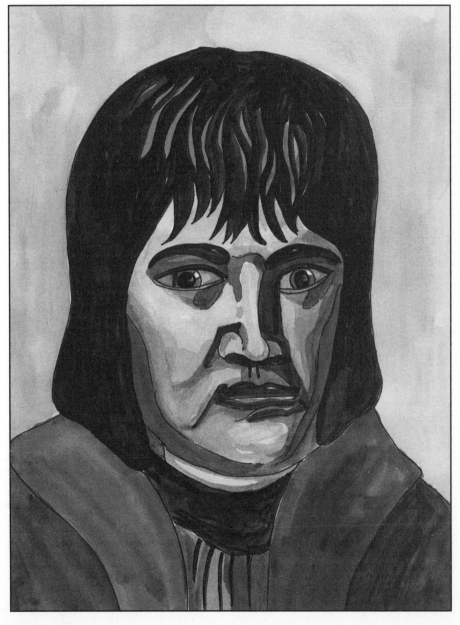

Kaspar Hauser.

However, the question of the continued expense of keeping Kaspar's guards on duty protecting him caused considerable dissension among the Nuremberg taxpayers. Did Kaspar justify what it was costing the city to maintain, guard, and educate him? There was a vociferous minority who felt that it did not. Far from the exciting and romantic theories of his origin spread by his supporters, these detractors suggested that he was either a foreign vagrant, or the discarded offspring of an overly large peasant family. There were also critics who thought that the whole thing was an elaborate hoax, perpetrated by Kaspar himself, to obtain the attention and free board and lodgings that he wanted.

Despite the arguments, Kaspar stayed at the home of his latest guardian, von Feuerbach, until the old man had a stroke and died in May 1833 — one of several people who had been in close contact with Kaspar and died unexpectedly. The circumstances of von Feuerbach's death were not, perhaps, sufficiently strange on their own to invite police investigation, but taken with a string of others, they were significant enough to deserve comment. It was known that — immediately before his death — von Feuerbach was in the process of compiling a detailed legal report on Kaspar, a report that might have contained a number of findings that some people might have wished to suppress.

The rather eccentric English aristocrat Lord Stanhope came on the scene next, took a keen interest in Kaspar, and said that he'd like to adopt him. The Nuremberg Council seemed not to want to lose their star attraction entirely, but they nevertheless negotiated a deal that allowed Stanhope to have temporary care and custody of the young man, provided that his Lordship contributed to the city's coffers to offset part of Kaspar's upkeep.

Stanhope took Kaspar on tour, showing him off to various minor royalty and his other friends among the European aristocracy. The tour was not an unqualified success. Rumours constantly linked Kaspar with the Royal House of Bavaria, and with the Grand Duchess Stephanie de Beauharnais of Baden. The deeply offended Royal Bavarians threatened a lawsuit. Predictably, the unusual Kaspar and the eccentric Stanhope quarrelled periodically, and, later in 1833, by arrangement between Stanhope and the Nurembergers, Kaspar was transferred to Ansbach, forty kilometres away, where he was placed in the care of Dr. Meyer. Just in case there were any further attacks on Kaspar, Stanhope arranged for him to be protected by Captain Hickel, a soldier who was working with the Ansbach police.

Whereas Daumer had been an enthusiastic Hauser supporter who had praised and encouraged him, and commented positively on the young man's intelligence, Meyer and Kaspar did not work harmoniously, and the doctor estimated that Hauser's mental age was no higher than eight or nine.

Things came to a violent and dramatic climax on Saturday December 14, 1833. Kaspar staggered home from the public park known as the *Hofgarten* clutching a wound in his chest and shouting, "Knife ... Man stabbed ... Gave purse ... Look quickly ... Go Hofgarten!"

Mrs. Meyer helped her husband to put Kaspar to bed and then sent for a doctor. When he arrived he confirmed that Kaspar had been stabbed, but did not think that the wound was unduly serious. Captain Hickel, meanwhile, had raced to the Hofgarten in pursuit of Kaspar's attacker. He failed to find him, but he did find the mysterious purse which Kaspar had shouted about. There was a note inside, but it was written in that odd back-to-front style thatVictorian children used to enjoy playing with, and which has to be held up to a mirror in order to read it. It said:

> Hauser can tell you who I am, what I look like and where I come from. To save him the trouble, I shall give you that information myself. I come from ... on the borders of Bavaria, on the River ... My name is M.L.O.

Anxiety was growing steadily about Kaspar's condition. He was failing to show any sign of improvement, and the wound soon proved fatal. He died on December 17. The subsequent post-mortem revealed that the knife had pierced the diaphragm and entered the lower part of his heart. All three medical examiners were certain that the assailant had been left-handed. Two were not sure whether the wound could have been self-inflicted: the third was adamant that it could not have been. Hauser's last words were, "I didn't do it myself."

Before he died, Kaspar had told a strange story about the attack, and told it repeatedly to the cluster of priests, medical men, local government officials, civic dignitaries, military and police officers gathered in his sick room.

In essence, Kaspar claimed that a man had arranged to meet him in the Hofgarten and had promised to reveal the secret of his true identity. When he arrived in the park, a tall man with dark whiskers who was wearing a black cloak came over and asked, "Are you Kaspar Hauser?"

When the young man said that he was, the sinister stranger had handed him a silk purse and then stabbed him. The purse had fallen in the snow, the attacker had disappeared, and Kaspar himself had struggled painfully back to Dr. Meyer's home.

Captain Hickel was doubtful because he had found only one set of prints in the snow — Kaspar's own — at the spot where the purse had been dropped. He and Dr. Meyer urged Hauser to confess and clear his conscience. This he stubbornly refused to do. He reminded those present of the previous attack that had been made on him in the cellar in Nuremberg.

He was buried in Ansbach Cemetery, where his grave marker still stands. It reads: "Here lies the Enigma of our Time — His Birth Unknown, his Death a Mystery."

What is the *truth* about Kaspar Hauser?

18 MYSTERIOUS PEOPLE

Giuseppe Balsamo, otherwise known as the Count of Cagliostro, was born in Palermo, in Sicily, on June 2, 1743. History tends to regard him as a suspected charlatan, a possible magician, and a wildly popular adventurer who was warmly acclaimed by Parisian society in the late eighteenth century. He reportedly died an ignominious prisoner in the Apennine fortress of San Leo on August 26, 1795.

Balsamo's many claims to fame included seances, soothsaying, alchemy, miraculous healing, and the production of aphrodisiacs and elixirs of youth. He also claimed that he knew the elusive Comte de Saint-Germaine, who had initiated him into a Masonic Order. If Cagliostro was telling the truth, for once, his evidence about Saint-Germaine is significant.

Saint-Germaine was variously known as "The Wonderman," and nothing reliable is known of his parents or his real place of origin. One of the wilder speculations about his origins identifies him with Cartaphilus, the Wandering Jew of legend.

In outline, that legend refers to a Jewish collaborator working as a door-keeper for Pontius Pilate and his Roman forces of occupation during the first century A.D. In another version, Cartaphilus is a bystander who spits on Christ as he journeys to Calvary. Either way, the heart of the legend is that Cartaphilus told Christ to hurry on, when he had stopped for a brief rest. Jesus looked steadily at him and said, "I will continue my journey — but you shall tarry in this world until I return."

The legend goes on to suggest that Cartaphilus had no idea what Jesus meant, until he noticed that all his friends and acquaintances were aging and dying, while he himself looked and felt no older than he had done on the day he had spoken so unsympathetically to Christ.

The Cartaphilus legend had become obscured and half-forgotten by the dawn of the thirteenth century, but it was suddenly revived by European travellers who came home with odd stories about their encounters with a curious-looking stranger who confessed to being Cartaphilus. In 1228, when an Armenian bishop visited St. Alban's in England, he claimed to have had a recent meal with Cartaphilus.

There was a surprisingly consistent general pattern to these reported sightings by European travellers: Cartaphilus seemed to be moving steadily westward. Was he the same man who called himself the Count of Saint-Germaine?

He turned up in Vienna in 1740, where contemporaries described him as a powerful and good-looking man, apparently in his thirties. The main talking point was his clothes. When all of fashion-conscious eighteenth-century society was wearing bright, almost gaudy, colours, Saint-Germaine always wore Hamletesque black, with white lace at his neck and cuffs. If his clothes were plain and sombre, his jewels compensated for their drabness. His fingers were encrusted with brilliant diamond rings and his shoe buckles were also decorated with diamonds. In addition, he had yet more diamonds studded all over his fob and snuffbox. If the seemingly more exaggerated versions of his arrival in Vienna are to be believed, he even carried tiny diamonds in his pockets to use instead of money.

During his time in Vienna, he made the acquaintance of Count Lobkowitz and Count Zabor, who were friends of the massively influential French Marshal de Belle Isle. The eminent Frenchman was far from well at the time, but Saint-Germaine used his mysterious powers to heal him. Overwhelmed with gratitude, de Belle Isle took Saint-Germaine to Paris as his protégé and provided him with luxurious living quarters and a lavishly equipped laboratory.

Doing the social rounds in Paris, Saint-Germaine attended a soiree arranged by the elderly Countess von Georgy. In the 1670s her now deceased husband had been an ambassador in Venice. She asked Saint-Germaine if his father had been there then. "No, Madame," he replied gallantly. "It was I, myself, who met you there, and I recall you most vividly as a very beautiful young girl."

"Utterly impossible!" the old countess retorted. "The Count Saint-Germaine whom I met was thirty or forty years old then. He could not possibly still be alive!"

The mysterious Count of St. Germaine.

"Gracious Lady," replied Saint-Germaine with an inscrutable smile, "I must confess that I am very old." He went on to tell her so many details of the Venetian society of the time that he convinced her that he really had been there in the 1670s.

"You're a most extraordinary man, a devil perhaps," she said, aghast. Her mention of the devil apparently had an electrifying effect on Saint-Germaine. According to the story, he began to shake as if he was having a spasm, winced with pain, made his excuses, and hurriedly left the party.

As tales of the count apparently grew with the telling, it was rumoured that he claimed to have met the Holy Family, that he had a particular respect and affection for St. Anne, mother of the Virgin Mary, and that he had been the one who proposed that she should be made a saint during the deliberations of the Council of Nicaea in A.D. 325. Saint-Germaine also claimed to have been a guest at the wedding in Cana of Galilee where Jesus turned the water into wine. But his claims went back farther than the Christian era: he said that he had known King Solomon and had met the Queen of Sheba.

ELIXIR OF LIFE

Saint-Germaine's claims to have the secret of great longevity — the legend-ary Elixir of Life — were substantiated by his valet, who was alleged to have been given it by his grateful master. Challenged by one of Saint-Germaine's guests to say whether or not the count really had known Solomon and Sheba, the valet replied gravely: "I'm afraid I cannot comment, sir. You see, I have been in the count's service only for the past century."

Jeanne Antoinette de Pompadour, mistress of Louis XV, was very impressed by Saint-Germaine, and so was Louis himself. Whether or not Saint-Germaine had any paranormal powers, he was certainly blessed with an above average level of normal human skill and intelligence. In 1760 he was Louis' trusted messenger to Austria.

His fortunes began to decline, however, when he made two powerful and energetic enemies: Casanova and the Duc de Choiseul. Choiseul was Louis's foreign minister at the time, and he managed to persuade the king that Saint-Germaine was betraying him to the English. In consequence, Saint-Germaine had to leave France in a hurry. He went first to England, then to Holland, where he took the title Count Surmont. For a time he appears to have busied himself as an industrialist, setting up factories, labo-ratories, and plants to process pigments and manufacture paints and dyes.

He left Holland as a wealthy man and established himself next in Tournai, where he changed his name again to the Marquis de Monferrat. In 1768 he turned up in Russia, where he came to the attention of Catherine the Great. Assisting his new patron against the Turks, Saint-Germaine employed his diplomatic skills once more, and soon became chief adviser to Count Alexei Orlov, chief of the Russian Imperial Forces. Things went so well for Saint-Germaine in this context that he was pro-moted to a very high position in the Russian army, where he adopted the British style of the time by calling himself General Welldone. At the Battle of Chesne, the Turks were resoundingly defeated, and, his duty in Russia done, Saint-Germaine set off on his travels again.

In 1774 he turned up in Nuremberg. Is there the remotest possibil-ity that he was connected in any way with Kaspar Hauser, the mysterious boy with no history who appeared in Nuremberg without explanation a few years later? Hauser caused some consternation and embarrassment by claiming to recognize the woman in a portrait in the Vienna Art Gallery: it had been painted in 1628. If old Countess Georgy really had seen Saint-Germaine in Venice many years before, was the bewildered Hauser telling the strange but simple truth when he claimed to have known a woman who had been dead for a century?

Saint-Germaine's 1774 visit to Nuremberg took him into the orbit of the Margrave of Brandenburg, Charles Alexander. Saint-Germaine asked the Margrave for funds to establish a laboratory. This time he was using the name Prince Rakoczy. There were three Rakoczy brothers from Transylvania (one-time haunt of the notorious Vlad Dracul, the impaler, the inspiration for Bram Stoker's Count Dracula), but unknown to the worthy Margrave Alexander all three were dead when Saint-Germaine arrived in Nuremberg. Count Orlov paid a visit while Saint-Germaine was there, embraced him warmly, thereby enhancing his status for some time with the unsuspecting Margrave. However, information about the deaths of all three Rakoczys finally reached Alexander. Saint-Germaine admitted his true identity — and prudently left Nuremberg at once.

Saint-Germaine's most powerful enemy in the French court, the Duc de Choiseul, had accused him of being a double-agent, working for Frederick the Great as well as the British, but when Saint-Germaine begged Frederick for help, his appeal went unanswered. Choiseul may have been wrong, of course, or Frederick may have employed Saint-Germaine on an "if-anything-goes-wrong-I've-never-heard-of-you" contract — said to be a popular device with politically astute potentates in turbulent times.

There is some evidence that Saint-Germaine's next stop was Leipzig, where he told Frederick Augustus, Prince of Brunswick, that he was a

---

DID SAINT-GERMAINE KILL KASPAR HAUSER?

If there was a connection between Hauser and Saint-Germaine's earlier visit to Nuremberg, might Saint-Germaine also have been the mysterious stranger who killed Hauser in the Hofgarten in Ansbach, because the boy knew too much — that same mysterious assassin who left no traces in the snow?

OLD SECRETS?

Frederick refused to recognize Saint-Germaine as a genuine Mason. The secret signs that Saint-Germaine used were not those used by the Prussian lodges which Frederick supervised. But was Frederick correct in his rejection? Is it possible that Saint-Germaine had learnt his ritual long before Frederick? Was it Freemasonry of an older and altogether more arcane type that Saint-Germaine had learned, something that had been largely lost and forgotten before the relatively new European lodges were founded in the eighteenth century, and presided over by aristocrats of Frederick's generation?

high-ranking Freemason, which links closely with Cagliostro's evidence. Frederick himself was the Prussian Grand Master, and Saint-Germaine may not have been aware of this when he made his claims.

The records of Saint-Germaine become cloudier over the next few years. He was cared for by the generous Prince Charles of Hesse-Cassel, and some of those who believe in Saint-Germaine's paranormal powers may have suspected a conspiracy between him and his patron to allow Saint-Germaine to assume a new identity. Many espionage stories use the device of a supposed death to enable an agent to take on a whole new character. Is that what Saint-Germaine and Charles did? According to the parish records and the stone that Charles erected for Saint-Germaine, the count died at Charles's castle on February 27, 1784. His monument reads: "The man who was known as the Comte de Saint-Germaine and as Welldone, and of whom nothing else is known, lies buried in this church."

The inscription is remarkably similar to the one raised for Kaspar Hauser half a century later. Whatever may have happened in the prince's castle, or whatever may lie buried in Saint-Germaine's coffin in the church at Eckenforde, the mystery did not die in 1784. For some reason only he knows — or perhaps with Saint-Germaine's connivance — Prince Charles burnt all the count's papers in 1784, giving his reason as "lest they be misinterpreted."

Baron Friedrich Melchior Grimm, the author (1723–1807), described Saint-Germaine as the most able man he had ever met. Horace Walpole wrote of him when he was in London in 1743: "He is called an Italian, a Spaniard, a Pole, a somebody who married a great fortune in Mexico and ran away with her jewels to Constantinople, a priest, a fiddler, a vast nobleman."

While in England in the 1740s, Saint-Germaine was arrested as a Jacobite spy, but released shortly afterward.

Stories of the count's appearances well into the nineteenth century and beyond fascinated Napoleon III, who organized a special inquiry team to investigate Saint-Germaine. Their report was destroyed by a mysterious fire at the Hotel de Ville in Paris in 1871. Those who believed that the count was still alive and as powerful as ever maintained that the fire had not been accidental, and that there were secrets in the report that he wished to conceal.

Just as there is a faintly possible link between Saint-Germaine and Kaspar Hauser of Nuremberg, so there is a far stronger link between Saint-Germaine and the mysterious treasure of Rennes-le-Château.

Bérenger Saunière, the enigmatic priest of Rennes-le-Château, became suddenly and unaccountably rich toward the end of the nineteenth century — not too many years after Napoleon III's report on Saint-Germaine vanished in the fire. Father Saunière seems to have spent money like water between acquiring his mysterious wealth in 1885 and his death in 1917. There are many and varied accounts of his life, and numerous theories abound as to the source of his wealth. Some of the wilder suppositions suggest that he acquired the secret of alchemical transmutation from somewhere, or that he possessed some other arcane method of *creating* wealth. There was talk of black magic, grave robbing, and murder. Some researchers believe that Saunière found an ancient Templar treasure, or even a Visigothic one, hidden below his ancient church.

EMMA CALVÉ

According to some chroniclers, the most intriguing part of Saunierè's story is that he had an illicit relationship with Emma Calvé, the famous French opera star, who was also reported to be involved in the magic and mystery that intrigued Parisian society at the time. There is an 1897 photograph in existence that Emma autographed to "The Count of St. Germaine, the Great Chiromancer who has told me many truths."

Another curious mystery attributed to Saint-Germaine after his supposed death was his appearance in Paris shortly before the French Revolution, where he warned Marie Antoinette of the danger to come. According to some accounts, she recorded in her diaries that she deeply regretted her failure to heed his warnings.

The count apparently turned up again in Sweden in 1789, where he tried to warn King Gustavus III of impending trouble. Saint-Germaine also told his friend, Madame d'Adhemar, that he would see her on five more occasions. She also noted that he seemed always to be in his mid-forties. According to her account, these five meetings took place as he had prophesied, and she was always totally surprised by them. The last of them was in 1820 on the night before the Duc de Berri was murdered.

In the 1970s a French alchemist named Richard Chanfray gave a demonstration on television during which he appeared to be able to turn lead into gold. Chanfray also claimed that he was the Count of Saint-Germaine.

Our good friend, Elisabeth van Buren, who has been a student of the Rennes-le-Château mystery and has lived in the vicinity of Rennes for many years, is convinced that Saint-Germaine is still very much alive and actively engaged in occultism and mysticism today. She believes that she has actually received messages from him.

The Count of Saint-Germaine may be no more than a relatively recent and singularly vivid example of the undying hero myth, a variant on the sleeper in the cave legends. But there are enough intriguing shreds of evidence and mysterious clues to suggest that he might just be more than that. If people such as him, with strange, time-defying powers, and other paranormal abilities, people such as the so-called gods of the ancient Greek, Roman, and Egyptian pantheons, are *more* than myth and legend, where did they come from originally, and what is their purpose here today? Could they be extraterrestrial aliens? Or survivors of an ancient and powerful quasi-human race that once occupied Atlantis, Lemuria, or the mysterious continent of Antarctica beneath its mile-thick shield of ice?

One of the strangest terrors of Victorian Britain, and especially Victorian London, was the amazing character known as Spring-Heeled Jack. Although there had been a few odd reports of a strange jumping man as early as 1817, it was not until September of 1837 that Jack made his first recorded appearances. Victoria had been queen for only a few months when Jack leaped over a cemetery wall near Barnes Common and frightened a businessman who was walking home after working late.

Very soon afterward, the same sinister leaping creature attacked a young London girl, Polly Adams, as she was coming home from Blackheath Fair. He tore the top of her dress away with hands, which she described as being more like iron claws. Three other victims of similar attacks all verified Polly's description of him: very tall and thin — but far stronger than such a lightly built man would have been expected to be. She also gave an account of a separate episode that had taken place a little earlier in which a man with bulging eyes had accosted her. Apart from commenting on those prominent eyes, the other witnesses said that Jack had pointed ears — and this was a century and a half before anyone saw Mr. Spock onboard the starship *Enterprise*. Spring-Heeled Jack's bulging, glowing eyes terrified the girls, who had probably filled their minds with images of medieval demons by this time. They all reported that he spat blue and white flames. Victims of some later attacks were blinded by them.

Spring-Heeled Jack.

Another young female victim was Mary Stevens, a servant who had been visiting her parents in Battersea and was walking back to her employer's home in Lavender Hill. At the entrance to the aptly named Cut Throat Lane, Mary was seized by a tall, thin attacker who threw his long arms around her and held her in a vice-like grip. Her screams and struggles attracted help. The mysterious attacker laughed demonically as it bounded away. A similar, sudden wild appearance by this grotesque jumping oddity a few days later terrified a pair of coach horses, which bolted, causing an accident in which the coachman was severely injured.

One of the most useful pieces of evidence Jack left was strangely deep footprints in soft, damp soil when he attacked a woman near Clapham Churchyard. It was suggested by a number of those who examined the marks that Jack had possibly fixed mechanical jumping devices to his shoes.

There was undoubtedly an imaginative streak in the Victorian public to which the character of Spring-Heeled Jack made a strong appeal. Several stories about him were featured in the popular Victorian "Penny Dreadfuls," and this no doubt added fuel to the speculative flames. Rumours, myths, and urban legends about Jack varied widely. He had been seen as a white bull in one area, a huge polar bear in another, and a gigantic baboon in a third. He was also said to have worn brightly polished brazen armour during one attack, and burnished steel armour during a different episode. One of his homelier pranks was to disguise himself as a London lamplighter and walk through the darkening streets on his hands, carrying his ladder on his long, wiry legs.

On one occasion, a victim who escaped from Jack's clutches without anything much worse than a fright said that she had seen the letter *W* emblazoned on the costume below his cloak. An elaborate crest and coat of arms were embroidered above it. Henry de la Poer Beresford, the Marquis of Waterford, had been an outstanding oarsman and boxer at Eton and Oxford. He had the kind of physique and coordination that would have enabled him to carry out at least some of Spring-Heeled Jack's minor feats.

It is also possible that his boxing career left him slightly brain-damaged, which could, perhaps, have accounted for some of his more eccentric behaviour. Beresford and some of his equally wild friends were notorious for throwing eggs at people as their coach galloped past, and in 1837 he literally painted not only a town, but one of its night-watchmen red as well! On another occasion he suggested to a railway company that they could arrange for two trains to crash head-on at his expense so that he could witness it. He was callous enough to evict thirty of his tenants on one occasion without providing either a valid reason or fair notice.

Physically and mentally, Waterford's character seems to fit in with Spring-Heeled Jack's performances as they were generally reported. Did the *W* on the tunic stand for Waterford? The problem with this theory, however, is that Waterford died following a riding accident in 1859, and Spring-Heeled Jack was still creating havoc until at least 1904.

Is there any possible connection between the Victorian sightings of the Spring-Heeled Jack phenomena and the reports of Owlmen and Mothmen that come mainly from the Canadian and American side of the Atlantic? Reported sightings of such beings abound.

A motorist travelling from Point Pleasant toward the Chief Cornstalk Hunting Grounds in West Virginia along Highway 2 suddenly spotted a very large humanoid figure blocking the road ahead of her. Its wings were so vast that the whole thing resembled a small aircraft, and it took off vertically just ahead of the car. In November 1966 it was seen again in the Point Pleasant area, this time by two couples, Mary and Steve Mallette and Linda and Roger Scarberry. Two strange red eyes, like those attributed to Spring-Heeled Jack in London more than a century earlier, were peering out at them from a derelict industrial area. The Mallettes and Scarberrys saw a grey, slow-moving humanoid creature more than seven feet tall, with large wings folded behind its back. They accelerated hard to get away from the thing, but it seemed able to fly alongside them without flapping its wings, even though they were travelling at 160 kilometres per hour.

SOME WILD THEORIES

Some of the wilder theories far surpassed pointing the finger of suspicion at young Waterford. Jack was alleged — among other things — to be a mentally ill circus acrobat, a fire-eater from a sideshow, even a kangaroo that had been trained and dressed up by a zookeeper with a bizarre sense of humour. To speculative thinkers of our own day, rather than those of the Victorian epoch, Jack seems more like an extraterrestrial than a kangaroo in fancy dress.

THE BIG BOOK OF MYSTERIES

In 1976, two teenaged girls saw something remarkably similar in the woods near Mawnan Old Church, in Cornwall, England — a creature that was later researched by leading cryptozoologist Jonathan Downes and recorded in detail in his excellent book *The Owlman and Others.*

Returning to the earlier British Spring-Heeled Jack exploits, by 1838 things had become sufficiently serious for the then Lord Mayor of London, Sir John Cowan, to declare Jack an official public menace. Vigilance committees were established to try to catch him, but none were successful.

On February 20, 1838, eighteen-year-old Jane Alsop was at home in her father's house in Bearhind Lane in Bow. Fortunately for Jane, her two sisters were there with her. She answered the door in response to loud, urgent knocking. A voice from the wintry darkness outside shouted excitedly: "Bring a light quickly. We've caught Spring-Heeled Jack." Jane ran to fetch a candle. As she stepped outside unsuspectingly with it cupped in her hands, the mysterious visitor grabbed her: it *was* Jack. The tough little East End teenager put up a superb fight and broke away from her mysterious attacker.

Her desperate screams brought one of her sisters racing to help. She got Jane away from the strange creature, pulled her inside, and slammed the door against their attacker. From the relative safety of an upstair window, the Alsop girls shouted for the police, founded by Sir Robert Peel's Metropolitan Police Act only nine years earlier. Spring-Heeled Jack was glimpsed by his pursuers as he bounded away through the February gloom of what were then open fields at the back of Bearhind Lane. He dropped his cloak as he ran, but someone retrieved it and escaped with it before the police could examine it. Was it possible that Jack had an accomplice? Was there, perhaps, a Spring-Heeled Jill?

Press reports on February 22 contained detailed descriptions given by the Alsop girls and other witnesses. Jack had been wearing a helmet together with a long cloak over a costume that resembled shiny, white oilskin. Another possibility was that Jack was not human at all but an extraterrestrial alien, or an unknown animal possessing shiny white skin like an amphibian or reptile. The press descriptions also referred to his blazing red eyes and his ability to spit dangerous blue and white flames.

Taking all the persistent reports together, there can be little doubt that Spring-Heeled Jack really existed, and that there was something abnormal and dangerous about him. His exceptional strength and speed and his ability to bound away effortlessly over high walls made him very difficult to capture.

In most of the early attacks reported between 1837 and the 1850s, Spring-Heeled Jack seems to have been satisfied with terrifying his victims, tearing off their clothes, and inflicting painful scratches with his cold, claw-like metallic hands — if, indeed, they *were* hands. No researcher has ever been able to decide exactly what sort of man, machine, alien, cyborg, or phenomenalist entity Spring-Heeled Jack really was.

As the years passed, however, the attacks grew more vicious, and the injuries Jack inflicted more severe — in some cases, permanent. Lucy Scales was a victim of one of these disabling attacks. Her father was a butcher in Limehouse. Lucy had been out to visit her brother, and was returning home through Green Dragon Alley when Spring-Heeled Jack appeared. He wore the same long cloak and tight-fitting, shiny white oilskin outfit that earlier witnesses had described. The blue and white fire which he spat into Lucy's face blinded the girl.

That was serious enough, but his next recorded attack, which took place in 1845, proved fatal for the victim. It happened in broad daylight in the Jacob's Island district of Bermondsey. Young Maria Davis was one of the sad little teenaged prostitutes who plied their trade in the area. Eyewitnesses described how Spring-Heeled Jack bounded at the girl as she was crossing a narrow wooden bridge. He seized her by the shoulders, breathed his vicious blue and white fire into her terrified face, and then flung her down into Folly Ditch — a deep, open sewer that oozed foully below the bridge. Maria drowned in it before passersby could get her out.

During the middle of the nineteenth century, Jack was reported to have been seen all over the place — but chiefly in the Midlands. In the 1870s he even attacked some military establishments, where tough veteran sentries were as startled by him as the girls he'd attacked in the London area. Some soldiers reported being slapped in the face by "a man with an icy hand — like the hand of a corpse." That compares interestingly with the descriptions of earlier victims whose clothes were torn off by "hands that felt like iron claws."

In Caistor, on the Norfolk coast, during the late 1870s, almost everyone in the village came out to watch Jack leaping from one cottage roof to another. This time the eyewitnesses commented on his large ears, and said that his costume was more like sheepskin than his normal shiny white oilskin.

BULLETPROOF?

At North Camp, part of the famous old military installation at Aldershot, Jack approached a sentry, ignored the formal challenge and leaped clean over the sentry box. The soldier did his duty and fired, reporting later that he was certain Jack had been hit. Hit or not, the strange creature bounded on its way as if nothing had happened. Jack had also been fired at by angry citizens in Lincoln, but their bullets and buckshot had had no apparent effect on him either, he merely leaped on his eccentric way through their historic city streets.

Ten years later he was observed in Cheshire — more than 480 kilometres away in the west of England. On this occasion, Spring-Heeled Jack leaped into a room where a girl sat playing the piano. He didn't touch her, but contented himself with sweeping all the ornaments from a shelf. Then he bounded away before anyone in the house had fully realized what was happening.

His last recorded British appearance was in Everton, in William Henry Street, in September of 1904. On September 25, *The News of the World* printed a story about this Everton appearance, reporting that Jack had amazed witnesses by jumping as far as seven metres. On this occasion, as with the pianist in Cheshire, Jack harmed no one, but seemed content to entertain the crowd with his phenomenal athletic powers. He ended the show by bounding clean over a house and disappearing. Although that was the last recorded sighting of Jack in England, something very much like him was reported in the United States.

One blistering hot June night in Texas during the summer of 1953, three Houston friends were sitting outside their apartment building in a vain attempt to get some relief from the intense heat. They reported seeing a huge shadow passing across the lawn in front them, then, in their words, it "seemed to bounce up into a pecan tree." The dim, greyish light revealed a strange shape in the tree, and it seemed to them to be a very tall, thin man wearing tight-fitting clothes under a large cape. Rather than bounding away, as Spring-Heeled Jack had done in most of his previous dramatic exits, the mysterious figure in the pecan tree seemed to gradually fade away. From the other side of the street, the Houston witnesses heard a weird swooshing sound and thought that they could see a rocket taking off from that vicinity. The investigating police officers to whom the witnesses reported this strange episode were of the opinion that their evidence had been given in good faith and that the witnesses were honest, well-intentioned, and genuinely frightened by whatever they thought they had witnessed.

As with most reported sightings of unexplained phenomena, there are numerous rational and logical explanations for Spring-Heeled Jack. In the Aldershot sentry episode, there is always the possibility that the sentry in question had been engaged previously in military training manoeuvres that had necessitated using blank rounds during the exercises. If his rifle still contained blanks when Spring-Heeled Jack leaped over his sentry box, that would account for the ineffectiveness of the shots that he reportedly fired at Jack at close range.

The episode in William Henry Street in 1904 was reported in the *Liverpool Echo*, which also mentioned a man in the area who suffered from some form of religious mania. He had accused his wife of being possessed by a demon, and was said to have leaped from rooftop to rooftop to escape from the police and fire brigade. Were the two stories compounded in some way, or did some of the superstitious residents of William Henry Street think they were watching the infamous Spring-Heeled Jack, when they were, in fact, watching the antics of a mentally ill neighbour?

There is compelling evidence on both sides of the argument: Jack could have been a series of errors of observation made in good faith, a cruel hoax begun by Waterford and improbably prolonged by a string of impersonators, an extraterrestrial cyborg or alien, or, just possibly, a very remarkable freak of nature — the springiest branch on Darwin's evolutionary tree.

Nikola Tesla was born on July 9, 1856, in Smiljan, in a part of the old Austro-Hungarian Empire that later became part of Yugoslavia. Nikola was the second son of Reverend Milutin Tesla and his brilliantly gifted wife, Djouka.

Milutin was a poet and philosopher as well as a priest. He was a deeply sensitive man who was easily offended and tended to bear grudges when that happened. His first profession before turning to the church was as an army officer, but the toughness of military life did not fit well with his sensitive character and he resigned his commission after only a short period of service. Milutin was as keenly interested in politics, economics, and social justice as he was in theology and religious history, and his sermons often had social or commercial themes.

Nikola Tesla.

Nikola's strange electrical engineering inventive genius seems more likely to have come down to him through Djouka's genes than through Milutin's. His mother had an exceptional, almost totally definitive memory. Amazingly, despite her brilliance and inventiveness, she was illiterate: perhaps her incredibly efficient powers of recall made literacy superfluous. She could recite all the old sagas, together with entire books of the Bible. She created many labour-saving household gadgets, including her own loom. Her weaving and needlework were legendary, and she could tie three knots in an eyelash using nothing but her hands until well into her sixties.

Djouka's phenomenal mind powers, inventiveness, and dexterity were clearly evident in her second son. Her first son, Dane, had them as well, but he died in a tragic accident when he was only twelve. The innate love of experimentation and discovery almost killed Nikola, as well. As a child he was very interested in birds, and especially in the mechanics of flight, and of air and wind resistance. Taking a large umbrella in both hands, young Tesla leaped from the roof of a barn, landing with a bone-jarring crash: he spent the next six weeks recovering.

One day, in the town of Gospic, Nikola was one of a large, happy crowd celebrating the inauguration of the new Gospic and district fire brigade and the first public demonstration of all their new technical equipment, which consisted of the latest pumps, reels, and hoses.

Music played. Speeches were made. Brawny firemen heaved away at the pumps — but nothing came out of the hose. Young Nikola shouted, "Please keep pumping," and raced down to the river, where he found that there was a kink in the hose. Heaving and straining at the heavy tubing, the lad finally managed to straighten it out: water gushed and spurted from the other end to the delight of the sweating firemen and the onlookers. In consequence, the ingenious young scientist became one of the heroes of Gospic.

At school, young Nikola's mathematical ability was phenomenal. He seems to have had the same powers as Trachtenberg — the brilliant mental mathematician who used his ability to calculate as a psychological escape from the horrors of a Nazi concentration camp, and who later founded the Trachtenberg Institute.

Tesla described the process by which he reached the answers to math problems as something that just unfolded by itself without any conscious effort on his part, other than reading and understanding the nature of the problems. He actually *saw* the answers, which seemed somehow to have sprung from his subconscious, and for him they had the same clarity, solidity, and definition as printing in the textbook or his math teacher's writing on the blackboard. Tesla's strange ability to create these visible forms and symbols — so real that he could walk round them and view them from other angles — was to play a vital part in his future career as an outstanding inventor in the field of electrical engineering.

In Edgar Allan Poe's "Fall of the House of Usher" there is a vivid description of the hypersensitivity and hyperacuity suffered by one of the major characters. The slightest noise sounds like an explosion to him; the lightest touch feels like an agonizing blow delivered by a heavyweight boxer. When Tesla was working in Budapest for the Central Telegraph Office, he was taken ill because of over-exertion and long hours without sleep. He suffered exactly the same symptoms as the Poe character. Tesla complained that he could hear a watch ticking loudly in a distant room, well away from where he was lying in bed. A friend or nurse speaking quietly sounded like thunder to him. Traffic in the street outside his home vibrated him so violently and painfully that rubber pads were placed beneath his bed: it was almost like the fairy tale of the real princess who could feel one hard, dried pea underneath six mattresses. Direct sunlight through the bedroom windows hurt his eyes, but in the dark he could locate objects on the far side of the room.

Another example of Tesla's strange mental powers was provided in Budapest in 1882 as he walked through the city with his friend Szigeti. Tesla seems to have switched into that special alternate reality mode for which he later became so famous. He saw a vision — for want of a better word — that showed him clearly how the alternating current electric motor could be constructed and made to function. Szigeti had to lead his excited friend out of the way of the city traffic.

Disappointed because he couldn't persuade European manufacturers to take up his new ideas for an alternating current motor, Tesla went to the United States in 1884, where he joined Thomas Edison for a brief period. The two brilliant inventors were poles apart in terms of personality, and a serious quarrel between them was inevitable. When it came, Tesla left Edison and set up on his own. Much of his laboratory work was aimed at demonstrating the superiority of alternating current.

One of the inventions for which he is best remembered is the Tesla coil, still frequently used in television and radio circuitry today. Tesla patented it in 1891. Basically, it consists of a central cylindrical core of soft iron, with an induction coil around it. There is an inner, primary

ALTERNATE REALITY

In H.G.Wells's short story "The Strange Case of Davidson's Eyes" a man has lost the ability to see what's close to him in his normal environment, but is watching a strange scene on an island on the other side of the world. As he ascends or descends slopes in Britain, so his strange visions of the unknown island ascend and descend as well, as though he was watching the scenes through a remote television camera. When Tesla went into his alternate reality, it was very similar to Davidson's unnerving experiences in Wells's story.

coil of just a few turns of copper wire, and an outer, secondary coil of many turns. Current in the primary coil is automatically stopped and started again by an interrupter. The current produced magnetizes the soft iron core and sets up a wide magnetic field in the induction coil. One of Tesla's many experiments with this coil provided the ancestor of the modern fluorescent tube.

Tesla worked with the Westinghouse Company for a while, where his motors were developed and used extensively in mining, printing, and ventilation.

A magazine interview in August 1894 included an interesting physical description of Tesla, who was typical of the tall, slim, hyper-energetic, brilliantly intellectual, ectomorphic body-type like Sherlock Holmes. The interviewer described Tesla as "very thin ... more than six feet tall ... less than 140 pounds.... He has very big hands.... His thumbs are remarkably big even for such big hands." The journalist went on to argue, somewhat quaintly, that big thumbs were a sign of extra high intelligence because apes had relatively small thumbs. His description of Tesla's head is particularly interesting. The eyes were deep-set and lighter than the interviewer had expected. He described Tesla's head as "spreading out at the top like a fan ... shaped like a wedge."

The miniature mummified humanoid body that we examined and photographed in the White's City Museum in New Mexico had a similar-shaped head, as did the aliens who were alleged to have crashed at Roswell — not far from White's City — in 1947.

Unlike his friend and contemporary, Marconi, the distinguished radio pioneer, Tesla was not interested solely in transmitting radio waves. His great interest was in finding ways to transmit huge amounts of electrical power. In 1899, using a huge coil generating millions of volts, he managed to pump millions of watts into the air before the generator burnt out. This amazing achievement took place in Colorado Springs. A copper ball about a metre in diameter was mounted at the top of a sixty-metre tower. Below this, Tesla had erected a square building, which contained two enormous coils — a primary and a secondary. His theory was that a resonating electrical and radio system would be created so that it would go on reinforcing itself and drawing current from the Earth.

Resonance can destroy a bridge, or keep a child's garden swing going, provided that the auxiliary push is applied in exactly the right place, at exactly the right time. In the briefest possible outline, the heart of Tesla's brilliant theory was that high-frequency radio waves would travel across the world and then return. Provided he had tuned them correctly to the natural frequency of the oscillation of the Earth's own electrical currents, he reckoned that they would reinforce the voltage pushes in his sixty-metre mast, and so increase the current being drawn from the Earth.

It worked only too well. Lightning bolts more than forty metres long crackled out of the copper ball atop Tesla's tower. It was undeniably spectacular. Then, just as suddenly as it had begun, the vast electrical firework display stopped. Tesla checked with his assistant, Czito, to discover what had gone wrong. They soon found out: the Colorado Springs' Generating Company's generator was burnt out. There was simply no more power available for activating Tesla's great tower, coil, and copper ball experiment. It was fortunate that Tesla had designed the Colorado Springs generator, and he had it up and running in a matter of days.

One of the greatest mysteries associated with Tesla and his globally effective electrical experiments concerns the great Siberian explosion that rocked Tunguska like a twenty megaton nuclear bomb on June 30, 1908. Some researchers accept that it was a meteorite — albeit an unusual one. Others suggest that a nuclear-powered alien spacecraft crashed there and exploded. A third theory concerns Nikola Tesla.

In 1935, Tesla, commenting on a mysterious secret electrical weapon that he had designed, said, "it will destroy anything, men or machines, approaching within a radius of two hundred miles." What had he invented? Would it really work in practice? There can be no doubt that

TUNGUSKA FACTS

- Energy generated by the blast was estimated at from ten to fifteen megatons, approximately one thousand times as powerful as the atomic bomb dropped on Hiroshima, Japan.

- The explosion knocked over approximately eighty thousand trees in a radius of forty kilometres from the blast site — an area measuring more than 2,150 square kilometres.

- Over the next few weeks, night skies over Europe and western Russia glowed brightly enough for people to read by.

- The blast remains the largest impact event over land in Earth's recent history.

his great electrical machine at Colorado Springs worked awesomely well. Is it remotely possible that Tesla, fascinated by the idea of transmitting vast amounts of power over huge distances, had caused the enormous Tunguska explosion of 1908 during some of his earlier experiments?

Tesla described the basic principles of a prototype laser, which would also have been applicable to a particle gun, as far back as 1900. Such beams consist essentially of wave energy in bundles or packets that are produced at precisely their own inherent frequency. This gives rise to a coherent emission, more or less equivalent to Tesla's ideas about standing waves in the paper he published at the turn of the century.

There were some serious speculations in the London *Evening Standard* in the 1970s referring to severe electrical storms over Canada, indirectly involving Tesla's last surviving assistant, Arthur Matthews, who, it was said, had been interviewed about Tesla's work by a mysterious Russian electrical engineer. The *Evening Standard* later reported that Major General George

Keegan, one-time chief of United States Airforce Intelligence, suspected that the Russians might have developed a particle gun that would have been able to destroy intercontinental ballistic missiles. Were experiments with that device based on Matthews's recollections of Tesla's work, and could experiments from inside the former U.S.S.R. have caused the severe electrical storms over Canada?

DID TESLA EXPERIMENTS AFFECT THE WEATHER?

Andrew Michrowski, one of the top scientists working in eastern Canada in the 1970s, was convinced that Russian experiments with Tesla's original ideas had produced traumatic meteorological effects. Watson Scott, who was then working in Ottawa with the Canadian Department of Communications, made several interesting suggestions. He wondered whether whatever the Russians might be doing with a Tesla-type particle beam had been responsible for the abnormal drought that plagued the British Isles in 1976, the surprisingly warm weather in Greenland, and the rare snowfalls in Miami.

Kit Pedler, writing in Colin Wilson's superb collection *Men of Mystery*, describes his interesting theory of an alternative framework of science, one in which the individual scientist is part of an integrated system in which he or she has a vital creative or formative role. This is remarkably close to the so-called "magical" theories put forward by Paracelsus and Crowley's Thelema school of thought. To what extent is the observer and measurer of phenomena an essential part of the phenomena themselves? Did Tesla create a purely internal type of alternative mental reality that was entirely his own, one that, although useful to him as an inventor and experimenter, had no tangible existence outside of his head? Or was there much more to it than that? Did he not so much invent something as get in touch with something that had an independent existence of its own? Just what are thought-forms, or *tulpas*, of the kind that Alex David-Néel believed she had made? Is there some alternative explanation perhaps? Can powerful thinkers like Paracelsus, Crowley, David-Néel, and Tesla create something inside their minds that then in some mysterious way goes on to acquire an objective, external existence?

St. Paul's letters strongly advised his readers in the early Church to think about things that were pure, good, and lovely. Was he hinting at the possibility that thoughts can acquire an objective reality and in that form can work more good or evil than the thinker dreams possible?

Tesla's inventions are far too numerous to list. Some were practical, readily applicable, and almost mundane. Others were much more advanced than the science fiction of Tesla's day. He patented an electric arc lamp, a commutator for dynamos, various electro-magnetic motors, electrical distribution systems and regulators, generators and alternators, control mechanisms for moving vessels or vehicles, a tele-automaton boat, a VTOL aircraft, and a machine that he believed could photograph thoughts. He also believed that he was receiving messages from intelligent beings on other planets — perhaps he was.

He also seems to have possessed some of the prophetic abilities of Mother Shipton, Nostradamus, and Coinneach Odhar, the Brahan seer. At one of his parties, for example, Tesla was almost obsessively determined that several of his friends should stay the night — the same guests who would otherwise have been travelling on a train that crashed later that night.

Other fascinating possibilities connect both Tesla and Einstein with the highly controversial Philadelphia Experiment, in which a ship and its crew were alleged to have travelled through the fourth dimension.

It was also rumoured that the FBI and CIA took a keen interest in the many scientific papers that were left in Tesla's home after he died. Were those officers, perhaps, looking for details of the formidable weaponry that Tesla claimed he could produce?

Surely, the great Nikola Tesla deserves a far more distinguished place in the hall of fame than history has granted him. His brilliant, innovative theories and inventions deserve further serious scientific investigation today: there is much conceptual gold still left in Tesla's deep intellectual mine.

If his alternate reality was not just a unique personal possession, a creation of his magnificent but eccentric mind, if, rather, it was reached via a *doorway* that he discovered and used, there is no reason why others cannot locate and use that doorway, too.

19 GLAMIS: THE CASTLE OF LEGENDS

Ever since King Robert II of Scotland (1316–90) gave Glamis to his son-in-law, Sir John Lyon, in 1372, the castle has remained with the family. They hold the title of Earls of Strathmore and Kinghorne. Their massive, picturesque castle stands in the vale of Strathmore in Tayside, Scotland, ringed by the villages of Jericho, Padanaram, and Zoar: all three names are biblical in origin, and this may hold historical and geographical clues to the mystery of Glamis itself.

The collapse of the walls of Jericho, when Joshua and the Israelites attacked the city, is often used as a symbol of the triumph of religious forces over their enemies. Padanaram was also highly significant in the story of Jacob, the Hebrew Patriarch, who went there to find a non-Canaanite wife from the family of Laban, his uncle. Zoar is featured in the biblical accounts of Lot's adventures when Sodom and Gomorrah were destroyed, and his wife was transformed into a pillar of salt (Genesis 19). All three locations are associated in different ways with conflicts: Joshua versus the Canaanites; Lot versus the men of Sodom and Gomorrah; and the fraternal quarrel between Jacob and Esau. Was it at the back of the minds of the pioneer inhabitants who named their Strathmore villages that there were strange psychic forces of good and evil in conflict in the vicinity of Glamis?

One of the first tragedies that occurred at Glamis was the murder of King Malcolm II (1005–34), who was butchered by rebels wielding claymores. As a result of his appalling injuries, almost all of his blood seeped out around his body, and the stain was said to have remained indelibly on the floor of the room in Glamis where he died. As the assassins retreated across a frozen loch, the ice broke and they all drowned.

Prior to 1372, the Lyon family had lived at Forteviot, where they were said to be the custodians of a very beautiful and ancient sacred chalice. This chalice, according to legend, was said to bring peace, safety, and good fortune to the Lyon family, provided that it was never moved. After being given Glamis, however, Sir John took the ancient Forteviot chalice with him. Whatever negative influences were supposed to follow the removal of the chalice, Sir John seems to have prospered and lived happily at Glamis for the next ten or eleven years. He died as the result of a duel in 1383.

Another of the great Glamis tragedies occurred in 1537, when the beautiful young Janet Douglas was burned at the stake in Edinburgh on charges of witchcraft and trying to murder King James V (1512–42). Her husband, who had been the sixth Lord of Glamis, had an unpleasant reputation, and nobody was surprised when he was found dead. Because he had been eating alone immediately prior to his death, Janet was accused of poisoning him. The trial collapsed through lack of evidence, but because she was a Douglas, James V detested her with a hatred that was less rational than the Shakespearean feud between the Capulets and the Montagues — but its outcome was even more tragic. Lady Janet was falsely accused and condemned on evidence extorted by torture.

Glamis Castle.

It is said that the spectral vision of the Grey Lady reported at Glamis on many occasions by reliable witnesses is the ghost of the brutally wronged and abused Lady Janet. She has appeared both in the chapel and above the clock tower.

Another horrific spectre appealing for sympathy and justice is the apparition of a woman with a mutilated face who is apparently tongueless. Little or nothing definite is known about her, but it is conjectured that she may be the ghost of an unfortunate servant who discovered the secret of Glamis, traditionally known only to the reigning earl and his chief steward. Rather than kill the woman, her tongue was cut out so that she could never tell what she had seen inside the forbidden chamber. She is occasionally glimpsed looking out from a barred window, but has also been reported moving about on the grounds.

The sad little apparition of a young black servant boy has also been reported at Glamis. It is thought that he was on the staff in the eighteenth century, when it was considered "fashionable" in some quarters to have Afro-Caribbean servants. According to the accounts of his appearances, he looks very unhappy, and is said to sit silently near the door of the royal bedroom.

A ghost named Beardie is a distinct contrast from that of the unhappy servant boy. He is said to be either one of the earls or an associate who was staying at Glamis as the earl's guest — versions of the legend differ slightly. In any event, a game of cards was in progress when a servant announced respectfully that it was almost midnight, and that as it would soon be the Sabbath, it would be wise for the game to end. Beardie shouted profane abuse and swore that he would rather play with the devil than abandon his game. The devil duly appeared, and accepted Beardie's offer of a game — with the gambler's soul as the inevitable stake. Needless to say, Beardie lost, and has been thumping, banging, and crashing his way around Glamis ever since. Another noise emanating from the region of the gambling ghost is the rattle of dice.

Glamis also has an emaciated, almost skeletal ghost who was, in life, locked in a dungeon and left to starve to death. This tale of a victim starved in a dungeon may be related to the tragedy of a group of Ogilvies who reportedly fled to Glamis seeking protection from their traditional enemies, the Lindsays. The then Lord of Glamis took them to a deep hiding place below the castle, secured the doors, and left them there to die.

The main legend of Glamis, however, concerns the occupant of a secret room. One relatively recent version of this secret room saga is that it dates back only as far as 1821, when the first son of the eleventh earl was said to have been born suffering from major deformities. According to this story, it was announced that the boy had died — when in reality he was concealed in a mysterious secret chamber deep within the castle. When another son arrived, his father kept the secret of the hidden elder brother from him until his twenty-first birthday.

In one variation of the story, the concealed brother has abnormal strength; in another, this is combined with extreme longevity; in a third version he has both these attributes. By an obscure and convoluted route, the child is said to have been so different from normal human beings because of an experiment with an alchemical elixir that bestowed superhuman strength and longevity — but at a terrible price as far as appearance went. An extension of this hypothesis postulates that the baby had been quite normal at birth, but became so ill that he was not expected to live — hence the announcement that he had died. The administration of the mysterious alchemical medicine was then a desperate last resort in a situation that seemed hopeless. According to this explanation, it saved the boy's life, but turned him into something barely recognizable as human.

Working on the simplest and broadest basic assumptions that at some period in the history of Glamis *something* was concealed in a secret room deep within the castle, seven hypotheses present themselves. First, it was just a sadly malformed but otherwise normal human being, and for reasons of their own the family decided to keep his existence secret. Second, as well as his strange appearance, he had attributes such as abnormal strength and longevity that enabled him to survive long enough for several generations of eldest sons to meet him on their twenty-first birthdays. Third, the occupant of the hidden chamber had no biological associations with the family — or, for that matter, with humans at all — he, she, or it was an alien visitor that had somehow reached Glamis. A fourth hypothesis suggests that the entity in the secret chamber was a strange-looking visitor from another dimension. A fifth supposition is that the mysterious occupant was from another probability track — one of the tantalizing *Worlds of If* — a realm in which evolution had taken a significantly different path, so that their equivalent of human beings was far removed from our experiences of terrestrial humanoids. The sixth hypothesis involves time-slips like the ones that J.W. Dunne envisaged in *An Experiment with Time* and *The Serial Universe*. Ever since the bizarre and conflicting reports of the

Philadelphia Experiment, a few serious scientists have wondered whether time and space may be more intricately interwoven than we have previously understood them to be, and more susceptible to warps and slips than was previously recognized. There are well-documented accounts of contemporary observers who *seem* to have moved through time, or who have reported encountering beings who have reached us from another time frame.

The seventh hypothesis centres on the opening decades of the nineteenth century, and Mary Shelley's fateful visit to Castle Frankenstein on the advice of her step-mother, Mary Jane Clairmont. Before writing her magnum opus about a creature constructed from parts of dismembered corpses and hurled back into the realm of the living at the whim of his creator and the power of a lightning flash, Mary had heard of a remarkable eccentric scientist named Johann Conrad Dippel. This strange man had lived in Castle Frankenstein, and, if half the stories about him were true, the real life Dippel had attempted many of the gruesome experiments that Mary laid at the door of the fictional Baron Frankenstein in her epic, published in 1816.

The tales of the "Monster of Glamis" began circulating at about the same time. Was there another Dippel, an eccentric Scottish surgeon, perhaps — someone like Dr. Knox, who was buying murdered corpses from Burke and Hare in Edinburgh in the 1820s? Had a successful version of

Lionel on roof of Glamis Castle.

the Frankenstein experiment been carried out — and then concealed and incarcerated for safety in the secret chamber of Glamis?

On one occasion, a workman carrying out repairs and refurbishments at Glamis accidentally broke through a partition wall that led to the secret room. Horrified at what he found in there, he spoke earnestly with Earl Claude, who rewarded him generously for his silence and paid for him and his family to start a prosperous new life in Australia.

HE KNEW THE SECRET

Claude Bowes-Lyon, who was the thirteenth earl, died in 1904 at the age of eighty. During his long life, he had been deeply involved with whatever mystery the secret chamber contained. On one occasion, he said with great solemnity and seriousness to an inquirer, "If you knew what the mystery was, you'd thank God that it wasn't yours."

In the 1920s, a period when rumours of the secret chamber and its mysterious occupant were at their height, a group of light-hearted young people from London were staying at Glamis as house guests. They decided to hang a sheet or towel from every window in the accessible rooms, reckoning that if a window had no indicator then it must be the window of the secret chamber. Perhaps a little more thought would have suggested to them that a genuine secret chamber would be singularly unlikely to have a window! According to reports of this adventure with the marker-linen at the windows, the Earl was absolutely furious and ordered his guests to leave. What did he know about the secret room that was so important to him to conceal? Is it still there? Is its mysterious occupant still there?

20 THE VERSAILLES TIME-SLIP MYSTERY

In November 2006, the authors made a special research visit to Versailles to study the site where Anne Moberly and her friend Eleanor Jourdain experienced what they firmly believed was a time-slip adventure first-hand, and to take essential photographs of the area. The two women had written everything up in considerable detail, and their research into the strange occurrence covered a period of some ten years, during which they made repeat visits to the site. Writing under the pseudonyms of Miss Francis Lamont (Jourdain) and Miss Elizabeth Morison (Moberly), they produced an accurate account of their experiences that was published as *An Adventure* in 1911.

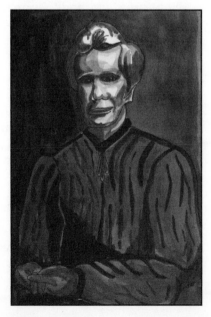
Miss Jourdain.

Miss Moberly.

The publisher's note among the preliminaries reads, "The signatures appended to the Preface are the only fictitious words in the book. The Publishers guarantee that the Authors have put down what happened to them as faithfully and accurately as was in their power."

The accuracy and validity of the account that the two women gave is supported critically and objectively by a hard-headed, contemporary scientist, Professor Sir W.F. Barrett, F.R.S. He read the independent accounts of their curious experiences, and they gave him access to letters from various friends to whom they had described their strange adventures at Versailles. Barrett said that following his perusal of the documents "no doubt whatsoever" was left in his mind that "the story was written substantially as it appears in this volume" (*An Adventure*).

Barrett was not prepared to accept that what had happened to the two women had been a genuine time-slip. He did accept, however, that the authors "had experienced a remarkable collective hallucination." Charles Fort would have smiled at Barrett's description of the womens' experience in Versailles as "a collective hallucination." In Fort's approach to the mysterious, what people tend to cling to for comfort and reassurance under the umbrella term "reality," may itself be only a collective hallucination.

Our own research visit to Versailles in November of 2006 enabled us to follow in Moberly and Jourdain's footsteps, and to absorb the atmosphere of these strange old buildings and the gardens and woodlands that surround them. Even with its twenty-first-century signposting and good, accurate maps and plans of the Versailles Estate, it is not an easy place to navigate. As we have noticed repeatedly during our research and analysis of these time mysteries, water seems to play a significant role in many of them, and Versailles was no exception:

The ladies began their August 1901 trip by describing how "a very sweet air" was blowing as they sat in the *Salle des Glaces* — the famous Hall of Mirrors. They walked from there until they reached the end of the Grand Canal that was nearer to the Château, and that the plan of Versailles describes as the *Embarcadere*.

They turned right from the Grand Canal along one of the many woodland paths through *Bosquets du Trianon*. Their comment on that day's weather is significant at this point in their narrative. The weather had been very hot, bright, and sunny up until their visit to Versailles, when it clouded over: "the sky was a little overcast and the sun shaded," they wrote.

Lionel at the Embarcadere.

THE TRIANON

Finding the meaning of the term "trianon" seemed relevant, but it did not appear as such in any French dictionary or Internet translation service to which we had access. However, further research seemed to indicate that the name was chosen because a village named *Trianon* had been bought by Louis XIV so that he could construct "a house for partaking of collations" — a quiet, informal place to which he could retreat with his family occasionally to get away from the demanding protocol of the court. It seems that even the redoubtable "Sun King" needed a little tranquility now and again!

Eventually they reached the *Petit Canal* close to the *Bassin du Fer-a-Cheval*, adjacent to the *Grand Trianon*. Miss Moberly and Miss Jourdain correctly identified the *Grand Trianon* and then did their best to get their bearings. Passing it on their left, they came to what is known today as *Allee des Deux Trianons*, which they described as "a broad green drive, perfectly deserted." Not realizing that it would have led them directly to the *Petit Trianon*, they crossed it, then turned right and saw some buildings. They were now well and truly inside the *Domaine de Marie-Antoinette*.

Miss Moberly was rather surprised that her friend Miss Jourdain failed to ask for directions from a woman whom Miss Moberly saw shaking a white cloth out of an upstairs window. Seeing three paths immediately ahead, they noticed that there were two men on the central one, and assumed at first they were gardeners because of a wheelbarrow and a spade nearby. They changed their opinion later when they realized that the men were wearing small tricorn hats, and long grey-green coats. This fact caused the women to assume that they were officials of some sort — perhaps garden supervisors or planners. The men directed the women to go straight on along this central path.

Miss Moberly then records that an unaccountable feeling of great sadness and depression came over her. She did her best to overcome it in order not to spoil the trip for her friend. As she struggled with these strange, melancholy feelings, they crossed another of the many paths that filled the wood.

The next thing they saw was what Miss Moberly described as "a light garden kiosk" with a sinister-looking man sitting beside it. He wore a cloak and a wide-brimmed hat and she described his face as "repulsive," and his complexion as rough. Her feeling of depression was now tinged with fear. She said later that things looked strange and unnatural. The trees behind the little wooden structure no longer seemed real. She described them as having the appearance of trees in a tapestry. She asked Miss Jourdain which way they ought to go, but was quite determined to go no closer to the dangerous-looking man near the kiosk.

The women's report of the strange arrival of another man at that moment adds further mystery to their account. He seemed to have emerged from the nearby rock, and was agitated and breathless as though he had been running fast to reach them in order to prevent some harm or danger to them — and they had, in fact, *heard* sounds of running just before he appeared. In stark contrast to the unpleasant-looking character near the kiosk, this newcomer was handsome. He wore a sombrero-style hat over his long curly black hair, and Miss Moberly commented particularly on his large, attractive, dark eyes. When she looked at him intently, as though trying to work out where he had come from, he gave her what she later described as "a most peculiar smile."

Like the man by the kiosk, their rescuer also wore a cloak. He urged them vehemently to take the path straight ahead, and it seemed to the ladies that he was most anxious that they should not turn left past the evil-looking man by the kiosk who had so unnerved Miss Moberly. As she had no intention of going to the left, she went straight ahead as their rescuer had directed them. Turning to thank him, she was very surprised to find that he was no longer in sight, although she could again hear the running sounds that she had heard immediately prior to his appearance.

The women continued along the path that the man had indicated, and found that it went over a small bridge crossing a miniature ravine. Once again, water appears to be an important aspect of time-slip mysteries. They reported a fine cascade descending into a tiny stream at the base of the ravine. The ladies also described ferns, but they could, perhaps, have meant rushes, and the authors certainly encountered a similar spot beside a small bridge, with a narrow path running behind it.

They proceeded through part of the forest and by the side of a meadow filled with long grass that gave them the impression of dampness and shadow. Trees obscured their view of the *Petit Trianon* until they were very close to the building itself. Miss Moberly described the building as smaller than she had expected, and commented on its square solidity. She noticed a terrace running around the north and west sides of the house, and a woman sitting there and sketching. Miss Moberly guessed that the woman was sketching trees, as there was nothing much else in front of her. She looked directly at Miss Moberly as she passed, and Miss Moberly saw her face clearly. She commented that the face — although quite pretty — was not a young face, and she did not feel attracted to the woman. If it was indeed Marie Antoinette whom the English visitor saw, it seems a little strange that Miss Moberly regarded her as "not young." Marie Antoinette was born in 1755 and was only 34 in 1789 when the Paris mob attacked Versailles. Perhaps the pre-revolutionary political strain and anxiety had aged her prematurely. As history proved, the ferocity of the Paris mob was a formidable thing.

In her account, Miss Moberly noted that the woman who she saw sketching close to the *Petit Trianon* was wearing a shady white hat over fair hair, fluffed around her forehead. With a keen eye for style and fashion, Miss Moberly commented on the woman's light summer dress arranged on her shoulders in what she called "handkerchief fashion." She also noticed particularly that there was "a little line of either green or gold near the edge of the handkerchief," which indicated that it was over the top of her low-cut bodice, not tucked inside it. The skirt was full and long-waisted, and, by Miss Moberly's rather prudish Victorian standards, "short."

It is more than a little surprising that when the women compared notes about what they had seen and experienced that August afternoon at the *Petit Trianon*, Miss Jourdain had not seen the woman whom Miss Moberly had seen sketching — although Miss Jourdain said that she had felt "as if there were people there whom she could not see."

Of particular interest was Miss Jourdain's feeling of sadness and depression that coincided with what her friend had also felt at the point where they had *both* seen the men whom they assumed to be gardeners.

As they talked through their experiences together, they wondered why the mysterious running man, who had seemingly rescued them, was wearing a cloak wrapped around him on such a warm August day. It even crossed their minds that he was about to fight a duel with the

THE STORMING OF THE TUILERIES

After the death of her husband, Henry II of France, in 1559, Catherine de' Medici arranged for the Tuileries Palace and grounds to be built close to the Louvre. Construction began in 1564. The name "Tuileries" is derived from the tile kilns (*tuileries*) that once stood on the site. Louis XIV, the Sun King, lived in the Tuileries while Versailles was being built. The hapless Louis XVI and Marie Antoinette and their family were forced to leave Versailles and were placed under house arrest in the Tuileries. On August 10, 1792, the Tuileries were stormed by the Paris mob, who massacred the Swiss guards while Louis XVI and his family ran for their lives through the gardens to the hall of the legislative assembly, where they took refuge.

odious-looking man beside the kiosk, and wanted to get them out of the way so that he could begin it without witnesses being present.

A few weeks after their adventure in Versailles, a friend of Miss Jourdain's told her that there was a persistent tradition in France that on a particular day in August (most researchers maintain that it is August 10) the ghosts of Marie Antoinette and several of her contemporaries are seen and felt in the area near the *Petit Trianon.*

She communicated this news to Miss Moberly, who did some additional historical research and discovered that on August 10, 1792, the Tuileries were sacked by the Paris mob.

Miss Moberly came up with an interesting theory to the effect that on that fateful day in August, 1792, Marie Antoinette might have been thinking deeply about happier days in Versailles, close to the Petit Trianon that had meant so much to her. Miss Moberly wondered whether she and Miss Jourdain had inadvertently walked into some strange projection of the doomed queen's vivid memory, and that this was what accounted for their feelings of deep sadness during their 1901 visit.

The idea of being caught inside someone else's dream is one that has been handled skillfully by a number of fantasy writers, and L. Ron Hubbard's *Typewriter in the Sky*, first published in serial form in 1940, has the hero trapped inside a story that one of his friends is writing.

The Reverend Charles Lutwidge Dodgson (1832–98), better known as Lewis Carroll, was a philosopher, logician, and mathematician, as well as an author, and *Alice's Adventures in Wonderland* had his young heroine involved in a brilliantly imaginative dream adventure. In view of Dodgson's academic powers, his second volume — in which Alice passes through a mirror into a back-to-front, future-to-past world — contains several extremely deep and serious ideas that touch on the nature and reversibility of time. It is by no means impossible that Miss Moberly's theory of being involved in a projection of Marie Antoinette's thoughts owed something to her reading of Carroll's works.

Miss Jourdain's second visit to Versailles, in January of 1902, took place on a cold, wet day, and because time was of the essence for her on that occasion, she went straight to both Trianons, also inspecting the Temple de l'Amour as part of her research. This inspection satisfied her beyond any reasonable doubt that it was *definitely not* the same place as the strange kiosk beside which they had seen the sinister man on their August visit. Up to this point in her January 1902 visit, she felt none of the unnatural fear and sadness — and the weird sense of unreality — that both ladies had experienced the previous summer.

Then she crossed the bridge leading to the Hameau. In her own words, she felt as if she had "crossed a line," and the unwelcome feeling of strangeness, sadness, and fear returned in full force.

She noticed two men loading sticks into a cart. Both were dressed in the characteristic tricorned hats and cloaks that the two women had seen on their previous trip. But instead of the grey-green colours that they had noticed then, one of these men was wearing dark blue; the other had a brownish-red cape. Miss Jourdain felt relieved to see them and thought that if she needed help with directions, she could ask them.

For scarcely more than a moment, she turned to look again at the quaint architecture of Le Petit Hameau, also known as *Le Hameau de la Reine*, meaning "the little hamlet belonging to the queen."

When she turned back, the men and the cart were nowhere to be seen — and there were no signs of any sticks on the ground at the place where the men had been loading them. With a great deal of courage and determination, she continued toward the Hameau.

Once again, water features prominently in the time-slip equation. As the authors noted on their research visit, the buildings in the Hameau are all on the edge of a landscaped pond. The architect responsible for it was

The Hameau Village at Versailles.

FANTASY FARM

The Hameau was what was known in France at the time as a *ferme ornee*, an ersatz or artificial farm, a place where wealthy aristocrats could play idyllic, romantic games dressed as milkmaids and shepherdesses. Handpicked and extra docile cows were washed and groomed there as an integral part of this fantasy farming. There were even monogrammed ceramic milk-churns, made in the royal porcelain works at Sèvres, in which the genteel milkmaids would store the milk the placid cows produced!

Ange-Jacques Gabriel (1698–1782), one of the greatest French architects of the eighteenth century. Louis XV had it built for his mistress, the beautiful and brilliantly intelligent Madame de Pompadour (1721–64). Louis XVI gave it to Marie Antoinette.

As Miss Jourdain walked from the Hameau through dense trees, she became aware, as before, that there were invisible people walking close to her — so close, in fact, that she could hear what they were saying to one another.

Another factor that struck the women as they pondered their strange adventure was that during their 1904 visit, the grounds and buildings were crowded with tourists (as they were when the authors went there in 2006) — whereas in 1901 Miss Moberly and Miss Jourdain had seen scarcely anyone. Was it a private royal precinct from the past that they had inadvertently stepped into? Or were they — in some incomprehensible way — wandering inside the powerfully projected thoughts and memories of the doomed Marie Antoinette?

Understandably, there was a great deal of controversy over the mysterious account that the women gave, but they steadfastly defended their version of the events and their interpretation of what they had seen and heard.

Charlotte Moberly saw a picture of Marie Antoinette and her children painted by the Swedish artist Adolph Ulrich Wertmuller (1751–1811) and recognized her as the woman she had seen sketching near the Petit Trianon.

They had also noticed a plough while they were walking through the grounds in 1901 — but no plough was there in 1901, although there *had* been one in the past. They never found the elusive bridge or the strange kiosk on later visits, but they did find an old map indicating that there *had* been a gazebo there at one time but that it had been demolished before 1901. They were more or less able to identify the sinister-looking man with the pock-marked face as the evil Comte de Vaudreuil, who had treacherously helped to bring about Marie Antoinette's downfall. Their researches also revealed that the men who they had seen in the tricorned hats were no part of the Versailles of 1901 — they were actually wearing a Swiss guards' uniform from the late eighteenth century. The mysterious breathless runner who had insisted that they did not go to the left could well have been a loyal servant of the royal family sent to warn Marie Antoinette that the Paris mob was approaching.

So what are the possible explanations of the Moberly and Jourdain "time-slip" experiences at Versailles, and what conclusions can be reached from their evidence? After both women had died, their real identities were revealed, and their academic status gave increased credibility to their evidence. If it was a straightforward time-slip that had taken them back from 1901 to 1789, that would account for the absence of visitors to the royal domain. The curious detachment of some of the people they saw, and the ways in which they either vanished rapidly or were not always visible to both ladies, might suggest that whatever glitch, or fault, had affected time that August day had irregular and inconsistent qualities — as though the edges of time had been roughly torn.

As Paracelsus taught, the power of the mind is vast, and emotion, such as Marie Antoinette must have felt in those terrifying days, *could* have been capable of creating a strange, quasi-realm into which Miss Moberly and Miss Jourdain were drawn.

BIBLIOGRAPHY

Asimov, Isaac. *Guide to Earth and Space*. New York: Fawcett Crest, 1991.

Asimov, Isaac. *The Universe*. New York: Avon Books, 1971.

Bacon, Francis. *Essays: The Wisdom of the Ancients and the New Atlantis*. London: Odhams Press Ltd., 1950.

Baring-Gould, S. *Historical Oddities and Strange Events*. London: Methuen and Co., 1890.

Begg, E. *The Cult of the Black Virgin*. Oxford: 1985.

Berlitz, Charles. *World of Strange Phenomena*. London: Sphere Books Limited, 1989.

Bernstein, Jeremy. *Einstein*. Glasgow: Fontana, 1978.

Blashford-Snell, John. *Mysteries: Encounters with the Unexplained*. London: Bodley Head, 1983.

Bord, Janet and Colin. *Mysterious Britain*. Southampton: Paladin, 1974.

Bord, Janet and Colin. *Modern Mysteries of the World*. London: Grafton Books, 1989.

Boslough, John. *Stephen Hawking's Universe*. London: Fontana Paperbacks, 1986.

Boudet, Henri. *La Vraie Langue Celtique et le Cromleck de Rennes-les-Bains*. Nice, France: Belisane, 1984.

Bradbury, Will, ed. *Into the Unknown*. Pleasantville, NY: Readers Digest Ass., 1981.

Bradley, M. *Holy Grail Across the Atlantic*. Toronto: Hounslow Press, 1988.

Brennan, J.H. *Time Travel*. Woodbury, MN: Llewellyn Publications, 2003.

Briggs, Katharine M. *British Folk Tales and Legends: A Sampler*. London: Granada Publishing in Paladin, 1977.

Brittman, Barry, and Anthony DeFail. *Maze of Life*. Meadville, PA: TouchStar Productions, 2007.

Brookesmith, Peter, ed. *Cult and Occult* London: Guild Publishing, 1985.

Brookesmith, Peter, ed. *The Enigma of Time*. London: Orbis Publishing, 1984.

Buren, Elizabeth Van. *The Dragon of Rennes-le-Château*. Vogels, France: 1998.

Butler, William Vivian. *The Greatest Magicians on Earth*. London: Pan Books Ltd., 1977.

Carey, Margret. *Myths and Legends of Africa*. London: Hamlyn, 1970.

Carroll, Latrobe. *Death and its Mysteries*. London: T. Fisher Unwin Ltd.m, 1923.

Cavendish, Richard, ed. *Encyclopaedia of the Unexplained*. London: Routledge & Kegan Paul, 1974.

Clark, Jerome. *Unexplained*. Farmington Hills, MI: Gale Research Inc., 1993.

Clarke, Arthur C. *Chronicles of the Strange and Mysterious*. London: Guild Publishing, 1987.

Clayton, Peter A. *Chronicle of the Pharaohs*. London: Thames and Hudson Ltd., 1994.

Crooker, William S. *Oak Island Gold*. Halifax, NS: Nimbus Publishing Ltd., 1993.

David-Neel, Alexandra. *Initiations and Initiates in Tibet*. New York: University Books, 1959.

David-Neel, Alexandra. *The Secret Oral Traditions in Tibetan Sects*. San Francisco: City Lights Publishing, 1964.

David-Neel, Alexandra. *With Mystics and Magicians in Tibet*. New York: Dover Publications, 1971.

Dunne, J.W. *An Experiment with Time*. London: Faber and Faber Limited, 1927.

Dyall, Valentine. *Unsolved Mysteries*. London: Hutchinson & Co. Ltd., 1954.

Eysenck, H.J., and Carl Sargent. *Explaining the Unexplained*. London: BCA, 1993.

Fairley, John, and Simon Welfare. *Arthur C Clarke's World of Strange Powers*. London: W. Collins Sons & Co. Ltd., 1985.

Fanthorpe, Lionel and Patricia. *The Holy Grail Revealed*. California: Newcastle Publishing Co. Inc., 1982.

Fanthorpe, Lionel and Patricia. *Secrets of Rennes le Château*. Maine: Samuel Weiser Inc., 1992.

Fanthorpe, Lionel and Patricia. *The Oak Island Mystery*. Toronto: Dundurn Press, 1995.

Fanthorpe, Lionel and Patricia. *The World's Greatest Unsolved Mysteries*. Toronto: Dundurn Press, 1997.

Fanthorpe, Lionel and Patricia. *The World's Most Mysterious People*. Toronto: Dundurn Press, 1998.

Fanthorpe, Lionel and Patricia. *The World's Most Mysterious Places*. Toronto: Dundurn Press, 1999.

Fanthorpe, Lionel and Patricia. *Mysteries of the Bible*. Toronto: Dundurn Press, 1999.

Fanthorpe, Lionel and Patricia. *Death the Final Mystery*. Toronto: Dundurn Press, 2000.

Fanthorpe, Lionel and Patricia. *The World's Most Mysterious Objects*. Toronto: Dundurn Press, 2002.

Fanthorpe, Lionel and Patricia. *The World's Most Mysterious Murders.* Toronto: Dundurn Press, 2003.

Fanthorpe, Lionel and Patricia. *Unsolved Mysteries of the Sea.* Toronto: Dundurn Press, 2004.

Fanthorpe, Lionel and Patricia. *Mysteries of Templar Treasure and the Holy Grail.* Maine: Samuel Weiser Inc., 2004.

Fanthorpe, Lionel and Patricia. *The World's Most Mysterious Castles.* Toronto: Dundurn Press, 2005.

Fanthorpe, Lionel and Patricia. *Mysteries and Secrets of the Templars: The Story Behind the da Vinci Code.* Toronto: Dundurn Press, 2005

Fanthorpe, Lionel and Patricia. *Mysteries and Secrets of the Masons.* Toronto: Dundurn Press, 2006.

Fanthorpe, Lionel and Patricia. *Mysteries and Secrets of Time.* Toronto: Dundurn Press, 2007.

Fanthorpe, Lionel and Patricia. *Mysteries and Secrets of Voodoo, Santeria, and Obeah.* Toronto: Dundurn Press, 2008.

Fanthorpe, Lionel and Patricia. *Secrets of the World's Undiscovered Treasures.* Toronto: Dundurn Press, 2009.

Faraone, Christopher A. *Binding and Burying the Forces of Evil: The Defensive Use of "Voodoo Dolls" in Ancient Greece.* California: Classical Antiquity Magazine, Vol. 10, No. 2. 1991.

Fowke, Edith. *Canadian Folklore.* Don Mills, ON: Oxford University Press, 1988.

Frazer, James George, Sir. *The Golden Bough.* New York: The Macmillan Co., 1922.

Gettings, Fred. *Encyclopedia of the Occult.* London: Guild Publishing, 1986.

Gettings, Fred. *Secret Symbolism in Occult Art.* New York: Harmony Books, 1987.

Gimbutas, Marija. *The Civilization of the Goddess.* London: HarperCollins, 1992.

Godwin, John. *This Baffling World*. New York: Hart Publishing Company, 1968.

Graves, Robert (Intro.). Larousse Encyclopaedia of Mythology. London: Paul Hamlyn, 1959.

Green, John. *On the Track of the Sasquatch*. New York: Ballantine Books, 1973.

Gribble, Leonard. *Famous Historical Mysteries*. London: Target Books, 1974.

Grimal, Nicolas. *A History of Ancient Egypt*. Oxford: Blackwell, 1988.

Guerber, H.A. *Myths and Legends of the Middle Ages*. London: Studio Editions Ltd., 1994.

Guiley, Rosemary Ellen. *The Encyclopedia of Ghosts and Spirits*, New York: Checkmark Books, 2000.

Guirdham, Arthur. *The Lake and the Castle*. Llandeilo, UK: Cygnus Books, 1992.

Guirdham, Arthur. *We Are One Another*. Llandeilo, UK: Cygnus Books, 1992.

Guirdham, Arthur. *The Cathars and Reincarnation*. London: Neville Spearman, 1970.

Haining, Peter. *The Restless Bones and Other True Mysteries*. London: Armada Books, 1970.

Harrison, Michael. *The Roots of Witchcraft*. London: Tandem, 1975.

Hay, George, ed. *The Necronomicon — The Book of Dead Names*. London: Skoob Books Publishing, 1992.

Heywood, Abel. *Mother Shipton's Prophecies*. U.K. George Mann, 1978.

Hieronimus, Robert. *America's Secret Destiny*. Vermont: Destiny Books, 1989.

Higenbottam, Frank. *Codes and Ciphers*. English Universities Press Ltd., 1975.

Hitching, Francis. *The World Atlas of Mysteries*. London: Pan Books, 1979.

Hogue, John. *Nostradamus and the Millennium*. New York: Doubleday Dolphin, 1987.

Hougham, Paul. *The Atlas of Mind, Body, and Spirit*. London: Octopus Publishing Group, 2006.

Knight, Gareth. *The Secret Tradition in Arthurian Legend*. Great Britain. The Aquarian Press, 1983.

Lacy, N.J. *The Arthurian Encyclopaedia*. Woodbridge, Suffolk, UK: Boydell Press, 1986.

Lampitt, L.F., ed. *The World's Strangest Stories*. London: Associated Newspapers Group Ltd., 1955.

Lawrence, Richard. *The Magic of Healing*. London: Thorsons, 2001.

Lemesurier, Peter. *Beyond all Belief*. Shaftesbury, Dorset, UK: Element Books Ltd., 1983.

Lewis, C.S. *The Abolition of Man*. London: Fount Paperbacks, 1978.

Mack, Lorrie, et al, eds. *The Unexplained*. London: Orbis, 1984.

Martin, Lois. *The History of Witchcraft*. Herts. Manchester: Pocket Essentials Publications, 2007.

Michell, John, and Robert J.M. Rickard. *Phenomena: A Book of Wonders*. London: Thames & Hudson, 1977.

Miller, G.H. *Dictionary of Dreams*. Bath, UK: Parragon Books, 1999.

Newton, Toyne. *The Dark Worship*. London: Vega, 2002.

Morison, E., and F. Lamont (actually Moberly, A., and E. Jourdain). *An Adventure*. London: Macmillan and Co. Ltd., 1913.

Nicholas, M. *The World's Greatest Psychics and Mystics*. London: Hamlyn Publishing Group, 1994.

Ogden, Daniel. *Magic, Witchcraft, and Ghosts in the Greek and Roman World: A Sourcebook*. Oxford: Oxford University Press, 2002.

Owen, Iris, and Margaret Sparrows. *Conjuring up Philip*. New York: Harper & Row, 1976.

Pearce, J. *The Crack in the Cosmic Egg. (Revised Edition of the Classic Back in Print Edition.)* South Paris, ME: Park Street Press, 2002.

Playfair, Guy Lyon. *The Unknown Power.* London: Granada Publishing Ltd., 1977.

Pott, Mrs. Henry. *Francis Bacon and his Secret Society.* London: Sampson Low, Marston, and Company, 1891.

Puharich, Andrija. *Beyond Telepathy.* London: Souvenir Press Ltd., 1974.

Priestley, J.B. *Man and Time.* London: Aldus Books Limited, 1964.

Rawcliffe, D.H. *Illusions and Delusions of the Supernatural and the Occult.* New York: 1959. (Republished Whitefish, MT: Kessinger Publishing, 2006.)

Read, Paul Piers. *The Templars.* London: Weidenfeld & Nicolson, 1999.

Reeves, Nicholas, and Richard H. Wilkinson. *Complete Valley of the Kings (Tombs and Treasures of Egypt's Greatest Pharaohs)* London: Thames & Hudson Ltd., 1966.

Rolleston, T.W. *Celtic Myths and Legends.* London: Studio Editions Ltd., 1994.

Russell, Eric Frank. *Great World Mysteries.* London: Mayflower, 1967.

Saint-Clair, David. *Drum and Candle.* New York: Bell Publishing, 1971.

Saltzman, Pauline. *The Strange and the Supernormal.* New York: Paperback Library Inc., 1968.

Sargant, William. *Battle for the Mind.* London: Penguin Books, 1961.

Schwartz, Gary E.R., and Linda G.S. Russek. *The Living Energy Universe.* Charlottesville, VA: Hampton Roads Publishing, 1999.

Seabrook, B. *The Magic Island.* New York: Harcourt Brace. 1929.

Sharper Knowlson, T. *The Origins of Popular Superstitions and Customs.* London: Studio Editions Ltd., 1995.

Shaw, Ian. *The Oxford History of Ancient Egypt.* Oxford: Oxford University Press, 2000.

Sinclair, Andrew. *The Sword and the Grail.* New York: Crown Publishers Inc., 1992.

Singer, Marian. *Everything You Need to Know about Witchcraft.* Newton Abbot, UK: David and Charles, 2005.

Snow, Edward Rowe. *Strange Tales from Nova Scotia to Cape Hatteras.* New York: Dodd, Mead and Company, 1946.

Spence, Lewis. *The Encyclopaedia of the Occult.* London: Bracken Books, 1988.

Spencer, John and Anne. *The Encyclopaedia of the World's Greatest Unsolved Mysteries.* London: Headline Book Publishing, 1995.

Spicer, Stanley T. *The Saga of the Mary Celeste.* Falmouth, NS: Lancelot Press Ltd., 1993.

Tomas, Andrew. *Atlantis: from Legend to Discovery.* London: Sphere Books, 1974.

Von Daniken, Erich. *The Gold of the Gods.* New York: Bantam, 1974.

Wilson, Colin, and Damon Wilson. *Unsolved Mysteries Past and Present.* London: Headline Book Publishing, 1993.

Wilson, Colin, and Christopher Evans, eds. *The Book of Great Mysteries.* London: Robinson Publishing, 1986.

Wilson, Derek. *The World Atlas of Treasure.* London: Pan Books, 1982.

Young, George. *Ancient Peoples and Modern Ghosts.* Queensland, NS: George Young Publishing, 1991.

Young, George. *Ghosts in Nova Scotia.* Queensland, NS: George Young Publishing, 1991.

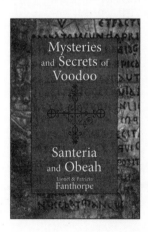